The Energy Gap
in Eastern Europe

The Energy Gap
in Eastern Europe

John M. Kramer
Mary Washington College

Lexington Books
D.C. Heath and Company/Lexington, Massachusetts/Toronto

Kramer, John M.
    The energy gap in eastern Europe / John M. Kramer.
        p.
    Bibliography: p.
    Includes index.
    ISBN 0-669-16756-8 (alk. paper)
    1. Energy policy—Europe, Eastern.   2. Energy industries—Europe,
Eastern.   3. Energy consumption—Europe, Eastern.   I. Title.
HD9502.E82K74   1989
333.79′0947—dc20   87-45583
                                                                                       CIP

Published simultaneously in Canada
Printed in the United States of America
International Standard Book Number: 0-669-16756-8
Library of Congress Catalog Card Number 87-45583

The paper used in this publication meets the minimum requirements of
American National Standard for Information Sciences—Permanence of
Paper for Printed Library Materials, ANSI Z39.48-1984. ∞ ™

Year and number of this printing:

90 91 92 10 9 8 7 6 5 4 3 2 1

To MLK

Contents

Tables

Preface

Eastern Europe experiences an "energy gap" in which it consumes more energy than it produces indigenously. This book examines how and with what consequences Eastern Europe has closed its energy gap. The subject is inextricably linked to broader political, economic, historical, and geographic conditions in the region.

Most fundamentally, the energy gap is a political phenomenon. This book demonstrates that political decisions created the energy gap and only political decisions can resolve it. That Eastern Europe traditionally has relied on importation from the Soviet Union to close much of its energy gap constitutes a seminal fact of political life in the region. An analysis of the energy relationship between the Soviet Union and Eastern Europe inevitably examines issues that are central to the overall political relationship between the two sides.

Homo politicus may have created the energy gap, but *Homo economicus* provides much of our understanding of why it continues to exist. Eastern European economies possess few economic incentives to limit the consumption of energy. Predictably, this circumstance makes them inordinate consumers of energy. The establishment of economic disincentives to overconsume energy—in particular, the formulation of prices for energy resources that reflect marginal costs—represents a sine qua non for an effective resolution of the energy gap. This book argues that such initiatives must be part of a comprehensive reform of the economic and political systems in the region.

These systems themselves are the progeny of the Stalinist era in Eastern Europe. Between 1948 and 1953, the late Soviet dictator imposed a model of economic and political development on Eastern Europe that replicated the one he had established in the Soviet Union. This Stalinist model persists to varying degrees in all Eastern European states. An historical analysis of its essential features is crucial to an understanding of the contemporary status of the energy gap in the region.

A focus on political, economic, and historical conditions must not obscure the geographic dimension of the energy gap. The paucity of high-quality energy reserves in the region almost ensures that the energy gap will remain a perennial problem. Coal, much of it brown coal and lignite of low caloric content, constitutes the primary energy resource in the region. Only Poland possesses significant quantities of higher energy yielding hard coal, and only Romania and Hungary possess appreciable reserves of liquid and gaseous fuels.

This book, like all books, results from the efforts of many people. Professors David Powell and Paul Shoup first kindled my interest in Soviet and Eastern European studies while a graduate student at the University of Virginia from 1966 to 1971. In my own work, I have sought, however imperfectly, to emulate their rigorous standards of scholarly excellence. David Powell, now of the Russian Research Center, Harvard University, merits special mention for his ongoing encouragement of, and substantive contribution to, my scholarship. I consider it a privilege to call David my friend as well as my colleague.

My association with Mary Washington College, where I have served as a professor of political science since 1971, has been a productive one both inside and outside the classroom. Lewis P. Fickett and Richard J. Krickus have been departmental colleagues throughout my tenure at the college. Like David Powell, they are more than colleagues; they are friends. Their considerable scholarly accomplishments continuously motivate me in my own work. Special thanks also to professor Stephen Stageberg of the Department of Economics for his valuable assistance in clarifying my sometimes muddled understanding of economic concepts and issues.

Philip L. Hall, vice president for academic affairs and dean of the college, has provided invaluable assistance in this project. He granted me a sabbatical in the 1986–87 academic year, which I spent as a senior fellow at the National Defense University in Washington, D.C. Much of the research for this book was completed during this year. Dean Hall also provided financial support for research and lectures in Eastern Europe in 1987. The ensuing discussions with members of the Institute for World Economics, Hungarian Academy of Sciences, materially contributed to my understanding of the energy gap in the region.

Dora Minor, my secretary for many years, performed admirably in typing and retyping (seemingly endless) drafts of the manuscript. I greatly appreciate her professional expertise and even more her unfailing good humor in dealing with a sometimes cranky author-to-be. Michele McClain, a senior undergraduate at the college, assisted in typing and proofreading this manuscript. I am pleased to acknowledge their contributions.

This book is dedicated to my wife, Mary Louise. She is a constant source of personal pleasure, emotional support, and professional respect in her capacity as a partner with the law firm of Sands, Anderson, Marks and Miller. She also is my toughest critic. I hope this book elicits her approval.

Glossary

Communist Europe. The USSR and Eastern Europe

Eastern Europe. Bulgaria, Czechoslovakia, Hungary, the German Democratic Republic, Poland, and Romania

Hard goods. Goods that can be sold on international markets for hard currency at world market prices (WMPs)

Soft goods. Goods that either cannot be sold, or can be sold only at subsidized prices, for hard currency on international markets

Transferable ruble. An accounting unit used in Council for Mutual Economic Assistance (Comecon) trade

1
The Energy Gap

The situation with regard to raw materials and fuels . . . is no
longer a laughing matter.
—*Zycie Warszawy*, 9 July, 1985

A ll states of Eastern Europe, except Poland, experience a negative
energy gap wherein primary energy consumption exceeds primary
energy production (Table 1–1). Eastern Europe as a whole has
experienced this gap since 1970, although it appeared in most states by
1960.

How to close the region's energy gap has become a question of paramount significance that is debated at the highest political levels of the
affected states. This debate has profound implications for their internal
political and economic welfare and for their relations with one another,
the Soviet Union, and nonsocialist states. This circumstance refutes the
assertion in a Radio Moscow broadcast that "Comecon is the only indus-
trially developed zone on this planet which has not been affected by the
energy crisis."[1] Ironically, Eastern Europe's energy problems persist even
though most industrialized states have recovered from the international
energy crisis of the 1970s.

Scope and Roots

Table 1–1 merits several comments. First, the scope of the energy gap
varies among countries, given their different natural resource endowments
and levels of economic and social development. Bulgaria and Hungary
consistently have experienced the largest negative energy gaps as a percent
of primary energy consumption. In contrast, a negative energy gap only
recently appeared in Romania, while Poland continues to enjoy a positive
energy gap. These differences must be remembered whenever generalizing
about the energy-gap in Eastern Europe.

Second, scope is only one of several variables determining the range
and severity of problems encountered in closing the energy gap. As we
shall see, these problems became acute in the 1981–1985 period, when

Table 1–1
Eastern Europe: The Energy Gap
(thousands of barrels per day of oil equivalent)

	Primary Energy Production[1]				Primary Energy Consumption[1]				Energy Gap[2]			
	1960	*1970*	*1980*	*1986*	*1960*	*1970*	*1980*	*1985*	*1960*	*1970*	*1980*	*1985*
Bulgaria	109	151	181	227	131	391	668	715	16.8	61.3	72.9	68.3
Czecho-slovakia	761	906	963	987	798	1,136	1,466	1,517	4.6	20.2	34.3	34.9
East Germany	1,027	1,172	1,213	1,471	1,166	1,491	1,827	1,978	11.9	21.4	33.6	25.6
Hungary	207	277	278	311	270	431	602	648	23.3	35.7	53.8	52.0
Poland	1,278	1,895	2,446	2,514	1,050	1,653	2,479	2,420	—	—	—	—
Romania	487	879	1,102	1,187	376	844	1,338	1,444	—	—	—	17.8
Eastern Europe	3,870	5,280	6,180	6,700	3,790	5,950	8,380	8,720	—	11.3	26.2	23.2

Source: Compiled from data in Directorate of Intelligence, *Handbook of Economic Statistics, 1987*, tables 96 and 97.
Note: Calculated only for countries with a negative energy gap.
[1]Data are for coal, crude oil, natural gas, natural gas liquids, and hydroelectric and nuclear electric power expressed in terms of oil equivalent. Data exclude minor fuels such as peat, shale, and wood.
[2]Difference between production and consumption as a percent of consumption.

the energy gap as a percent of primary energy consumption was either declining or essentially unchanging in most Eastern European states.

Third, the energy gap is not a static phenomenon. It emerged in the 1960s, expanded dramatically between 1960 and 1980, and contracted somewhat between 1981 and 1985. The numerous variables affecting supply and demand make forecasting the status of energy in any society a speculative exercise. Consequently, the present study eschews long-term prognostications on this subject. It seems clear that no major changes in supply and demand for energy will occur through 1990. In the longer term, the demand side should prove the key variable affecting the energy gap. If, for example, reformers successfully reverse the stagnant or declining performances of most Eastern European economies in the 1980s, then the concomitant increase in demand for energy could again widen the energy gap.

Fourth, the energy gap for oil and (in most states) natural gas is even greater than the overall energy gap (tables 1–2 and 1–3). This circumstance determines the decisive role that the Soviet Union, the principal supplier of these fuels to Eastern Europe, plays in closing the gap.

Several interrelated factors contribute to the energy gap. Eastern Europe possesses relatively limited reserves of primary energy, especially of

Table 1–2
Eastern Europe: The Energy Gap in Oil

	Production[1]		Consumption[2]		Energy Gap[3]	
	1976	1986[4]	1976	1986[4]	1976	1986
Bulgaria	3	6	265	295	98.9	98.0
Czechoslovakia	3	3	353	358	99.1	99.2
East Germany	1	1	315	333	99.7	99.7
Hungary	43	40	227	204	81.0	80.4
Poland	9	3	322	351	97.2	99.1
Romania	308	212	319	324	3.4	34.5
Eastern Europe	367	265	1,801	1,865	79.6	85.8

Source: Directorate of Intelligence, *International Energy Statistical Review*, 17.
[1] Thousands of barrels per day.
[2] Thousands of barrels per day crude oil equivalent.
[3] Difference between production and consumption as percent of consumption.
[4] Estimated.

liquid and gaseous fuels.[2] The reserves themselves are distributed unevenly in the region. The structure of primary energy production in the region reflects the distribution of primary energy reserves (table 1–4).

Brown coal and lignite of low caloric content are the only fossil fuel reserves found abundantly in all states. East Germany, with upward of forty billion tons of brown coal and lignite, including twenty-two billion to twenty-five billion tons suitable for open cast mining, possesses the

Table 1–3
Eastern Europe: The Energy Gap in Natural Gas

	Production[1]		Consumption[1]		Energy Gap[2]	
	1976	1986[3]	1976	1986[3]	1976	1986
Bulgaria	—	—	5.7	16.0	100	100
Czechoslovakia	2.8	2.0	14.2	32.0	80.3	93.7
East Germany	22.7	23.0	34.0	40.0	33.2	42.5
Hungary	17.0	19.0	19.8	31.0	14.1	38.7
Poland	17.0	16.5	25.5	31.5	33.3	47.6
Romania	93.4	101.5	93.4	107.5	0	5.6
Eastern Europe	152.9	162.0	192.6	258.0	20.6	37.2

Source: Directorate of Intelligence, *International Energy Statistical Review*, 18.
[1] Millions of cubic meters per day.
[2] Difference between production and consumption as percent of consumption.
[3] Estimated.

Table 1–4

Eastern Europe: Structure of Primary Energy Production, 1985
(percent of total production)

	Coal	Natural Gas	Oil	Primary Electricity[1]
Bulgaria	89.1	0.1	—	10.8
Czechoslovakia	95.6	1.3	0.3	2.8
East Germany	93.2	5.0	—	1.8
Hungary	44.3	36.7	15.6	3.5
Poland	95.6	4.0	0.2	0.2
Romania	22.6	59.1	16.8	1.6

Source: United Nations Economic Commission for Europe, *Economic Survey of Europe in 1986–1987*, 199.
[1] Primarily nuclear power and hydropower.

largest such reserves in Eastern Europe. Poland possesses more than 90 percent of the reserves of hard coal. Only Czechoslovakia and Poland have reserves of coking coal.

More than 90 percent of the proven oil reserves are located in Romania. Czechoslovakia, East Germany, and Poland possess limited reserves of oil and Bulgaria almost no reserves. Romania (28 percent), East Germany (27 percent), Poland (24 percent), and Hungary (17 percent) possess approximately 97 percent of the known reserves of natural gas in the region. Romania, traditionally the leading producer of natural gas in Eastern Europe, experienced a decline of 22 percent in known reserves of this fuel between 1983 and 1988. At current rates of extraction, Romania could exhaust these reserves within five years. In the same period, both East Germany (by 188 percent) and Poland (by 41 percent) experienced substantial increases in their known reserves of natural gas. Presumably, some reserves now classified as "probable" or "possible" will continue to augment known reserves of natural gas in the region. If this fails to occur, production of natural gas in Eastern Europe could cease as early as the first quarter of the next century.

Commercially exploitable hydroelectric resources are concentrated primarily in Bulgaria, Romania, and the Carpathian Mountains along the border between Czechoslovakia and Poland. Romania alone possesses approximately 40 percent of these reserves. Czechoslovakia and Hungary are now jointly constructing (amid considerable technical and political difficulties) the huge Gabcikovo–Nagymaros barrage system to exploit the hydroelectric potential of the Danube River. Finally, the scanty data available publicly indicate that Czechoslovakia and Hungary, in that order, possess the largest reserves of uranium in Eastern Europe.

Table 1–5
Eastern Europe: Primary Energy Production and
Consumption
(average annual percentage change)

	Production[1] 1971–1985	Consumption[2] 1971–1984
Bulgaria	0.5	4.3
Czechoslovakia	0.8	1.8
East Germany	1.7	1.9
Hungary	1.4	3.3
Poland	2.2	2.9
Romania	2.2	3.8

Source: United Nations Economic Commission for Europe, *Economic Survey of Europe in 1986–1987*, 197, 200.

[1]Calculated from data on primary energy production converted into standard coal equivalent (coefficients vary across countries). Due to the methodology applied, the figures in this table may differ from national or other sources.

[2]Tons of oil equivalent.

After World War II, the Soviet Union imposed the Stalinist model of economic development on Eastern Europe. This greatly exacerbated the energy gap. Chapter 5 examines this subject in detail. In brief, this model (the so-called command economy) sought economic development primarily through *extensive* growth (quantitative increases in factor inputs, including energy) rather than *intensive* growth (qualitative increases in factor productivity). The model emphasized the development of energy-intensive industries such as steel, chemicals, and machine building as the foundation for constructing a Communist society. The ensuing increase in consumption of energy typically far outstripped the indigenous production of energy (table 1–5). A prominent Hungarian economist has argued that extensive growth still prevails throughout Eastern Europe: "The question whether an alternative growth path requiring less energy and raw material inputs is at all feasible has not even been seriously raised. If (this is so) more than a decade after the first oil price hike . . . it does not require much imagination to understand how strong and widespread this approach was in the 1960's and 1970's."[3]

Finally, Eastern European states are wasteful consumers of energy. Official data indicate that on average states of the Council for Mutual Economic Assistance (Comecon) consume between 30 and 50 percent (and some countries upward of 80 percent) more energy than do industrialized capitalist states to produce similar units of national income.[4] Their consumption of coal with a low caloric content, their obsolete machinery, the predominance of energy-intensive industries among power consumers, and the imperatives of economic plans that emphasize the production of goods rather than the conservation of inputs largely explain this circumstance. Indeed, Hungarian economists identify the "insatiable appetite" for fuels and energy, engendering a "persisting propensity to overconsume" these resources as the root cause of the region's energy gap.[5]

The Questions

The energy gap is an *ante factum* phenomenon. By definition, consumption cannot exceed supply of energy. How and with what consequences Eastern European states have closed the energy gap comprises the subject matter of this book.

Supply side initiatives to increase the amount of energy predominate in efforts to close the energy gap. These initiatives include importation of fuels and energy from the Soviet Union and the international energy market, as well as the expanded exploitation of indigenous reserves of energy. Eastern European states have yet to enact meaningful *demand-side* initiatives to regulate the consumption of energy. These initiatives raise critical questions of public policy.

These questions in the Soviet–Eastern European energy relationship relate primarily to the price and quantity of Soviet energy exports to its allies and to joint Comecon projects to develop the region's reserves of fuel and power. Most importantly, should the Soviet Union price its energy exports to Eastern Europe at world market prices (WMPs) and demand that its allies pay for these exports with hard currency and/or goods competitive on international markets? If not, then what should be the price, and how should it be computed? To the extent that the Eastern Europeans must allocate more resources to pay for Soviet energy, what consequences will this have on their capacity to import from the West advanced technology to modernize their economies and consumer goods to placate their populations? Concomitantly, such imports also can increase the capacity of Eastern Europe to produce more of the high-quality industrial and consumer goods that the Soviet Union increasingly demands in payment for energy. How does the Soviet Union assess the costs and benefits—in both economic and political terms—of its energy exports to Eastern Europe, and what are the policy implications of such an assessment? Does the Soviet Union increasingly see Eastern Europe as an economic liability that imports huge amounts of Soviet energy at subsidized prices? In contrast, does the Soviet Union view Eastern Europe as providing political and economic services—for example, diplomatic and material support for Soviet foreign policy initiatives or participation in joint pro-

jects to develop energy and raw material reserves in the Soviet Union—
that mitigate the cost of whatever subsidy it extends to the region?

What will be the future quantity of Soviet energy exports to Eastern
Europe? Will the Soviet Union maintain the present level of these exports
if its own production of oil does not increase and depressed WMPs for
energy impel it to export more of its total energy output to capitalist
countries to earn requisite sums of hard currency? Or will the Soviet
Union behave as it did in 1982 when these same circumstances impelled it
to reduce oil exports to Eastern Europe by approximately 10 percent?
How does the Soviet Union assess the opportunity costs of these policy
options? Does it perceive that reductions in vital supplies of energy could
engender in Eastern Europe economic and political dislocations deleterious
to the interests of both itself and its allies? Should the Soviet Union
maximize its petroleum exports to capitalist countries, currently the Soviet
Union's single largest source of hard currency, and then help the Eastern
Europeans in other ways to resolve their energy problems, or should it
simply accept the existence of these problems and their attendant economic and political dislocations?

What are the optimum strategies within Comecon to close the energy
gap? Should Comecon emphasize the production of energy through joint
projects or the conservation of existing reserves? How can creditors (typically Eastern European states) determine the economic efficiency of joint
projects when their contributions are valued in the arbitrarily established
domestic prices of the debtor state (typically the Soviet Union)? What
would "real" prices in joint projects reveal about the distribution of benefits and burdens among creditors and debtors? Would it be better to
allocate some portion of the huge requisite resources for joint projects to
the importation of advanced technologies from the West to modernize
obsolete production processes and concomitantly reduce consumption of
energy?

Eastern Europe's effort to close part of its energy gap through purchases on the international energy market also engenders questions. First,
how much energy can and should Eastern Europe purchase on this market? Will OPEC (Organization of Petroleum Exporting Countries) nations
demand hard currency or accept barter in payment for these purchases? If
payment is in hard currency, where will Eastern Europe acquire the necessary reserves? Will they acquire them primarily through borrowing on
capitalist markets, and, if so, what will be the policy implications of this
indebtedness on East–West relations and relations between individual socialist and capitalist states? Will they be more likely to seek this hard
currency through increased trade with capitalist states, and, if they do,
what political and economic implications arise from diverting domestic
reserves to the export market? Will the Soviet Union, which charges

WMPs for its energy exports to capitalist states, pursue its own economic and political self-interest and support OPEC when it raises prices, even though Eastern Europe must now pay more for energy imported from this source and for many goods imported from the West?

What will be the political implications of importation from the international energy market? How will the Soviet Union and its allies react if instability threatens a politically conservative regime—Iran under the Shah, for example—that nevertheless supplies Soviet bloc countries with oil? Will they seek to exacerbate this instability to enhance their own influence in the country and their revolutionary image among radical forces? Or will they view the instability as threatening their economic self-interest and seek to support the regime and/or provide little, if any, encouragement to the forces opposing it? Will Eastern European states pursue multilateral or bilateral approaches to expand energy importation from the international market? If the approaches are bilateral, will these states become competitors of one another for the same markets? Could such competition accelerate centrifugal forces within the bloc itself?

A final series of questions relates to domestic initiatives to close the energy gap. In the conservation of energy, these questions concern the economic and political feasibility of altering those features of the command economy that promote the excessive consumption of energy. Where will Eastern Europe in an era of severe budgetary constraints acquire the requisite investment monies (especially hard currency) to replace energy-inefficient production technologies and transform industrial infrastructures now dominated by energy-intensive industries? Can political elites muster the will to acquire these monies primarily by using investments now devoted to expanding the production of energy? These investments currently make up between 40 and 45 percent of total investments in industry in all Eastern European states.[6] How can consumers be provided with a monetary incentive to conserve energy resources when prices for these resources do not reflect marginal costs? Will increases in retail prices for commodities to reflect the marginal costs of energy contained therein spark the type of political turmoil found in Poland in 1970 and 1976? In 1970, the announcement of such increases precipitated riots that toppled Polish United Workers party (PUWP) leader Wladysaw Gomulka, and in 1976 a similar announcement again led to rioting that almost ousted Gomulka's successor, Edward Gierek. In lieu of monetary incentives to conserve energy, how can consumers realistically be compelled to pursue this end?

The production of energy engenders equally difficult questions. Most importantly, is it economically rational to devote 40 to 45 percent of all investments in industry to exploiting energy reserves such as brown coal and lignite that are of low, and continuously declining, quality? Should Eastern Europe reconsider its overwhelming reliance on low-quality solid fuels in primary energy consumption, given the enormous deterioration in the quality of the environment and the ensuing threat to public health attendant upon their exploitation? What is the future status of nuclear power in the region, especially after the explosion at the Chernobyl nuclear power station (NPS) in the Soviet Union? Chernobyl graphically refuted the official contention that nuclear accidents could occur only under capitalism, where the rapacious pursuit of profit compromised safety. How should governments respond to strident critics of nuclear power who demand that ambitious nuclear programs either be abandoned or substantially scaled back? And if this demand is met, where will Eastern Europe find the energy reserves to compensate for the loss of nuclear power capacities?

These provide only a suggestive list of the policy questions with which Eastern Europe's political leaders must now and in the future grapple. All answers to these questions engender painful policy dilemmas, entail obvious costs, and provide no panacea to resolve the region's energy problems.

Methodology

The scope of this study is *comprehensive*: It encompasses the energy gaps of all Eastern European states. The analysis is *comparative* and explicitly seeks to identify similarities and differences among regimes of the region. The study firmly roots its contemporary analysis within an *historical* context. It assumes that understanding the past constitutes the sine qua non for apprehending the present and future. The study asks questions that are *policy oriented*. The subject matter is *interdisciplinary*, involving the disciplines of economics, geography, history, and political science.

Chapters 2 through 5, which examine the principal supply- and demand-side initiatives to close the energy gap, compose the core of the study. Chapter 2 examines the Soviet–Eastern European energy relationship from its inception to the present and assesses its probable future evolution. Chapter 3 examines indigenous programs to expand the production of energy. Chapter 4 details efforts to close a portion of the energy gap through importation from the international market. Chapter 5 focuses on nascent efforts to limit the demand for energy through energy conservation programs. The concluding chapter assesses the future status of the energy gap through a retrospective analysis of the principal findings of this study.

Professor George Hoffman, former director of the East European Program at the Woodrow Wilson Center for International Studies, has lamented that in the United States, "we know absolutely nothing about Eastern Europe."[7] Professor Hoffman's own writings illustrate that this criticism is not always warranted. Nevertheless, it is a truism that empirically oriented comparative analyses of the Eastern European polities are not abundant.

The absence of comprehensive and reliable data contributes to this circumstance. Eastern European scholars themselves recognize the difficulty of verifying economic and political hypotheses about their region "empirically, on a systematic basis."[8]

The present study also has encountered this problem. I have already noted the limited data available on primary energy reserves in the region. Another aspect is the key issue of the volume of Soviet oil exports to Eastern Europe. The Soviet Union did not publish official statistics on this subject between 1977 and 1987. Bulgaria continues to withhold data on the volume of both its exports and imports of oil. Data also may be falsified. For example, Polish sources now admit that official data deliberately overstated by upward of 20 percent output of coal in the late 1970s.[9]

Of course, if complete data on a subject constituted the sine qua non for publication, then relatively few books would ever be written. I have drawn upon an extensive body of both primary and secondary sources in my research. Detailed discussions with scholars in both the United States and Eastern Europe supplemented this research. The following analysis demonstrates that an adequate base of data exists to examine comprehensively the energy gap.

2
The Supply Side:
Importation from the Soviet Union

> During the years of the energy and raw material crisis Comecon was the only group in the world to overcome its distressing consequences relatively painlessly. This was achieved first and foremost by means of fuel, power and raw materials . . . from the USSR. (The USSR) in doing this often restricted its own growing requirements in the interests of raising the level of economic development and cooperation of the fraternal countries.
>
> —TASS, 14 November 1985

This statement contains an accurate, an incorrect, and a debatable proposition. That exportation from the Soviet Union has been the "first and foremost" means of closing the energy gap is undeniable. Eastern Europe imports almost all of its natural gas, 80 percent of its imports of crude oil and petroleum products, and more than 70 percent of its imports of hard coal from the Soviet Union. In 1985, all Eastern European states except Romania derived more than 75 percent of their total imports of energy from the Soviet Union (the figure for Romania was approximately 19 percent).[1]

However, the Soviet Union has not closed Eastern Europe's energy gap "relatively painlessly." Numerous disputes and acrimonious debates, veiled (and sometimes explicit) criticism of the Soviet Union, and the overall vigorous explication of individual national interests have characterized Soviet–Eastern European energy relations. Many Eastern Europeans also would contend that the Soviet Union has not "often" subordinated its own interests to those of the "fraternal countries." For example, a Hungarian commentary argues that economic self-interest prevails when the Soviet Union prices its energy exports:

> We have to be aware that cooperation is not an altruistic thing; it is not a matter of sentiment. If something justifiably costs more to someone . . . the extra cost is an objective fact. In other words, it cannot be expected that someone should one sidedly bear this extra cost. Since we import a significant part of our raw material and energy sources from the Soviet Union, we have to pay more for these.[2]

Table 2–1

Eastern Europe: Volume and Geographic Distribution of Gross Imports and Exports of Solid and Liquid Fuels by Area of Origin and Destination

East Europe's Trade with Listed Area	Solid Fuels (MT of hard coal equivalent)			Liquid Fuels (MT) Total			Refined Fuels		
	1955	1960	1965	1955	1960	1965	1955	1960	1965
Total (in weight units)									
Imports	18.3	22.0	31.4	4.1	10.6	25.0	1.7	3.7	4.9
Exports	34.3	30.7	34.4	7.4	7.7	10.4	7.0	7.3	9.3
Areas (in percentages)									
Eastern Europe (intra-area)									
Imports	72.3	50.6	42.3	26.8	7.9	3.9	39.8	17.2	16.6
Exports	38.2	35.9	38.0	11.2	9.1	8.4	8.4	6.8	7.8
Soviet Union									
Imports	19.8	45.1	53.2	52.1	88.6	91.9	29.5	78.5	82.0
Exports	25.1	16.8	20.7	49.5	39.2	15.6	51.0	39.1	17.5
Other Communist countries									
Imports	*	*	*	*	0.1	*	*	0.4	*
Exports	—	—	—	0.4	4.4	11.6	0.4	4.3	9.2
Other world									
Imports	7.8	4.3	4.4	21.1	3.4	4.2	30.7	3.8	1.4
Exports	36.6	47.3	41.3	38.9	47.4	64.7	40.2	49.7	65.9
Western Europe									
Imports	5.1	2.8	1.5	4.3	0.5	0.3	9.4	1.4	1.4
Exports	31.4	42.1	39.9	28.5	33.6	31.3	29.4	35.1	33.6

Source: Polach, "The Development of Energy in East Europe," table 18.
*Negligible.

Energy Relations: 1960–1985

Eastern European states have closed their energy gaps since the 1960s primarily through importation from the Soviet Union. Whereas in 1955 the Soviet Union was still a net importer of both solid and liquid fuels from Eastern Europe, by 1960 it had become a net exporter of these fuels to the region. By 1960, the Soviet Union accounted for 52 percent of Eastern Europe's importation of solid fuels and 89 percent of its importation of liquid fuels. However, through the 1960s, Eastern Europe remained a net exporter of both solid and liquid fuels to the world market, especially to Western Europe (table 2–1).[3] This was due largely to exports of coal and coke from Poland and Czechoslovakia and exports of crude oil and petroleum products from Romania.

The construction of crude oil and natural gas pipelines and a uniform electric power grid in the 1960's considerably augmented the capacity of the Soviet Union to export to Eastern Europe. Political considerations largely determined these initiatives. Soviet Communist party leader Nikita Khrushchev sought after the uprisings in Hungary and Poland in 1956 to mitigate the economic exploitation of the satellites. In particular, Soviet oil would provide the raw material base to develop petrochemical industries in Czechoslovakia, East Germany, Hungary, and Poland. The emphasis on petrochemicals also reflected Soviet priorities because Khrushchev simultaneously sought the "chemicalization" of Soviet industry. Ironically, then, Eastern Europe's energy gap, which has become such a contentious issue, originates in part from initiatives designed to foster political harmony and economic prosperity within the "socialist commonwealth."

These projects became public in 1958 when Soviet first deputy premier Anastas Mikoyan announced that the Soviet Union would construct a "gigantic" pipeline to bring "millions of tons of oil" annually from fields in the Volga region to Eastern Europe. The Druzhba (Friendship) oil pipeline network transmits this oil through a northern branch to Poland and East Germany and through a southern branch to Czechoslovakia and Hungary. Each of the participating states was responsible for construction of the pipeline on its territory and purchased much of the necessary equipment from the Soviet Union. By 1967, the Druzhba network was carrying approximately 18 million tons (MT) of crude oil annually from the Soviet Union to Eastern Europe.[4]

The energy relationship already exhibited tension. Thus, the group that ousted Khrushchev from power in 1964 accused him of incorrectly excluding Romania from the Druzhba project.[5] The project also strained relations with the West. The United States sought unsuccessfully to delay or prevent completion of the pipeline by banning the use of Western equipment and technology in its construction.

The Soviet Union concluded agreements with Czechoslovakia in 1966 and East Germany in 1967 for even more Soviet oil. The agreement with Czechoslovakia obligated the Soviet Union to deliver annually between 1973 and 1984 5 MT of crude oil at 15 transferable rubles (TR) per ton in exchange for a 500 million TR credit from Czechoslovakia to purchase machinery, materials, and consumer goods. Apparently, the agreement also provided for additional deliveries of at least 30 MT of oil, but terms for such deliveries remain unpublished. Even fewer details are available regarding the agreement with East Germany, but its main provisions appear similar to those concluded with Czechoslovakia. Obviously, both countries benefited enormously from these agreements, for they each received 60 MT of crude oil at far below WMPs. Whether this circumstance represented a conscious decision by the Soviet Union to subsidize these countries or whether the Soviet Union simply failed to predict accurately the future course of world oil prices remain moot questions. During the Prague Spring in Czechoslovakia in 1968, critics rejected the former inter-

Table 2–2
Eastern Europe: Importation of Energy, 1970
(percent)

	Importation as Share of Consumption	Importation from Soviet Union as Share of Importation
Bulgaria	63	86
Czechoslovakia	29	80
East Germany	26	66
Hungary	43	66
Poland	14	87
Romania	11	19

Source: National Foreign Assessment Center, *Energy Supplies in Eastern Europe: A Statistical Compilation*, tables 15 and 16.

pretation and alleged that the agreement revealed the exploitive nature of the Soviet policy because the contract price was above the WMP for oil.[6]

Exports of natural gas to Eastern Europe developed far more slowly. The Soviet Union began exporting small quantities of gas via border-crossing pipelines to Poland in the late 1950s and to Czechoslovakia in 1967. In July 1968, the first section of the Bratstvo (Brotherhood) natural gas pipeline network linking gas fields in Soviet Ukraine with Czechoslovakia and Austria became operational. In 1968, both Czechoslovakia and East Germany—in agreements similar to those they had concluded for oil—extended loans to the Soviet Union for the construction of natural gas pipelines in return for Soviet deliveries of this fuel after 1970. Significant deliveries of Soviet natural gas awaited the expansion of the Bratstvo network that occurred in the 1970s.[7]

Finally, in the 1960s, the European states of Comecon began linking their electric power grids through the Mir (Peace) uniform power grid network. In 1962, Comecon established the Central Dispatching Administration for the Joint Power System of Comecon Countries. The Mir network lowered the unit cost of transferred electricity and enhanced the capacity of these states to meet peak demands for power. In 1967, the member states exchanged approximately 8.7 billion kwh of electricity through the system compared to 708 million kwh exchanged among themselves in 1956.[8]

Thus, by the end of the 1960s, the infrastructure that permitted the substantial expansion of Soviet energy exports in the following decade was in place. Table 2–2 indicates the role that importation played in closing Eastern Europe's energy gap as of 1970.

The Soviet Union subsequently expanded energy exports to Eastern

Europe despite admonitions that its allies should rely more on indigenous reserves and on importation from the world market to close their energy gaps. In a harbinger of arguments made even more insistently in subsequent years, Soviet analysts asserted that escalating costs incurred in exploiting and transporting energy reserves located increasingly in remote and inhospitable regions of western Siberia made their export to Eastern Europe too expensive.[9] However, an Eastern Europe less dependent on the Soviet Union for vital raw materials—and commensurately less susceptible to political pressure—was probably unappealing to Soviet leaders after the turmoil in Czechoslovakia in 1968.

At any rate, Soviet energy exports to Eastern Europe increased at annual rates of 9.5 percent and 6 percent, respectively, in the periods 1971–1975 and 1976–1980. Between 1976 and 1980, to Eastern Europe the Soviet Union sent more than 370 MT of crude oil and oil products, 98 billion m³ of natural gas, 57 billion kwh of electricity, and 41 MT of coal and coke. Exports of natural gas increased rapidly during these years as East Germany (1973), Bulgaria (1974), and Hungary (1975) began importation. Natural gas grew from 3 percent to 16 percent of total Soviet energy exports between 1970 and 1980, whereas exports of crude oil and oil products declined from 78 percent to about 73 percent.[10] Importation of fuels and energy from the Soviet Union in 1979 constituted more than 90 percent of net energy imports in Bulgaria, East Germany, and Hungary and approximately 85 percent of these imports in Czechoslovakia. Poland was still a net exporter of energy in 1979, while Romania imported no oil from the Soviet Union before 1979.

The information available publicly indicated that Soviet energy exports to Eastern Europe would continue to increase during the period 1981–1985. Thus, in 1979, Soviet premier Aleksey Kosygin announced that these exports would increase by approximately 20 percent during this period, although their rate of increase would be lower than, and their composition different from, those in the two previous five-year plan periods. Annual exports of crude oil would remain at approximately the level attained in 1980, while exports of natural gas would increase substantially. From 1981 to 1985, exports of crude oil and natural gas would make up 69 percent and 21 percent, respectively, of total Soviet energy exports to the region, versus 75 percent and 16 percent, respectively, from 1976 to 1980.[11] As late as 1981, official statements reflected these plans. For example, Erich Honecker, the East German Communist party leader, speaking at the party's national congress in April 1981, asserted that annual deliveries of oil from the Soviet Union "have been securely agreed upon on a long term basis." Similarly, the secretary general of Comecon reiterated that "under no circumstances" would Moscow reduce oil deliveries to Eastern Europe before 1985.[12]

Table 2–3
Soviet Union: Exports of Crude Oil to Eastern Europe
(millions of metric tons)

	1981[1]	1983[1]	1987[2]	1983 as Percent of 1981	1987 as Percent of 1981
Bulgaria	12.3	11.2	11.5	91.1	93.5
Czechoslovakia	18.1	15.0	16.9	82.9	93.4
East Germany	19.1	17.1	19.8	89.5	103.6
Hungary	7.2	6.5	7.4	90.2	102.8
Poland	13.5	12.5	13.7	92.5	101.5
Romania	2.6	NA[3]	4.6	—	177.0

Sources: Data for 1981 and 1983 compiled from *Magyar Hirlap*, 1 February 1984; *Svet hospodarstvi*, 1 October 1985; *Trybuna ludu*, 13 March 1984; *Plan Econ Report: Developments in the Economies of the Soviet Union and Eastern Europe*, 1, nos. 17–18 (30 December 1985). Data for 1987 from *Vneshniaia torgovlia SSSR v 1987*, table 17.

[1] Estimated.

[2] Actual.

[3] Not available. Romania did not report any data on importation of crude oil for 1983 in the official Comecon statistical yearbook. It has reported data for all other years in the 1980s.

Suddenly, in 1982, the Soviet Union announced an approximately 10 percent reduction in its planned oil deliveries to Eastern Europe between 1982 and 1985. This decision apparently affected Czechoslovakia and East Germany most. Soviet oil deliveries to Bulgaria and Czechoslovakia have never again reached the level they attained in 1981. By 1987, however, these deliveries to East Germany, Hungary, and Poland were slightly above the 1981 level of importation (table 2–3).

On the one hand, a Western source predicted that the 1982 reduction in exportation "could push a number of countries in Soviet Europe to the brink of economic insolvency and political collapse. . . . Moscow may be forced to reckon with a mass revolt the likes of which it has never seen."[13] This assessment proved overly pessimistic, although several Eastern European states experienced considerable economic difficulties in the 1982–1985 period. Many variables, such as political turmoil in Poland, undoubtedly contributed to this circumstance. However, a Hungarian economist asserts that cutbacks in Soviet oil deliveries "played a decisive role" as well.[14]

On the other hand, some reduction in Soviet oil supplies could prove salutary to future economic growth by forcing officials to undertake economically necessary, but politically distasteful, measures (such as price increases for fuels) to stimulate the more efficient use of energy resources. Predictably, Eastern European officials, grappling with the immediate dislocations attendant upon sudden reductions in oil deliveries, derived little solace from this prospect. Even normally pro-Soviet officials expressed their concern. For example, Premier Lubomir Strougal of Czechoslovakia, quoted in *Rude pravo*, asserted that the realization of economic plans during 1984 and 1985 would depend "to no small extent on the fulfillment of agreed upon contracts within the Comecon framework." Strougal added "that the experience of recent years" clearly demonstrated that "the economies of our individual states react very sensitively to shortcomings in the development of mutual trade," and he pointedly noted that "any difficulties and complications in this sphere would have a chain reaction."[15]

Soviet policy toward Poland suggests the limits of the oil card to achieve political ends. That the Soviet Union has played this card in the enduring Polish crisis seems clear. A Western source reports that the Soviet Union curtailed deliveries of petroleum to Poland whenever it "stepped too far out of line." Polish leader Wojciech Jaruzelski recently justified his 1981 decision to impose martial law and ban Solidarity, the trade union movement, by asserting that the Soviet Union had threatened to cut off supplies of fuel and raw materials if he refused to do so.[16] Yet the setting in which Jaruzelski made this disclosure graphically symbolizes the failure of the oil card and martial law to crush Solidarity and stem the tide of reform in Poland. The disclosure came as Jaruzelski campaigned for the post of president before members of Solidarity who had been elected to the Sejm (the Polish parliament) in Poland's first free elections since 1945.

Romania: A Special Case

The Romanian–Soviet energy relationship remains sui generis in Eastern Europe. A shortage of hard currency to purchase crude oil on the world market for its petrochemical industry has led Romania since at least 1973 to seek a portion of its crude oil imports from the Soviet Union in guaranteed volumes and with payment in soft goods.[17]

The Soviet Union has not acceded to these demands, although it has sold crude to Romania for hard goods (principally foodstuffs and equipment for the oil and gas industries) since 1979.[18] Further, the Soviet Union has sought political advantage from this situation. At one point, Radio Moscow's Romanian service informed its listeners that the Soviet Union's "friends" in Comecon would receive adequate deliveries of crude oil on advantageous terms—a not very subtle hint that Romania could receive similar treatment if it became one of the Soviet Union's friends. In early 1984, news leaks from the Soviet Embassy in Bucharest (which Romania emphatically denied) alleged that the Soviet Union was selling Romania crude oil on "preferential conditions" with repayment in "closer foreign policy cooperation."[19]

These disputes have continued since Mikhail Gorbachev achieved power in 1985. Nicolae Ceausescu, head of the Romanian Communist party (RCP), charges that the Soviet Union has reneged on promises made in 1984 at the Comecon summit of political leaders to meet "in a better way" the requirements for raw materials and fuels of the member states. This pledge, Ceausescu contends, is "not being attained" in the coordination of Romanian–Soviet economic plans for 1986–1990.[20] Reportedly, the Soviet Union has agreed to sell Romania 5 MT of crude oil annually during these years.[21] In 1988, Radio Moscow's Romanian service also asserted that the Soviet Union would increase deliveries of electricity, coal, and natural gas over the levels attained in 1987 and over the levels called for in the 1986–1990 trade protocol between the two countries. However, Romania apparently continues to pay with hard commodities for all these deliveries.[22]

Soviet Energy Policy

Several factors will determine whether the Soviet Union might reduce energy supplies to Eastern Europe despite potentially serious political and economic costs. In particular, observers both inside and outside the Soviet Union repeatedly have expressed skepticism that indigenous energy production is sufficient for the Soviet Union simultaneously to satisfy internal demand, meet requirements for hard currency through energy exports to the world market, and continue as the primary source to close Eastern Europe's energy gap. The opportunity costs of pursuing these objectives concurrently are "extremely high," a Hungarian source has contended. This circumstance imparts a "firefighting mode" to energy policy as the Soviet Union continuously seeks to reconcile competing demands on its scarce resources.[23]

In one of the more pessimistic assessments of Soviet capabilities, the Central Intelligence Agency (CIA) predicted that sharply declining oil production in the 1980s could impel the Soviet Union to become a net importer of oil—a circumstance with ominous implications for Eastern Europe. Subsequently, the CIA, while retaining its generally conservative view of Soviet production capacities, amended this estimate and predicted that increased investments would permit the Soviet Union to meet its energy needs in the 1980s without net importation of oil. Several studies sharply challenged the CIA's prognoses. One study by the Defense Intelligence Agency (DIA) assesses Soviet energy prospects as "highly favorable," thereby permitting the Soviet Union to increase oil production and exports for the foreseeable future.[24]

Numerous Western analyses of the status of and prospects for Soviet energy make a similar exercise here superfluous.[25] However, several observations germane to this study are necessary. First, all Western prognoses of Soviet energy prospects are, at best, informed judgments based on key assumptions that are either controversial (for example, the size of Soviet petroleum reserves, which the Soviet government considers a state secret) or subject to changes in public policy (for example, the overall amount and distribution of resources invested within the energy sector). Typically, such imponderables have made Western assessments of the prospects for Soviet energy, in the words of one respected analyst, "pathetically wrong."[26]

Second, while mindful of these caveats, the prospects for a substantial increase in production of either petroleum or coal appear limited. Both the petroleum and coal industries failed to fulfill their annual production targets throughout the 1976–1985 period. In fact, the Soviet Union actually extracted less petroleum in 1985 than in 1980 (595 MT and 603 MT, respectively). While gross output of coal in 1985 exceeded the 1980 level by 10 MT, the declining caloric content of mined coal yielded almost 8 percent less energy in 1985, than in 1980.[27]

The performance of these industries revived somewhat in 1986 and 1987. The Soviet Union set records for extraction of petroleum in both years (615 MT and 624 MT, respectively). Extraction in 1987 even exceeded the plan target by 7 MT. This improved performance continued in the first quarter of 1988, when output was 2 percent higher than in the corresponding period for 1987. The coal industry also increased production in both 1986 and 1987. In 1987, gross coal production of 760 MT exceeded the plan target by 16 MT. However, the caloric value of mined coal continued to decline, so the energy yield from 1987 output was less than the comparable yield in 1980.

These developments indicate that both the petroleum and coal industries are likely to fulfill their production targets for 1990 of 635 MT and 795 MT, respectively.[28] Yet these targets must be placed in perspective. The 1990 target for both fuels falls within the range of output previously planned for these commodities in 1985. Whether the petroleum and coal industries can sustain their performance beyond 1990 also is questionable. For example, several initiatives that have increased the output of petroleum, including an extensive program of well repair and mechanization, likely will stimulate production only in the short run.

In contrast, the problems besetting the petroleum industry are manifest and seemingly intractable. These include:

- poor management
- peaking or declining output at major fields
- limited discovery of new reserves
- enormous costs in exploiting reserves located predominantly in western Siberia
- severe labor shortages in western Siberia
- a premium system that promotes production at the expense of sound mining practices.

A Western student of these issues accurately commented that a catalogue of problems plaguing the petroleum industry "would run to many pages."[29]

Third, nuclear power will not in the foreseeable future, as many once thought, prove the panacea of the country's energy problems. The Soviet nuclear industry had encountered considerable problems in fulfilling its production targets even before the explosion at the Chernobyl NPS on April 26, 1986. Whereas by 1985 nuclear power was supposed to account for 14 percent of total electricity production, by 1988 it actually accounted for only 12.7 percent of such production.[30]

The disaster at Chernobyl only exacerbated these problems. The Soviet Union is spending as much as $5 million for additional safety systems on every operational reactor. Henceforth, the Soviet Union will equip all reactors with steel containment vessels to control meltdowns. Previously, it had argued that its fail-safe technology made such vessels (standard features on Western reactors) superfluous. The Soviet Union also has announced that all new power blocks will be equipped with the pressurized-water reactors standard throughout Eastern Europe rather than the graphite-moderated reactors of the type installed at Chernobyl. And, most significantly, the Soviet Union, citing dangers posed by nuclear facilities located in areas of high seismicity and dense population, has halted construction at six NPS's with planned capacities of 28 million kw. The now abandoned capacities were equal to installed nuclear capacity in 1985.[31]

Public opposition to nuclear power—undoubtedly facilitated by Communist party leader Mikhail Gorbachev's stress on *glasnost* (openness) in public discussion—also emerged in the wake of the Chernobyl disaster.[32] This is especially true in the Ukrainian Republic where the Chernobyl plant is located. Prominent Ukrainian scientists and literary figures have lobbied vigorously to halt, or at least slow down, the ambitious program to develop nuclear power in the republic. (At present, five NPS's, accounting for 40 percent of installed nuclear capacity in the Soviet Union, operate in the republic, and four more NPS's are currently under construction.) A public letter from thirteen leading Ukrainian scientists embodies many arguments of the opponents of nuclear power.[33] The scientists chastise the Ministry of Atomic Energy for a "belligerent and bureaucratic" attitude that seeks only to expand the production of nuclear power, that ignores the "bitter lessons of Chernobyl," that is indifferent to the valid concerns of the public regarding the safety and impact on the environment of NPS's, and that typically locates these stations in conurbations. Critics also charge that Ukraine is being exploited to benefit Eastern Europe, since several of these NPS's, including Chernobyl, supply electricity to the Mir network.

Many ordinary citizens express similar concerns. Reportedly, since Chernobyl doctors in some areas spend "most of their working time" in "combating radiation phobia" among citizens fearful of contamination from nearby NPS's.[34] Readers of *Izvestiia* raise what the newspaper itself labels the "difficult and very acute" question of the location of NPS's contiguous to, or even within, conurbations. These readers, *Izvestiia* reports, say "that the public is indignant; it protests, but no one takes any notice. Power engineers are building nuclear installations wherever it suits them."[35] Other citizens, particularly religious believers, view Chernobyl (which means "wormwood") as a harbinger of the Apocalypse. They note that in St. John the Divine (Rev. 8:10–11), a great star fell from heaven upon the waters of the earth, "and the name of the star is Wormwood; and the third part of the waters became wormwood; and many people died of the waters, because they were made bitter."

One should not summarily dismiss public opposition to nuclear power as ineffectual. The Soviet Union has now established an Interdepartmental Council for Information and Ties with the Public in the Nuclear Power Sphere. The council seeks to "analyze public opinion, ensure **glasnost**, and monitor the safety of nuclear plants' work." Soviet sources themselves contend that public opinion played an important role in recent decisions to suspend construction at several NPS's.[36] Admittedly, the secrecy (even in the era of glasnost) surrounding the Soviet policy-making process prevents outside observers from verifying this contention.

Fourth, natural gas has become a key component of the Soviet energy balance. The share of oil in domestic energy consumption declined from 39 percent in 1980 to 32 percent in 1987, while consumption of natural gas increased from 27 percent to 37 percent. Natural gas was the only energy resource that met its plan production targets in the 1976–1985 period, and it is the only major fuel whose production target was substantially raised in the current five-year plan. Production of natural gas increased by approximately 60 percent between 1981 and 1987. In the first half of 1988, production was 7 percent higher than in first half of 1987 and 3 percent above the plan target. As noted, Soviet exports of natural gas to Eastern Europe have increased rapidly since the 1970s and continue to make up a larger share of total energy exports to the region.

Unlike oil, already known reserves of natural gas—which compose almost 40 percent of proven natural gas reserves in the world—are ample to meet projected production targets. Moreover, new discoveries of economically exploitable deposits continue to add to proven natural gas reserves. But like oil, natural gas development encounters the same imposing technological, infrastructural, locational, and environmental problems associated with the exploitation of reserves located primarily in Siberia.[37] The Yamburg natural gas field, which is scheduled to provide the entire increment in natural gas production in the current economic plan, is one example. The word for Yamburg in the native Nenets language means "great marshland," an accurate designation for the geography of the region under exploitation. The area has no indigenous population, housing and a transportation infrastructure were nonexistent before exploitation began, the temperatures are extreme for most of the year, and much of the work can proceed only in winter when heavy machinery will not sink in the marshy land. Environmentalists warn that the exploitation of oil and gas "at any cost" is creating a "catastrophe" in the fragile ecosystem of the region. Development at Yamburg already has fallen behind schedule, requiring increased output at other fields to meet production targets.[38]

Finally, in this entire debate about the prospects of Soviet energy production, the fact of paramount significance for Eastern Europe is that it is unlikely to receive any appreciable increase in crude oil from the Soviet Union. In 1985, the Soviet Union exported to socialist (mostly Eastern European) countries approximately 11.25 percent less crude oil and petroleum products than it did in 1980. In both 1986 and 1987, Soviet deliveries of crude oil to all Eastern European states except Romania remained essentially unchanged.[39] Reports from Hungary and Poland indicate that the Soviet Union intends to maintain its present levels of exportation to them through 1995.[40]

Soviet Energy Trade with the West

That exports of energy to capitalist countries are the primary source of hard currency for the Soviet Union also affects Soviet willingness to export energy to Eastern Europe. The Soviet Union uses this hard currency to purchase Western technology and machinery to modernize its industry and grain to feed its people. Between 1976 and 1981, the volume of Soviet oil exports to capitalist countries actually declined slightly, but escalating WMPs for this commodity provided the Soviet Union with almost three times as much hard currency from its sale in 1981 as in

1976. This circumstance, combined with increases in indigenous energy production during these years, then permitted the Soviet Union to expand its energy exports to Eastern Europe.[41]

The Soviet Union has exported energy to Western Europe for decades, but this trade expanded after 1970. Between 1970 and 1980, exports of Soviet oil to Western Europe rose from 33 MT to almost 54 MT, and gas exports grew dramatically to approximately 20 MT of oil equivalent. This trend continued, and in 1986 exports of oil (crude and products) and natural gas to Western Europe were 35 percent and 51 percent higher, respectively, than the level attained in 1980.[42]

The increase in Soviet gas deliveries and the concomitant need to construct a new pipeline on Soviet territory (the so-called Siberian gas export line) for their transmission provoked a bitter controversy between the United States and several of its allies in Western Europe. The export line transmits natural gas from the world's largest gas field, located at Urengoi in western Siberia, over more than 4,500 km of Soviet territory, much of it rugged terrain filled with marshes, ice fields, and forests. The line crosses eight hundred waterways and the Ural Mountains and exits the Soviet Union at Uzhgorod, where it connects with pipelines in Czechoslovakia to bring the gas to markets in Western Europe. The need to import more than $5 billion in wide-diameter pipe, compressor stations, and turbines from Japan and Western Europe made the project the largest East–West trade deal in history.[43]

The United States—arguing that the West should not provide the Soviet Union with a hard currency windfall through gas sales, that Western credits and loans for the project carried overly lenient terms, and that the Soviet Union could exploit Western European dependence on Soviet gas to its political advantage in a crisis—sought unsuccessfully to prevent or delay construction of the pipeline. Proponents of the pipeline argued that the United States greatly exaggerated the degree of dependence on the Soviet Union that the pipeline would bring. Proponents also reversed the argument regarding dependence by contending that the pipeline would give Western Europe leverage over the Soviet Union because the latter needed hard currency earned from energy exports far more than the former needed Soviet natural gas. Finally, proponents saw sanctions as futile because the Soviet Union possessed the requisite capacities to build the pipeline itself. If anything, proponents argued, sanctions would be counterproductive, since they would force the Soviet Union to develop its own capacities in these fields and thereby lessen its dependence on the West for sophisticated technologies.[44]

Developments on the international energy market in the 1980s mitigated much of this controversy. A complex of well-known factors—economic recession in the West, successful efforts aimed at conservation of energy in key importing states, and the expanding role of energy exporters such as Britain and Norway—drove the WMP for oil down from approximately $34 per barrel in 1981 to under $15 per barrel in 1986 (and even less on the spot market). This development also adversely affected the export price for natural gas, which was tied to the WMP for oil. According to one Western analyst, the Soviet Union responded to this situation by "frantically trying to remain in the market, even at the expense of its allies." Thus, in 1982 and 1983, it increased its exports of crude oil and petroleum products to nonsocialist states by 25.9 percent and 17.4 percent, respectively, while simultaneously cutting crude oil exports to Eastern Europe by 10 percent.[45] The Soviet Union, which traditionally charges capitalist countries the WMP for oil, even risked alienating its political friends (and foes) in OPEC by engaging in a price war that saw it slash its price for crude in 1983 below the official OPEC price in a desperate attempt to retain hard currency customers in Western Europe. The Soviet Union also sought this end by seeking (unsuccessfully) to create a spot market for natural gas in which it could sell this fuel at below official OPEC prices. Reportedly, these initiatives sparked "grave concern" among OPEC officials, who thereupon initiated a "dialogue" with the Soviets about honoring OPEC benchmark prices.[46]

An export strategy of maintaining hard currency earnings through increases in volume rather than price proved effective through 1984. These earnings actually peaked in 1983 at $23.6 billion. However, this strategy was unsustainable after 1984 as WMPs continued their decline (from around $29 per barrel in 1984 to between $15 and $17 per barrel in 1987). In both 1986 and 1987, the Soviet Union established records for volume of energy exports to nonsocialist states, but its earnings from these exports were only $13.5 billion and $16 billion, respectively. The declining value of the dollar (by which international oil sales are denominated) made the loss in hard currency purchasing power even greater than these data suggest. For instance, in constant prices, one barrel of Soviet crude oil in 1987 could purchase from West Germany approximately two–thirds less goods than it could in 1984.[47] These developments prompted critics to argue that the Soviet Union must reduce its reliance on energy resources to earn hard currency. One critic asserted that the Soviet Union has become merely a "raw materials appendage" to the West, and another castigated those officials "who do not understand that the 'oil El Dorado' cannot go on forever, that prices in the world market are unstable, and that it is necessary to prepare for less favorable times."[48]

The energy glut in the short run clearly redounded adversely on Eastern Europe. Eastern European states suffered directly from depressed prices for oil and petroleum products because they also export these commodities to the world market.[49] More importantly, the Soviet decision to divert oil supplies from Eastern Europe to hard currency markets fostered both economic dislocations and tensions in managing the energy gap in the region. The Soviet leadership has been sensitive to these attendant costs of its policy. It has sought, with seeming success to date, to reduce oil exports to the lowest level compatible with maintaining requisite economic and political stability in the region.[50]

Yet the energy glut also benefits Eastern Europe. Lower WMPs for energy have already made Soviet energy cheaper for Eastern Europe. The Soviet Union also may export more natural gas to Eastern Europe than originally contemplated if its gas exports to Western Europe fall significantly below initial projections. Analysts in both the East and the West predict that in this century the supply will exceed the demand for Soviet natural gas in Western Europe.[51] Then, too, less demand for oil on the world market enhances Eastern Europe's prospects for concluding deals on favorable terms with noncommunist states anxious to reduce surplus stocks. Finally, Eastern European states benefit to the extent that they respond to reduced deliveries of Soviet oil by enacting effective measures to reduce their excessive consumption of energy.

The world energy glut also may not persist, and the present incentive and means to acquire hard currency may change in the Soviet Union. The former condition could arise if several developments—such as rapid economic expansion in major industrialized countries that engenders increased demand for energy or conflict in the Middle East that reduces or cuts off supplies of oil from that politically volatile region—occur either singly or in combination. This scenario, with its attendant increase in WMPs for energy, might then allow the Soviet Union to pursue its export strategy of the late 1970s, when escalating WMPs permitted it to earn sufficient hard currency while simultaneously holding energy exports to capitalist countries relatively constant and increasing exports to Eastern Europe. The latter condition could materialize if Mikhail Gorbachev's program of *perestroika* (restructuring the national economy) substantially increases both the quantity and quality of foodstuffs and industrial products. This would then permit the Soviet Union to reduce importation of foodstuffs and machinery from the West and increase exportation of high-quality manufactured commodities to that part of the world. Concomitantly, this scenario would lessen the imperative to export energy to the West and provide more energy for export to Eastern Europe. Naturally, neither scenario will likely emerge in pure form, and neither may emerge at all, but this analysis does suggest that the Soviet–Eastern European energy relationship is not impervious to change.

The Price Issue

What the Eastern Europeans pay for Soviet energy also determines the course of their relationship. Between 1958 and 1975, prices in Comecon trade followed the so-called Bucharest formula—that is, prices for individual commodities were established for a five-year period and based on the average WMP ("cleansed" of the effects of "monopoly," "speculation," and other "distortions" found in the capitalist economic system) for that commodity in the preceding five-year period. In a provision that became relevant when world energy prices began skyrocketing after 1973, the Bucharest formula permitted ad hoc adjustments in contract prices if unanticipated developments in international trade necessitated them.[52]

Considerable controversy exists over whether the Soviets or the Eastern Europeans benefited more from this formula. As noted, this subject arose in 1968, when reformers in Czechoslovakia accused the Soviet Union of exploiting that country by charging above WMPs for oil. A careful Western study of the subject not only supported this charge but found that during the 1960s the Soviet Union consistently charged customers in Eastern Europe more for all fuels than it charged capitalist customers. Yet Eastern Europeans also exploited the Soviet Union by paying with soft goods for most Soviet exports and by charging the Soviet Union above WMPs for exports of machinery, equipment, and energy resources such as coal from Poland.[53]

The rapid escalation in world energy prices after the October 1973 war between Israel and the Arab states temporarily suspended this debate and permanently ended the Bucharest formula. Eastern European officials initially argued that higher energy prices would not affect them because prices in Comecon trade were not scheduled for revision until 1976. However, by March 1974, the official Comecon price for oil was already 80 percent below the comparable WMP. This circumstance prompted intensive discussions and threatened deep divisions within Comecon as the Soviet Union demanded an immediate revision of the Bucharest formula. The ensuing revision entailed a special price increase for 1975 (reportedly the Soviet Union unsuccessfully sought a retroactive increase to 1974) and thereafter annual adjustments in prices based on average WMPs for individual commodities in the preceding five-year period. This formula represented a compromise between the divergent economic interests of the Soviet Union and Eastern Europe: By bringing Comecon prices for energy closer to WMPs but by delaying increases in WMPs for up to one year in Comecon prices, it benefited the Soviet Union and Eastern Europe, respectively.[54] Table 2–4 illustrates how these changes affected the official Comecon price for oil between 1978 and 1984.

Table 2–4
Eastern Europe: Estimated Price of Soviet Oil
(dollars per barrel)

Year	World Market Price	Comecon Price	Comecon Price as Percent of World Price
1978	12.70	11.39	90
1979	17.26	13.89	80
1980	30.22	14.01	46
1981	32.50	15.67	48
1982	34.00	21.91	64
1983	29.00	25.89	89
1984	28.20	27.28	97

Source: RFE *Background Report*, no. 155 (24 August 1984).

If one interprets these data literally, prevailing prices for oil in Comecon trade through 1984 represented an economic windfall for Eastern Europe. This circumstance arose, in part, because of the one-year lag between increases in WMPs and those in Comecon prices. Eastern Europe especially benefited from this delay through 1978, when the Comecon price included the relatively lower WMPs for oil existing before 1974.

Eastern Europe actually benefited even more than these data suggest. In reality, table 2–4 overstates the price of Soviet oil because it uses the artificially high official exchange rate to convert rubles into dollars. Table 2–5 presents an attempt, based on computations by Hungarian foreign trade experts, to determine the real price of Soviet oil to Eastern Europe by using more realistic exchange rates.[55]

Table 2–5
Eastern Europe: Estimated Price of Soviet Oil Using Realistic Exchange Rates
(dollars per barrel)

Year	World Market Price	Comecon Price	"Real" Comecon Price as Percent of World Price
1978	12.70	6.78	53
1979	17.26	8.23	48
1980	30.22	7.74	26
1981	32.50	8.79	27
1982	34.00	11.26	33
1983	29.00	11.52	40
1984	28.20	11.58	41

Source: RFE *Background Report*, no. 155 (24 August 1984).

Eastern Europe also pays for most Soviet energy in soft goods. This condition persists despite repeated demands by the Soviet Union that Eastern Europe improve the quality of goods it exchanges for Soviet energy.[56] Analysts differ over whether many of these goods are sold at inflated prices in Comecon trade; if they are, Eastern Europe derives even greater benefits from this trade.[57] Finally, since 1975, Eastern Europe as a whole has experienced a huge (although declining) trade deficit with the Soviet Union—attributable primarily to the price of imported Soviet energy and raw materials—thereby making the former an involuntary creditor to the latter.[58]

However, other factors increase the price that Eastern Europe pays for Soviet energy. First, the Eastern Europeans claim that they too must buy soft goods from the Soviet Union at inflated prices to compensate the latter for losses it allegedly incurs in energy sales. A Hungarian source explained: "The profits of our Soviet partner derived among other things from the fact that it was able to sell commodities which it would have been unable to sell on the world market, or at least not at the same price. . . . [I]t was able to have costs acknowledged by the socialist countries which were not accepted at all or to a smaller degree by other nonsocialist partners."[59] The Eastern Europeans also claim that the Soviet Union seeks to exchange soft goods for hard goods in Comecon trade. This applies particularly to trade in agricultural products and foodstuffs imported from Eastern Europe. Bulgaria, Hungary, and Romania have demanded that the Soviet Union "harden" the terms of trade in these commodities.[60] The Soviet Union may be meeting this demand in part in the present plan period.[61]

Second, the Eastern Europeans purchase above plan deliveries of—and Romania purchases all of its—petroleum from the Soviet Union with hard currency at WMPs.[62] This circumstance assumes increasing salience as the Soviet Union refuses to increase its planned deliveries of crude to the region.

Third, the Soviet Union has imposed a de facto increase in price on its energy exports by tying their availability to Eastern European participation in the development of energy resources located in the Soviet Union. Participation in these so-called joint development projects represents a hardening in terms of trade because it obligates Eastern Europe to supply the Soviet Union with hard goods either produced domestically or purchased on capitalist markets. Further, the creditor extends to the debtor in these projects (typically Eastern European states and the Soviet Union, respectively) an implicit subsidy through the artificially low interest rate of 2 percent charged on credits.[63]

Finally, the one-year lag in Comecon prices behind WMPs for energy hurts Eastern Europe in periods—such as the present one—when WMPs are declining. Thus, in 1986 and 1987, the official Comecon price for oil was anywhere from two to three times greater than comparable prices charged on world markets.[64] Of course, the real price is considerably less than the official price. The latter price is based on the artificially high official rate of exchange and does not indicate that Eastern Europe pays with soft goods for most of this oil.

Then, too, the official price itself is declining, as it now includes the lower WMPs for energy since 1985.[65] Western analysts calculate that in the 1986–1990 period, Soviet ruble earnings from exports of energy to Eastern Europe could decline by 17 to 18 percent from comparable earnings in the 1981–1985 period.[66] This calculation assumes that oil exports remain relatively constant in volume and that natural gas deliveries double in volume through 1990. In 1987 compared with 1986, Soviet exports of crude oil to Eastern Europe (excluding Romania) increased by 0.7 percent, while ruble earnings from these exports declined by 10.7 percent.[67] In this same period, the value of total trade turnover between the Soviet Union and Eastern Europe declined by 0.7 percent and the value of Soviet exports to Eastern Europe declined by 4.2 percent.[68]

Soviet premier Ryzhkov, speaking at the 1988 session of the Comecon Council in Prague, bluntly asserted that the traditional pattern of trade in Comecon is now obsolete: "The earlier model of the division of labor, based primarily on the exchange of fuel and raw materials for finished articles, had drained the potential for the dynamization of trade turnover. Today the situation is made even more difficult by the fall in contract prices for oil, energy resources, and other types of raw materials." The premier concluded that "prompt and vigorous measures" must be taken to rectify the situation.[69]

Western analysts differ regarding the distribution of benefits and burdens in Comecon trade. In one of the prominent studies on this subject, Jan Vanous and Michael Marrese estimate that between 1972 and 1984, the Soviet Union deliberately extended to Eastern Europe an "implicit trade subsidy" of $115 billion by charging less than WMPs for its exports.[70] Vanous and Marrese argue that the Soviet Union exacted political charges from Eastern Europe—for example, support among these states for its boycott of the 1984 Olympics or their diplomatic and material support for Soviet foreign policy initiatives in the Third World—in compensation for making it a winner in Comecon trade. Critics question both the size of and the reasons for the subsidy found by Vanous and Marrese.[71] They identify a cyclical pattern of alternating winners and losers in Comecon trade caused by the delayed appearance of changes in WMPs in this trade.

The absence of relevant data (for example, precisely what is the real price that Eastern Europe pays for Soviet energy) prevents a definitive resolution of this debate. However, two aspects of the subject do seem clear.

First, the exchange of soft goods for energy represents the key to understanding the Soviet–Eastern European energy relationship. That Eastern European states (excluding Romania) continue to import oil almost exclusively from the Soviet Union, despite the fact that the official Comecon price for this commodity is substantially above the comparable WMP, reflects this circumstance.[72]

Second, this circumstance provides the Soviet Union with a powerful instrument that constricts the overall economic and political independence of Eastern European states. Recently, the official organ of the PUWP rebuked unnamed "voices" in Poland that made this argument: "What is this dirty laundry? It is voices attempting to impute that under 'Moscow's dictate' we are limiting economic relations with capitalist countries. Moscow also 'imposes' on us its scope of trade with Comecon and binds us with the threads of raw materials supplies . . . to subordinate Poland politically as a consequence."[73] It is this broad process whereby energy dependence on the Soviet Union limits the autonomy of Eastern Europe (more so than the inclusion of explicit political charges in Comecon prices) that constitutes a principal nexus between politics and energy in Communist Europe.

Price issues continue to generate conflict within Comecon. A Polish source reports that "some members" of Comecon wish to bring the organization's prices closer to WMPs, "especially for oil."[74] These unnamed members argue that the present price formula, with its one-year lag behind WMPs, is hurting oil-importing states in this period of declining international oil prices. Soviet officials may well respond (not unfairly) that these same members did not advocate WMPs in Comecon during the oil price explosions of the 1970s. The Soviet Union itself may be seeking to revise the price formula to prevent or limit any further decline in the Comecon price for oil. Thus, Miklos Nemeth, premier of Hungary, indicated that the decline in world oil prices would soon be reflected in lower prices for Soviet oil "on the condition that the principles of price formation already operating within the Comecon framework are strictly observed," thereby raising the possibility that this condition may not be strictly observed.[75]

Joint Development Projects

Joint projects involve the participation of interested Comecon states in the exploitation of fuel and raw material reserves located primarily in the Soviet Union.[76] Participating states provide investment credits, personnel, equipment, and technical assistance, with repayment in the product of the project. Joint projects represent an overall hardening in Soviet–Eastern European terms of trade, since hard goods and hard currency compose a publicly undisclosed portion of the assistance provided. A Hungarian scholar sees this hardening, absent real prices in Comecon trade, as "seemingly the sole effective means" whereby the Soviet Union can simultaneously reduce demand for exportation of fuels and raw materials to Eastern Europe and also increase importation of agricultural products and high-quality consumer and industrial goods from this region.[77]

Joint projects have their origins in the late 1950s, when the Soviet Union made incremental increases in exports of fuels and raw materials to Eastern Europe contingent upon the extension of investment credits.[78] The ensuing credit arrangements typically were bilateral, involved relatively small sums, and sought to expand the productive capacity of existing facilities. The aforementioned agreements that Czechoslovakia and East Germany concluded with the Soviet Union in 1966 and 1967, respectively, represented the first large–scale exchange of investment credits for energy. These agreements proved a harbinger of subsequent developments.

In 1971, Comecon elaborated the Comprehensive Program for the Further Extension and Improvement of Cooperation and the Development of Socialist Economic Integration by the CMEA Member-States. This program sought to foster both political cohesion and economic intercourse among members of the socialist commonwealth. It endorsed joint projects as one means to this end.[79]

The Comecon states concluded agreements between 1972 and 1974 for seven joint projects (two of which involved energy resources) to be undertaken between 1976 and 1980. These agreements envisioned investments totaling thirteen billion to fourteen billion TR between 1976 and 1985. However, only nine billion TR were actually invested in joint projects during this period.[80] Analysts differ over the financial burden these investments imposed on Eastern European states. A Hungarian economist estimated that during the period 1976–1980, Czechoslovakia and Hungary each devoted about 4 percent of their total national investments to joint projects, while the comparable figure for the other states ranged between 2.5 and 3 percent. This source contended that these sums "represent transfers of resources that can be regarded as substantial." In contrast, a Western analysis of this subject concluded that Eastern European states allocated only 1 percent of their overall investments to joint projects between 1976 and 1980.[81] These conflicting estimates may arise from different methods of calculating the volume and value of contributions to joint projects.

The Orenburg natural gas complex and associated Soyuz (Union) pipeline and a 750 kv electric power grid were the two joint projects initiated in the 1970s to develop energy resources. The former project, based on a 1974 agreement signed by all European members of Comecon, entailed expansion of productive capacity at the Orenburg gas fields in the Urals and construction of the Soyuz pipeline from Orenburg to the Soviet–Czechoslovak border, where it connects with existing pipelines.[82]

The Soviet Union, with the aid of equipment purchased by Romania from capitalist states, was responsible for work at Orenburg itself. The Eastern European states, excluding Romania, were each responsible for financing and constructing one of five roughly equal segments of the pipeline, including requisite compressor stations. The agreement provided that each of the Eastern European contractors on the pipeline would receive 2.5 billion m³ of natural gas annually for a twenty-year period. Romania would receive 1.5 billion m³ of natural gas annually over the same period for its role at Orenburg. The actual volume and duration of deliveries can vary, however, since Comecon values both credits and payments at time of delivery. Consequently, credits are either devalued or inflated depending on subsequent market conditions.

The project had a nominal cost of between $4.6 billion and $5.8 billion to the Eastern European states. Western manufacturers provided upward of $2 billion in materials and equipment for the project. All wide-diameter pipe used in the pipeline and all requisite equipment for the compressor stations were of Western manufacture. Eastern European states financed hard currency purchases primarily (and perhaps exclusively) through credits raised on the Eurocurrency market by Comecon's International Investment Bank.

Eastern European states failed to fulfill many of their obligations for the pipeline. A severe shortage of skilled labor (especially in laying pipeline) proved a major impediment to their work. Only Poland managed to meet all obligations on its respective section of the pipeline. Other states were forced to subcontract work (usually to the Soviet Union) to meet their responsibilities. The Soviet Union, which in the original agreement had no responsibility for construction, actually laid almost 70 percent of the total pipeline. It also assisted in the installation of compressor stations on the first (Hungarian) section of the pipeline. Terms of payment for this subcontract work remain unpublished. The Soviet Union did, however, receive hard goods for at least some of this work.[83]

The 750 kv power grid project entails the construction of high-tension transmission lines and NPS's in the Soviet Union to augment the capacity of the Mir network. The first of these transmission lines, the Vinnitsa-Albertirsa line, is now completed. It links power stations in Soviet Ukraine with the power grids of Hungary and Czechoslovakia. Hungary has become the Eastern European state most dependent on the Mir grid for electricity. It now derives almost 30 percent of its electricity from this source.[84] Both Czechoslovakia and Hungary reported a temporary reduction in supplies of electricity after the accident at the Chernobyl NPS. The Soviet Union compensated these states for the reduction with increased deliveries of natural gas.[85]

Part of the power grid project involves construction of the 4,000 MW Khmelnitsky NPS in Ukraine. Czechoslovakia, Hungary, and Poland are financing half of the estimated $2.2 billion cost of the project, with Poland contributing more than $600 million and Czechoslovakia more than $350 million. These figures represent only nominal, not overall, costs. The total cost to the Eastern Europeans may be more than double the published figure. The project also includes construction of a high-tension transmission line from the NPS to Rzeszow in southern Poland. Participants were to receive electricity from the station between 1984 and 2003 as repayment for their contributions,[86] but construction is far behind schedule. Original plans called for two reactors to be fully operational by 1985, but only one reactor was even in limited operation at the end of 1987.[87]

Fewer details are available concerning a similar agreement for participation by Bulgaria and Romania in the construction of another NPS (designated South Ukrainian) located on the bank of the Bug River in Ukraine and a high-tension transmission line from the plant across Romania to Bulgaria. The first block of the plant, with a 1,000 MW reactor, was installed in 1982, and a similar reactor became operational in 1985. During the 1986–1990 period, four additional 1,000 MW reactors are to be installed.[88] The precise contribution of the Eastern European participants to this project and the terms for their repayment have not been published.

The 1984 session of the Comecon Council announced an ambitious program for more joint projects worth between 45 billion and 55 billion TR, sums that greatly exceeded those either planned or actually invested for this purpose since 1976.[89] To date, however, only the Progress natural gas pipeline project, worth an estimated twenty billion TR, has been initiated.

All Eastern European states are participating in the construction of what will be the world's longest pipeline (4,605 km) when completed.[90] The pipeline, stretching from the Yamburg gas field to the Soviet–Czechoslovak border, will have an annual capacity of twenty billion to twenty-two billion m^3. The forty compressor stations on the pipeline will be fully fitted out with equipment of Soviet manufacture.[91] Eastern European participants in the project will receive annual deliveries of natural gas over a twenty-year period in proportion to their respective contributions. Soviet and Eastern European sources offer sharply contrasting assessments of the pace of construction on Progress. The Soviets report that construction is ahead of schedule and the pipeline may become operational before its target date in 1989. The Eastern Europeans indicate that contractors are encountering numerous difficulties in construction and have fallen far behind their projected schedule.[92] Whether gas deliveries through Progress will produce a net increase in Soviet energy exports to Eastern Europe also remains uncertain. Thus, a respected Western source hypothesized that upon completion of the pipeline, the Soviet Union will probably make more crude oil available for export to capitalist markets by reducing supplies to Eastern Europe.[93]

Individual Eastern European states also participate in numerous projects to develop natural resources in the Soviet Union. Poland illustrates the magnitude of this cooperation. Poland has already constructed a section of a natural gas pipeline between Kobryn and Brest. It has started construction on a similar section of the Tula–Kiev pipeline. Poland is participating in the expansion of several gas industry installations located near Kiev, Lvov, and Minsk. Polish workers also are assisting in the construction of NPS's, including those at Khmelnitsky, Kursk, and Smolensk. Repayment for this work, as with other joint projects, comes from output of the completed facility.[94]

Joint projects engender considerable criticism and conflict. Some Eastern Europeans fear that joint projects further undermine their already limited political sovereignty. A Polish source, writing in a Soviet journal, admitted that "there is still some feeling that the formation of the international division of labor in socialist countries . . . cannot be based upon supranational principles," but he assured his readers that in all joint endeavors, "each partner's national interests are respected."[95]

Yet the reconciliation of divergent national interests has proven almost impossible to achieve. Many Eastern Europeans remain unconvinced that joint projects represent the optimal economic method to close their energy gaps. The Hungarian state secretary for foreign affairs recently charged that many joint projects have "no economic foundation" and only "the primacy of politics and the interest of demonstrating unity with the USSR" justify their existence.[96]

Several factors explain this circumstance. First, joint projects typically are agreed upon without aid of technical documentation and realistic projections of cost. For example, Czechoslovak workers, arriving in Soviet Kazakhstan to help build a natural gas complex, found the site without fuel, water, heat, electricity, boiler rooms, and even nails. A Czechoslovak source asserted that "such a lack of preparation ties our hands and this increases costs."[97]

Second, the method for valuing credits in joint projects usually benefits the debtor over the creditor. I have noted that the artificially low interest rate charged on credits in joint projects represents an implicit subsidy from creditor to debtor states. More importantly, official prices of the debtor state are used to value credits in joint projects. The ensuing valuations are arbitrary, since official prices in all Comecon states are determined administratively and bear little relationship to the dictates of supply and demand. Soviet and Eastern European sources agree that (1) the present system of valuation benefits the debtor over the creditor in joint projects located in the Soviet Union; (2) the use of WMPs to value credits in the projects would reverse the situation. A Hungarian official has bluntly warned that the interest of Eastern Europe in joint projects "will be eliminated" if valuation of credits in domestic prices continues.[98]

Third, Eastern European creditors express concern over provisions for repayment in joint projects. The policy of valuing repayment at the time of delivery prevents creditors at the beginning of a project from determining actual rate of return on investment.[99] As noted, this provision also devalues credits in periods of inflation: "This gives the debtor a one-sided advantage in that the credit fixed in terms of its nominal value has a lower real value with each year, and an even smaller performance is needed to service the debt."[100]

After repayment of credits, creditors have no right (as is usual in international practice) to preferential terms of purchase from completed facilities. The debtor assumes complete ownership of jointly constructed facilities upon repayment of credits. Reportedly, the Comecon Executive Committee, meeting in Moscow in October 1988, made "no progress" in resolving problems of repayment in joint projects. Its work on this subject will "continue."[101]

The uncertain economic benefits of joint projects contrast with the certain opportunity costs incurred in allocating hard commodities to these endeavors. Hard commodities allocated to joint projects are commodities unavailable for trade with Western states. Prime Minister Dascalescu of Romania, speaking at the 1986 session of the Comecon Council in Bucharest, urged that Comecon states "should no longer resort to hard currency imports for targets being built with joint efforts."[102]

In contrast, the Soviet Union contends—and some Western analysts agree—that an objective assessment of costs and benefits in joint projects reveals that it shoulders a disproportionate share of the former while Eastern Europe enjoys a disproportionate share of the latter.[103] Eastern European states have not only failed to fulfill many of their commitments to joint projects, but they have run up huge trade deficits with the Soviet Union. Soviet economists argue that the latter circumstance especially makes joint projects economically unfeasible: "When most European Comecon states are permanently indebted to the Soviet Union as a result of clearing their commodity trade, their deliveries to the Soviet Union under special purpose credits no longer make economic sense."[104]

Consequently, one Western study bluntly asserts that the "Soviets have completely abandoned a multilateral approach to solving Comecon energy and raw materials difficulties."[105] While the Progress pipeline demonstrates that this is not completely so, Progress does remain the only major joint project initiated in the 1980s. In the opinion of one Hungarian economist, the new emphasis will be on the "coordination of investments" among Comecon states to promote conservation of energy and the production of hard goods that can be exchanged for energy.[106]

Prospects: Gorbachev and the Energy Relationship

The future status of energy relations in Communist Europe is inseparably linked to Mikhail Gorbachev's overall drive to restructure Comecon.[107] Gorbachev seeks to create a self-styled unified socialist market among the Comecon states based on the mutual development and exchange of commodities and technologies that match or exceed prevailing world standards for excellence. Failure to realize this goal would relegate these states to permanent status as technological appendages of the developed capitalist countries. This circumstance, a leading Soviet specialist on Comecon argues, might even threaten the very existence of the socialist system: "It is true that in this respect we find ourselves in a very difficult situation. I may be using strong words here, but I feel that indeed the future of socialism is at stake. If we are unable to catch up in this respect, the entire socialist system may be endangered. We can see this very clearly."[108]

The Comprehensive Program for the CMEA Countries' Scientific and Technological Progress (1985) embodies Gorbachev's ambitious effort to restructure the organization. This program identifies five priority areas—electronics, automation, nuclear power, new materials and technologies, and biotechnology—where the Comecon states will jointly cooperate in research, design, and production of commodities to narrow the East–West technological gap. "Leading" or "chief coordinating" organizations (all of which are located in the Soviet Union) will supervise newly created international associations, joint enterprises, and direct links between manufacturers in different countries to pursue this end.

Both Soviet and Eastern European officials argue that the establishment of real prices both within and between the Comecon states represents the indispensable precondition for the success of the Comprehensive Program.[109] Premier Strougal voiced the assessment of many officials when he contended that it is an "illusion" to believe that this condition can be realized without "basic changes" in the domestic economies of the member states.[110]

It lies beyond our purview to examine the considerable difficulties that the Comprehensive Program has encountered in its implementation. Suffice it to note that, according to an official commentary, deliberations at the 1988 session of the Comecon Council on the status of the Comprehensive Program were conducted in a "sharp, critical, and self–critical spirit; in an atmosphere of absolute openness and healthy dissatisfaction with the fact that the results achieved . . . do not correspond with the extended effort."[111]

Nevertheless, the Gorbachev strategy to resuscitate Comecon raises significant issues for the energy gap. The Soviet–Hungarian energy relationship, characterized by a Hungarian source as "tension filled,"[112] provides illustration. Hungarian Socialist Workers party (HSWP) leader Karoly Grosz indicates that "above all" Hungary seeks "to restore the 1981–1982 level" of oil deliveries in trade with "our Soviet partners." Grosz has reiterated this position on several occasions, including a banquet at the Kremlin held in his honor on a state visit to the Soviet Union.[113] Yet the Gorbachev strategy seeks precisely the opposite end: to alter what Premier Ryzhkov has called the "archaic" commodity structure of Soviet trade with Eastern Europe by dramatically increasing the exportation of machines and other industrial manufactures.[114] Simultaneously, the Soviet Union insists that Eastern Europe must provide more hard goods in payment for existing deliveries of energy.

An impasse has ensued. The Soviet Union refuses to increase its oil exports to Hungary, although it apparently has pledged to maintain the present level of exportation through 1995. Hungary refuses to import more low-quality industrial manufactures from the Soviet Union. An authoritative article in *Pravda* admits that only one-half of Soviet exports of machinery to Hungary "meet modern technical standards."[115] Hungary and the Soviet Union encountered considerable difficulty in concluding bilateral contracts for many projects envisioned in their 1988 trade pact. The 1989 trade pact between the two states calls for Hungary to import 7 percent less from and export 11 percent less to the Soviet Union in comparison to the 1988 trade targets.[116] Grosz stresses that the two countries must work together to avoid a decrease in the level of trade turnover. Hungary will not, however, sacrifice its national interest to this end: "At the same time, what the contents of trade turnover are is not a matter of indifference. Obviously, we must go in the direction of the most economic cooperation which expresses the interests of both sides. . . . It is hardly possible nowadays to conclude deals out of sympathy or friendship. It is only possible on the basis of interests."[117]

National self-interest also has led Hungary to review its 1985 agreement to construct processing facilities and a desulphurization plant at the Tengiz natural gas complex in the Soviet Union in return for two billion m³ of natural gas annually between 1992 and 2008. The president of the Hungarian National Bank asserts that projects such as Tengiz "practically burst the seams of our monetary possibilities and for this reason their review cannot be avoided."[118] Party leader Grosz has admitted that a decision to cancel the project might prove a "grave mistake," but Hungary had "justified anxiety" over whether its "straitened financial circumstances" would permit its participation.[119] Grosz added an intriguing but publicly unelaborated upon observation that "political motivation" also was part of Hungary's objections to the project.[120]

Key questions remain unanswered in the Gorbachev strategy. First, will the "basic changes" (to use former premier Strougal's term) needed to restructure domestic economic systems and produce more hard goods for the Soviet market engender unacceptable political costs? In remarks applicable to all of Eastern Europe, a Czechoslovak source candidly admitted that many enterprises will "soon find themselves face to face with a complicated situation" if they cannot sell their "run-of-the mill but fully obsolete" production on the Soviet market.[121] How will Gorbachev and the Eastern European leaders respond when (and if) this complicated situation threatens stability within the polity? That the Czechoslovak leadership has now removed Strougal, the most prominent proponent of restructuring in its ranks, from the premiership suggests the turmoil likely to accompany the Gorbachev strategy.[122]

Second, will the diversion of hard goods to the Soviet market restrict the capacity of Eastern European states to trade with the West? Ironically, such trade represents one means whereby these states can acquire the sophisticated technologies their economies so desperately need and concomitantly enhances their capacity to produce the very hard goods that the Soviet Union so desires. A Hungarian economist has predicted that this circumstance will compel the Soviet Union, as it has in the past, to moderate its demands for hard goods from Eastern Europe.[123]

Third, is the interest of the Soviet Union in maintaining political control in the region promoted if Eastern Europe must pay in hard goods for much of its energy? After all, it is precisely the willingness of the Soviet Union to accept payment in soft goods that has proven so attractive to Eastern Europe and thereby provided the Soviet Union with a carrot to extend to loyal regimes and a stick to withhold the carrot from disloyal regimes in the region.

Finally, can the Soviet Union realistically expect to revitalize Comecon trade, especially in the short run, through the Gorbachev strategy of increasing exportation of machinery and industrial commodities? The available evidence warrants a negative response. Concomitantly, does the continued stagnation in Comecon trade serve the economic and political interests of the member states? Soviet spokesmen themselves argue that it does not. If Comecon cannot be revitalized, one of them predicts, "then the very foundation of economic cooperation between socialist states will be severely damaged, and this is fraught with the most serious dangers that are not only economic in nature."[124]

3

The Supply Side: Production of Energy

The future does not offer a realistic foundation for the raw material and energy intensive growth pursued in the 1950's, 1960's, and 1970's. Thus far, there is no indication of this recognition in announced economic policies.

—*Kozgazdasagi Szemle*, no. 12, 1987

Eastern Europe traditionally has pursued an extensive strategy of economic development based on quantitative increases in factor inputs rather than qualitative increases in factor productivity. Ipso facto, substantial increases in the production of energy are a key component of this strategy. That Eastern European states devote between 40 and 45 percent of all investments in industry to expanding the production of energy reflects this circumstance. When expenditures devoted to energy projects in Comecon are included, this percentage is even higher. Eastern Europe responded to the increasing unwillingness or incapacity of the Soviet Union to close its energy gap primarily through efforts to increase the indigenous production of energy. These efforts inevitably concentrated on the development of nuclear power and coal, given the paucity of alternative energy reserves in the region.

Nuclear Power

Nuclear power, once considered by many a panacea to meet the world's demand for energy in an inexpensive, safe, and environmentally sound manner, is now more often associated with soaring costs and interminable delays in the construction of new plants, apprehension regarding the reliable and safe operation of existing plants, and fear that governments might use the nuclear energy industry to acquire, and even employ, nuclear weapons. Such concerns have prompted many governments to reassess, reduce, or largely abandon their hitherto ambitious plans for the development of nuclear power.

To paraphrase Mark Twain, however, news of the death of nuclear power may be greatly exaggerated if one considers its projected status in

Table 3–1
Eastern Europe: Installed Nuclear Capacity*

Plant	Installed Capacity		Reactors under Construction		Planned Reactors	
	Reactors	Megawatts	Reactors	Megawatts	Reactors	Megawatts
Bulgaria						
Kozloduy	5	2,760	1	1,000	—	—
Belene	—	—	1	1,000	3	3,000
Czechoslovakia						
Jaslovske Bohunice	4	1,760	—	—	—	—
Dukovany	4	1,760	—	—	—	—
Mochovce	—	—	4	1,760	—	—
Temelin	—	—	4	4,000	—	—
Kecerovice	—	—	—	—	2	2,000
East Germany						
Rheinsberg	1	80	—	—	—	—
NORD	4	1,760	4	1,760	—	—
Stendal	—	—	—	—	4	4,000
Hungary						
Paks	4	1,760	—	—	2	2,000
Undesignated	—	—	—	—	4	4,000
Poland						
Zarnowiec	—	—	4	1,860	—	—
WARTA	—	—	—	—	4	4,000
Undesignated	—	—	—	—	2	2,000
Romania						
Cernavoda	—	—	4	2,640	1	660
Moldava	—	—	—	—	3	3,000
Transylvania	—	—	—	—	5	3,300
Total Eastern Europe	22	9,880	22	14,020	30	27,960

Sources: Official publications of the respective countries.
*On line as of January 1989 and projected.

Eastern Europe. All governments there have announced plans to establish or substantially augment existing nuclear power capacities. At present, NPS's are in commercial operation in Bulgaria, Czechoslovakia, East Germany, and Hungary and are under construction in Poland and Romania. Installed nuclear capacity in the region now totals 9,880 MW, versus 80 MW of installed capacity in 1970, and could approach 42,000 MW by the year 2000 if projected targets for nuclear power are realized (tables 3–1 and 3–2).[1] The 1985 Comecon Comprehensive Program identified nuclear power as one of five priority avenues for scientific and technical cooperation among the member states.

In the wake of the disaster at the Chernobyl NPS, the Comecon states reiterated their commitment to nuclear power. Present plans, announced at the 1986 session of the Comecon Council held in Bucharest, envision that by the year 2000 Eastern Europe will have an installed nuclear power plant capacity of 50,000 MW and an installed nuclear heating plant

Table 3–2
Eastern Europe: Electricity from Nuclear Power
(percent)

	1985/1986	*1990*[1]	*2000*[1]
Bulgaria	32	44	60
Czechoslovakia	20	30	50
East Germany	11	15	30
Hungary	25	NA[2]	40
Poland	—	—	13
Romania	—	18	NA

Sources: Official publications of the respective countries.

[1]These projections should be treated cautiously because, as the present study clearly demonstrates, all of these countries have a record of substantial underfulfillment of their nuclear plans.

[2]Not available.

capacity of 7,000 MW. Nuclear power will generate between 30 and 40 percent of the electricity then being produced.[2] Such projections reflect the official position that Eastern European governments have adopted since Chernobyl. These governments acknowledge that the accident was serious and that it is essential to enhance safety standards to avoid its repetition. They assert, however that Chernobyl will not affect their nuclear plans, in part because the damaged Soviet reactor differs in design from all operational or planned reactors in Eastern Europe and in part because they see no alternative to the atom as an important source of power to meet their needs for energy.[3] Of course, *Homo politicus* in any political system often makes public statements that belie private beliefs. We shall see that Chernobyl has fostered or reinforced reservations about nuclear power among the elites in Eastern Europe.

The Rationale for Nuclear Power

Proponents frequently argue that nuclear power is essential to close the region's energy gap. A Czechoslovak proponent of nuclear power has pointed out that "our country is not exactly awash in fuel and energy resources," while a Polish counterpart sees nuclear power as the "only realistic source of additional energy." A citizen of East Germany colorfully captured the essence of this argument: "Unless we want to turn off the lights, we just have to live with nuclear power."[4]

Proponents also see nuclear energy as a cost-effective source of power, compared with nonnuclear sources. A Czechoslovak analyst, while admitting that the question of costs is a "complicated" one, nevertheless accepts this rationale "even after including the costs connected with solving problems of the external fuel cycle, such as storage of spent fuel, its transport and reprocessing, and neutralization of radioactive wastes."[5] Presumably, these calculations include only the cost of operating, not constructing, nuclear and nonnuclear plants. Nuclear plants typically entail far greater construction costs than do nonnuclear power plants of comparable capacity.[6]

Supporters also contend that greater reliance on nuclear power and a concomitant reduction in reliance on brown coal and lignite in primary energy consumption would significantly enhance the overall quality of the region's environment. "Nuclear plants will be much better for the environment than coal," a Polish source argued, adding that "more and more people understand this." Undeniably, Eastern Europe suffers from exceedingly high levels of environmental pollution, much of it caused by the overwhelming reliance on heavily polluting solid fuels. This circumstance may explain why many environmentalists in the region, notably in Hungary, have voiced little opposition to nuclear power.[7]

Finally, proponents of nuclear power, particularly before Chernobyl, have usually summarily rejected fears about the danger of nuclear power. "Nuclear power is probably the best thing that humanity has ever had from the point of view of avoiding risks," proclaimed a ranking official of the Czechoslovak Atomic Energy Commission in a typical exposition of this argument.[8] If nuclear power represents any danger, proponents say, it does so only under capitalism, where the insatiable pursuit of profit could lead the power industry to subordinate safety considerations to its own selfish economic interests. The Soviet Union and Eastern Europe have pursued a prophylactic approach to nuclear safety—through, for example, excellence of design, reliability of equipment, and careful operational procedures—rather than the approach prevalent in the West of developing contingency plans for worst case scenarios, including meltdowns. For example, the Soviet Union has argued that its nuclear technology is so reliable that standard safety features in the West (such as containment vessels to control meltdowns) are superfluous. These features are merely "placebos to placate the people" under capitalism, several Soviet scientists once contended, made necessary by "negative dramatizations" in the press.[9] Such hubris has been less common (but not totally absent) since Chernobyl.[10] Indeed, the chairman of the Soviet State Committee for the Utilization of Atomic Energy has acknowledged that Chernobyl represented a "severe blow" to the development of nuclear power but that the Soviet Union had "no intention" of abandoning it, "given, of course, the essential condition that a higher level of safety is ensured."[11]

All these rationales for nuclear power have been challenged by both political elites and private citizens. I shall return to their criticisms when I assess the prospects for nuclear power in Eastern Europe. Before doing so, it is useful to trace the development of nuclear power in the region from its inception in the mid-1950s to the present.

Nuclear Power: 1955–1970

On January 17, 1955, the Soviet Union announced that it would cooperate with its allies in the "peaceful development of atomic science, technology, and national economy." Shortly thereafter, the Soviet Union concluded agreements with Eastern European states to aid in the conduct of research on nuclear energy. The agreements with Czechoslovakia, East Germany, and Hungary also provided technical assistance and equipment, including reactors, to construct NPS's.[12]

The emphasis on nuclear power had both ideological and economic foundations. Ideologically, communist planners, remembering Lenin's famous dictum that communism "equals Soviet power plus electrification of the country," historically had identified electricity generation as a key measure of communist society. Further, communist planners were aware that economic development in the region was substantially increasing demand for energy. As early as 1952, planners in Czechoslovakia had recommended the development of nuclear power in response to this circumstance.[13]

Under terms of the research agreements, each Eastern European state received a 2 MW research reactor fueled with enriched uranium and cooled and moderated with light water. All states except Romania also received small capacity cyclotrons and related equipment. Even more significant aid involved the training of Eastern European scientists and technicians at nuclear research centers in the Soviet Union, primarily at the preeminent Soviet center located at Dubna. In 1956, this center was renamed the Joint Institute of Nuclear Research.

The agreements for technical assistance and equipment were to provide Czechoslovakia with a 150 MW reactor to be made operational by 1960 (the so-called A-1 plant at Jaslovske Bohunice) and East Germany and Hungary with 80 MW and 100 MW reactors, respectively, for NPS's to be made operational in the mid-1960s. Czechoslovakia and East Germany devised additional plans for nuclear power that substantially exceeded the capacities envisioned in the 1955 agreements. Poland sought a course then unique among Eastern European states: to rely almost exclusively on its own resources, including the development of a reactor fueled by natural uranium, to have an installed nuclear capacity of 200 MW in commercial operation by 1965 (table 3–3).

In fact, for political, economic, and, perhaps, technological reasons, the Soviet Union honored only its agreement with East Germany, whose

Table 3–3
Eastern Europe: Projected Nuclear Capacity by 1970

	Projected Capacity (Megawatts)	Actual Capacity (Megawatts)
Bulgaria	0	0
Czechoslovakia	3,000	0
East Germany	3,000	80
Hungary	100	0
Poland	600	0
Romania	0	0
Eastern Europe	6,700	80

Source: Computed from data in Polach, "Nuclear Power in East Europe," 6.

NPS at Rheinsberg became operational in 1966. Politically, the upheavals in Hungary and Poland in 1956 and the growing rift between the Soviet Union and the People's Republic of China reminded the Soviet leadership of the tenuous allegiance of its ostensible allies and of the potential use of nuclear energy for other than peaceful purposes.

These concerns applied especially to Czechoslovakia. Czechoslovakia wanted a Soviet-designed reactor using gas as the coolant, heavy water as the moderator, and natural uranium as the fuel. From the Czechoslovak standpoint, this type of reactor had the great advantage of permitting Czechoslovakia to use its own abundant indigenous reserves of natural uranium for fuel. From the Soviet perspective, the reactor had two disturbing features that ultimately led the Soviet Union to withhold assistance. First, the reactor's use of indigenous natural uranium would eliminate an important mechanism whereby the Soviet Union hoped to exercise control over the nuclear programs of Eastern Europe: reliance on the Soviet Union as the sole source of enriched uranium. Second, a heavy-water reactor is capable of producing fissionable material that can be used for military purposes, including the production of nuclear weapons. Reportedly, the Soviet Union "advised" Poland to abandon its plans for an independent nuclear program based on reactors fueled by natural uranium. In contrast, in the agreement that the Soviets did honor, East Germany opted for a light-water reactor not well suited to the production of fissionable materials and fueled by enriched uranium supplied by the Soviet Union.[14]

Economically, the Soviet Union may have feared that an extensive nuclear power capacity in Eastern Europe would lessen the economic rationale for the region to import large quantities of liquid fuels from the Soviets. Technological considerations also might have influenced the Soviet position. The type of reactor that Czechoslovakia requested was not then operational in the Soviet Union, and Soviet scientists knew relatively little about it. Conversely, East Germany requested the type of reactor that the Soviets themselves were relying on for the development of their own civilian nuclear power program. The Soviet Union reportedly honored its agreement with East Germany in part to undertake joint experiments with German nuclear scientists to benefit the Soviet domestic nuclear program.[15]

While the precise combination of factors that influenced Soviet policy remains unclear, its consequences were devastating to the development of nuclear power in Eastern Europe. Without prospect of Soviet aid, Hungary abandoned its initial plans for nuclear power. Czechoslovakia continued the development of the A-1 plant by relying primarily on internal resources for expertise and technology. Predictably, these efforts were enormously costly, wasteful of resources, and duplicative of research in other countries. The A-1 plant was finally completed in 1972 (twelve years behind schedule), but problems continued to plague its operation, and it was permanently closed in 1977. The history of the A-1 project refutes the recent contention of one Western analyst that the plant was "duly built with the active assistance of the Soviet Union."[16]

In a seeming reversal of previous policy, in 1965–66 the Soviet Union concluded a new set of agreements to develop nuclear power with all Eastern European states except Romania and Poland. The agreements with Bulgaria, East Germany, and Hungary obligated the Soviets to provide each of them with technical assistance and equipment, including two 440 MW pressurized light-water reactors fueled with lightly enriched uranium for NPS's to be completed by 1975. The type of reactor to be provided— now standard throughout Eastern Europe—was patterned after a model produced by Westinghouse (in fact, it is often referred to as Eastinghouse) and at the time was considered reliable and economical by nuclear experts in the West.[17] The agreement with Czechoslovakia envisioned construction of the A-2 and A-3 nuclear plants with reactors of the same type, albeit of a larger capacity, as those used in the A-1 plant. Finally, in 1970, the Soviet Union concluded an agreement with Romania similar to the ones it had concluded with Bulgaria, East Germany, and Hungary.

Several considerations led to these agreements. First, the Soviet Union sought to prevent Eastern European states from seeking assistance in nuclear development from capitalist countries. In 1964–65, Czechoslovakia approached Britain and France, and later Canada, about the purchase of a reactor and other equipment for the completion of the A-1 project. Of course, the initiative derived precisely from the Soviet refusal to honor its obligations to complete this project. Romania, wishing to achieve some degree of independence from the Soviet Union, also sought nuclear aid from several capitalist states, including Britain, Canada, and Sweden. None of these initiatives succeeded, largely because the United States, for security reasons, prevented much of the necessary equipment from being exported to communist countries.[18]

The agreements also enhanced Soviet political control in the region by binding the Eastern European states closely to the Soviet Union in an important area of technology. The Soviets sought this end by supplying the Eastern Europeans with a reactor fueled by lightly enriched uranium and by requiring them both to export their indigenous reserves of uranium for enrichment in the Soviet Union and to return all spent fuel rods for reprocessing there.

These policies again created conflict with Czechoslovakia. The history of the A-1 plant repeated itself as the Soviets refused to supply Czechoslovakia with heavy-water reactors fueled by natural uranium for the A-2 and A-3 projects. Finally, after the Soviet Union invaded Czechoslovakia in 1968, the latter opted (or was coerced) to adopt the same type of reactor as that used by other Eastern European states. Consequently, Czechoslovakia in effect lost its ability to develop an independent nuclear program. The former director general of the Czechoslovak uranium industry (who escaped to the West after the invasion) said of this decision, "Our children will condemn us for it some day." This same official also charged that the Soviet Union maintained a "colonial relationship" with Czechoslovakia (and, presumably, other Eastern European states) by ruthlessly exploiting indigenous reserves of uranium primarily for its own use.[19]

Economic self-interest also may have motivated the Soviet Union. By including Eastern Europe as a market for reactors, the nascent nuclear power industry in the Soviet Union achieved economies of scale in production that domestic demand alone would not have engendered. The Soviets apparently did not feel that the Eastern Europeans, even under optimal circumstances, would soon achieve sufficient nuclear power capacities to threaten the Soviet Union's current and projected exports of liquid fuels to the region.

In any event, the Soviet Union did honor its agreements with Bulgaria and East Germany for the delivery of reactors that permitted these countries in 1974 and 1975 to open the Kozloduy and Nord NPS's, respectively. The agreements with Czechoslovakia and Hungary were substantially modified and implemented only after protracted delays; the agreement with Romania was never fulfilled, and the entire project was eventually abandoned.

In sum, the story of nuclear power in Eastern Europe during this period is one of frustration, broken promises, and both latent and manifest acrimony between the Soviets and their nominal socialist allies. The overall record of achievement fell far short of initial expectations. By 1970, only one NPS in Eastern Europe, at Rheinsberg in East Germany, was in commercial operation.

The Role of the Soviet Union

Political and economic factors contributed to a renewed emphasis on nuclear power in the 1970s. Politically, the Soviet Union saw nuclear power as an instrument to foster the integration of economies—and thereby attenuate fissiparous political forces—in the region. This task was to be pursued primarily under the auspices of Comecon, which in 1971 promulgated its Comprehensive Program, which included measures to develop nuclear power.

Economically, the Eastern Europeans began to view nuclear power as a cost-effective substitute for increasingly expensive oil imported from both the Soviet Union and the international energy market. "Acceleration of the nuclear construction program in the Comecon states was projected as a response to changing oil prices," a Comecon Council communiqué asserted shortly after the October 1973 war between Israel and the Arab states.[20]

In 1974 and 1975, the Soviet Union signed bilateral agreements with all Eastern European states to provide nuclear equipment for NPS's and other uses.[21] The agreement with Czechoslovakia also permitted that state to manufacture, under Soviet license, Soviet-designed equipment and components, including reactors, for both domestic use and export. In its 1977 and 1979 sessions, the Comecon Council announced ambitious plans to develop nuclear power. During the 1979 session, the council projected that nuclear power in the Comecon states would generate more than one-third of the electricity in 1990 and one-half of the electricity ten years later.[22]

The establishment of Interatominstrument in 1972 and Interatom-energo in 1973 also represented visible institutional commitments to nuclear power.[23] Interatominstrument, a legally autonomous international association composed of the Soviet Union and all Eastern European members of Comecon except Romania, has its headquarters in Warsaw and coordinates industrial production, scientific research, and technical collaboration among fifteen producers of components for nuclear engineering in the member states. In 1975, the association established branches in Bulgaria, Poland, and the Soviet Union. Although initially heavily subsidized, the association reportedly had become economically self-sustaining by 1978.[24] The planned value of equipment produced under its auspices between 1986 and 1990 exceeds 600 million rubles, compared with a figure of approximately 450 million rubles between 1981 and 1985.[25]

Interatomenergo, founded by the members of Comecon and Yugoslavia, coordinates the design, production, delivery, construction, and safe operation of equipment for NPS's. The organization conducts annual seminars for specialists concerning questions of nuclear safety and has established a data bank to gather and disseminate information about this subject. Under its auspices, each member state assumes responsibility for producing specific components for reactors and other nuclear equipment. A Soviet publication boasts, albeit with some exaggeration, that the socialist countries themselves produce all equipment for NPS's "down to the last nut."[26]

Czechoslovakia plays a key role in this activity, under terms of the agreement it signed with the Soviet Union in 1974. At present, Czechoslovakia exports to Comecon states approximately one-half of all such equipment and components that it manufactures, and it has already supplied reactors for NPS's in East Germany and Hungary. In the 1986–1990 period, Czechoslovakia was scheduled to supply two reactors each for NPS's in East Germany, Poland, Bulgaria, and Romania. To date, all reactors exported are of the standard 440-MW capacity, although Czechoslovakia is manufacturing 1,000-MW reactors for Bulgaria and Romania. Czechoslovakia also supplies the Soviet Union with special equipment for fast breeder reactors whose construction is to begin in the 1990s.[27]

The Soviet Union controls the nuclear activities of the Comecon states behind this veneer of multilateral cooperation. As noted, it requires these states to obtain enriched uranium for their reactors from the Soviet Union and to return spent fuel for reprocessing to that country. Within the multilateral nuclear programs of Comecon, the Soviet Union also controls the division of labor among the member states, the design and standardization of nuclear equipment, the advanced training of scientists and other specialists, the export of nuclear technologies, the dissemination of technical information, and myriad other activities that ensure that these states cannot develop independent nuclear programs.

The Soviet Union also is a major supplier of components, including reactors, for NPS's in Eastern Europe.[28] In the 1970–1980 period, the Comecon states ordered nineteen reactors, from the Soviet Union which delivered eleven on schedule. The Soviet Union henceforth will specialize in the delivery of 1,000 MW reactors, while Czechoslovakia will become the primary supplier of 440 MW reactors. Bulgaria was the first Eastern European state to install the 1,000 MW reactors. In 1979, it ordered two such reactors for the fifth and sixth power blocks at the Kozloduy NPS and plans to install four similar reactors at a plant currently under construction in the Belene region. Overall, between 1986 and 1990, the Soviet Union is to supply approximately 50 percent of the requisite equipment for construction of NPS's in the Comecon states.

The participating states openly criticize nuclear cooperation in Comecon. These criticisms evoke a sense of déjà vu among those familiar with the problems of Comecon in other functional areas of cooperation.

A common complaint focuses on delays in fulfilling contractual obligations by the participating states. Thus, Premier Lubomir Strougal of Czechoslovakia, after noting that his country has important cooperative agreements with the Soviet Union and other Comecon states for the delivery of components for reactors, charged that its "partners" are "lagging behind" in meeting their obligations. Other Comecon states have made similar accusations against Czechoslovakia. This criticism relates above all to delays in the production and delivery of the 440 MW reactors and related equipment.[29]

Both Czechoslovakia and the Soviet Union complain that they suffer substantial economic losses when other Comecon states renege on agreements to purchase nuclear equipment. Romania recently cancelled an order to purchase two 1,000-MW reactors while they were under construction in Czechoslovakia. Czechoslovakia estimates that cancelled or delayed orders will idle about twenty percent of the reactor manufacturing capacity at the Skoda works. Premier Ryzhkov, speaking at the 1986 session of the Comecon Council, urged the member states to guarantee that they would honor contracts concluded with the manufacturers of nuclear equipment. Such guarantees, he said, are an "indispensable condition" to providing manufacturers with requisite financial incentives to expand their capacities.[30]

Complaints also involve the quality and price of commodities in cooperative projects. Premier Strougal asserted that the Comecon states have addressed these subjects "very frankly and sometimes very critically, and I believe with justification." A Western source added that Eastern Europeans privately complain that Comecon's nuclear policy creates "inflexible links to outdated Soviet technology," which are a "sure recipe" for maintaining the "inefficiency and declining technological competitiveness Eastern Europe is struggling to overcome."[31] An accord, adopted at the 1987 session of the Comecon Council, seeks to "overhaul dramatically" the production of equipment for NPS's and to "develop the nuclear power industry at priority rates." This overhaul will include the creation of a "new generation" of pressurized-water reactors (VVER's) with more "technical safety devices" and greater "economic viability" than their predecessor.[32]

An unusually frank article in a Slovak publication provides insights into the difficulty that Czechoslovakia (and, presumably, other Comecon states) has experienced in ensuring that Soviet nuclear equipment meets national safety standards. This difficulty is "frequently criticized but nevertheless deeply rooted in practice," the article declares. It creates "enormous difficulties" and represents a "fundamental shortcoming" in the completion of new power projects. The article adds that "increased nuclear safety demands new elements, new design solutions" and that the "frequent and favorite argument" of the Soviet Union that "power blocks are identical no longer applies." According to Stanislav Havel, chairman of the Czechoslovak Commission for Nuclear Energy, in an interview shortly before the disaster at the Chernobyl NPS, one of the primary goals of Comecon is to achieve "considerably greater reliability for nuclear facilities and the safe operation of NPS." His statement came nearly two years after Czechoslovakia already had "significantly altered" Soviet-designed reactors to enhance their "reliability, safety and technical production characteristics"—alterations also accepted by East Germany, Hungary, and Poland.[33]

Comments by Polish officials suggest unhappiness in general with the self-styled "informal" procedures Comecon has developed to exchange information regarding accidents at NPS and in particular with how the Soviet Union transmitted such information about the incident at Chernobyl. Jerzy Urban, the official press spokesman for the Polish government, informed listeners that following "difficulties in the way of responding to certain facts" about Chernobyl, the Soviet Union and Poland have agreed "to more precisely define" procedures for reporting emergencies that have "not been precise up to now."[34]

Several recent initiatives denote an expanded role for Comecon in nuclear cooperation. In 1987, all European Comecon states except Bulgaria and Romania adopted rules for the safe carriage of spent nuclear fuel by rail and sea. The rules include a convention on liability for damage caused by a radiation accident in the international transportation of this fuel.[35] Bulgaria, Czechoslovakia, and the Soviet Union have established within Comecon's International Investment Bank a common fund to finance research on problems of decommissioning obsolete NPS's. Research institutes from these countries have formed an international economic association for this purpose.[36] Finally, in 1988, Comecon established a Standing Commission for Cooperation in the Sphere of Electrical Energy and Nuclear Power. This commission combines the functional responsibilities of now abolished individual commissions for electrical energy and nuclear power.[37]

National Nuclear Programs Since 1970[38]

Bulgaria. Bulgaria is among the six leading nations in the world, and the leading nation in Eastern Europe, in the percent of its electricity generated by nuclear power. Its installed nuclear capacity of 2,760 MW, in five reactors at the Kozloduy NPS, ranks it behind only Czechoslovakia and East Germany in installed capacity in the region. Kozloduy is being expanded with another 1,000 MW reactor supplied by the Soviet Union. Excavation work has begun for another NPS, equipped with four similar reactors supplied by Czechoslovakia, to be located in the Belene region and made fully operational by the mid-1990s.

Bulgaria, where nuclear power in 1988 generated more than 30 percent of total domestically produced electricity, hopes to increase this to 44 percent and 60 percent in 1990 and 2000, respectively. The plants at both Kozloduy and Belene also will provide for the centralized supply of heat to nearby population and industrial centers. In the "near future," Bulgaria will begin construction of the country's first NPS devoted solely to the production of heat. The plant, with an initial heating capacity of 500 MW in each of two blocks, will be expanded "at a later stage" to an overall capacity of 2,000 MW. By 1995, Bulgaria hopes that such plants will supply upward of 17 percent of the "general heating consumption" in the country.[39]

These ambitious projects likely will not be completed on schedule. A joint decree of the highest bodies of the Communist party and the government has harshly criticized the pace of construction on the fifth and sixth blocks at Kozloduy. These blocks were originally scheduled to be fully operational in 1986 and 1988, respectively. A special committee, headed by a member of the Politburo of the Communist party, now oversees construction of the project, but work continues to "develop at an extremely slow pace." The fifth block became operational in 1988, but the status of the sixth block remains unclear. Official publications, although typically reticent in providing detailed information, identify labor shortages (especially of highly skilled technicians), related personnel problems, and delays in the supply of essential equipment as among the primary culprits fostering delays. To mitigate the labor shortage, Bulgaria has imported guest workers from Cuba, Ethiopia, Nicaragua, Poland, and Vietnam for work on the project. The plant at Belene has experienced similar delays in construction, apparently for many of the same reasons as in Kozloduy. In the 1986–1990 period, work there must proceed under "tense conditions of organization and planning" if the project is to be completed on schedule. Bulgaria and Czechoslovakia are engaged in a dispute over the price of reactors for Belene. Czechoslovakia, charging that Bulgaria is unable to pay for it, has delayed delivery of the plant's first reactor. Bulgaria countered that it would purchase reactors from other (unspecified) suppliers whose prices were more competitive than those of Czechoslovakia.[40]

Czechoslovakia. The future of nuclear power in Czechoslovakia seemed problematic when the trouble-plagued A-1 reactor at Jaslovske Bohunice, the country's only operational NPS, was finally closed (allegedly temporarily for repairs) in 1977, never to reopen.[41] Yet only a decade later, Czechoslovakia had the largest installed nuclear capacity in Eastern Europe and will maintain that status through the rest of this century.

Czechoslovakia has two NPS's in commercial operation: one at Jaslovske Bohunice (on the same site as its predecessor, the A-1 reactor) and the other at Dukovany in southern Moravia. Both plants are equipped with 440 MW reactors. The Soviet Union supplied the first two reactors for the plant at Jaslovske Bohunice, and Czechoslovakia supplied all the subsequent reactors for both plants.

According to a Western source, the projected status of nuclear power in Czechoslovakia will create a " 'nuclear state' in the truest sense of the word."[42] By the year 2000, Czechoslovakia plans to commission four reactors each at two NPS's currently under construction at Mochovce in western Slovakia and Temelin in southern Bohemia. Reactors at the latter plant will be the first of 1,000 MW capacity in Czechoslovakia and, more significantly, the first to be protected by a containment vessel. Three other NPS's, each equipped with 1,000 MW reactors, will be built at Kecerovice in eastern Czechoslovakia, Blahutovice in northern Moravia, and Tetov in eastern Bohemia. If plans for the Mochovce, and Temelin plants materialize, Czechoslovakia will have 9,280 MW (or even 11,280 MW if two reactors at Kecerovice become operational) of installed nuclear capacity by the turn of the century. Nuclear power is planned to generate approximately 30 percent of all electricity in 1990 and more than 50 percent by the year 2000, compared with 20 percent in 1986. However, planned nuclear power capacities will still provide only 7.2 percent of primary energy consumption.[43] Additionally, all NPS's will supply heat and hot water to industrial and municipal customers. By the year 2000, nuclear plants are to supply approximately 15 percent of the heat generated in the country. Between 1986 and 1990, investments in the construction of NPS's will more than double similar investments in the previous plan period. Fifty percent of all industrial investments are earmarked for the development of nuclear power up to the year 2010.[44]

Whether these goals will be met is questionable. Indeed, a Czechoslovak source claims that previous targets were devised "without regard to the actual capacity" to realize them.[45] For example, in 1978, Czechoslovakia projected that by 1990 it would possess 10,800 MW of installed nuclear capacity, yet actual capacity by that date will not exceed 4,400 MW. Even this projection may prove overly optimistic, since it includes 880 MW of installed capacity at the Mochovce NPS. Already an official publication has called the plant at Mochovce "the worst prepared building project of its kind" and added that "mistakes in and modifications to the early stage of the project will probably take ten years to rectify." That the site of the plant has proved geologically unstable, thereby creating an "unavoidable need to reinforce the seismic protection," is one of several problems confronting the builders at Mochovce.[46]

Critics have been outspoken regarding delays in commissioning nuclear power facilities. One commentary called it "staggering" that builders have not met even extended deadlines for commissioning reactor blocks. The highest bodies of both the Communist party and the government have issued detailed critiques on the subject.[47] Taken together, these criticisms provide revealing insights into the problems that Czechoslovakia (and, undoubtedly, other Comecon states) are encountering in constructing NPS's.

A shortage of qualified specialists appears to be a major cause of delays. This circumstance above all is the reason for the complicated and extended process of preparation for new nuclear facilities. Skilled blue-collar workers are particularly scarce. At one point, the Skoda works, the principal industrial manufacturer of nuclear equipment, had only six individuals qualified to perform highly exacting hand-welding work on nuclear components. The failure to provide adequate housing, cultural and educational facilities, and other amenities impedes efforts to attract qualified personnel for work at construction sites of new NPS's. Approximately twelve thousand construction and assembly workers are needed at the Mochovce site, while more than ten thousand workers will be deployed during the peak period of construction at Temelin.[48]

Bureaucratic infighting and conflicts are another major source of delays. There have been "repeated failures" to prevent "fundamental conflicts" among designers, suppliers, and builders, who often "subordinate deadlines, the quality of supplies, and other planned parameters to narrow economic viewpoints." There is a "conflict ridden" relationship between participating Soviet and Czechoslovak organizations that often requires discussions between the two sides in an "exacting spirit." These circumstances cause numerous alterations in design, failure to provide requisite equipment and materials to the builders on schedule, and low morale and productivity among the work force.[49] If an account in *Rude pravo* is accurate, then construction of NPS's borders on the farcical:

> Once upon a time, when they began construction there (i.e., Dukovany), they first laid a foundation stone and functionaries descended on the place in nearly 70 cars. Only much later almost without blueprints, a few dozen people started the building process in earnest. Many of them had been recruited from a local brick kiln factory which happened to have closed down recently. The first machinery at their disposal they borrowed from the neighboring agricultural cooperative.[50]

A Western source bluntly assessed these conditions: "More convincingly than any other undertaking, the Czechoslovak nuclear energy program exposes the creeping crisis in the country's neglected economic system." Responsible officials in Czechoslovakia voice similar sentiments in more circumspect language. Thus, Deputy Premier Ladislav Gerle, the official in charge of the nuclear program, during "frank and critical deliberations" with representatives of the nuclear power industry, pointed out "specific shortcomings" in their work. Sounding like Soviet Communist party leader Mikhail Gorbachev in his calls for extensive economic reform, Gerle stressed that the "way out of the situation" demands "an increase in the productivity of all participants in the construction and in the improvement of organization and management work."[51]

East Germany. This country has traditionally been a leader in nuclear power among Eastern European states. Its NPS at Rheinsberg was the first commercial nuclear facility in the region. Between 1974 and 1979, its second NPS (referred to as Nord or Bruno Leuschner) began commercial operation with four reactors. By 1980, East Germany possessed 1,840 MW, the largest installed nuclear capacity in Eastern Europe. In that year, nuclear power generated 12 percent of all indigenously produced electricity.

The assessment that East Germany is "firmly committed" to the development of nuclear power merits caution however. Erich Honecker, the secretary general of the Socialist Unity party (SED), believes that "atomic energy is not the last word" and that coal should remain the principal source of power.[52] Initial forecasts projected that by 1985, East Germany would install an additional 3,520 MW of nuclear power by commissioning another four reactors at the Nord facility and by opening a third NPS (called Stendal or Magdeberg), also with four reactors. By 1985, nuclear power would generate between 12 and 14 percent of indigenously produced electricity. Between 1986 and 1990, expansion of the Stendal plant with four more 440 MW or 1,000 MW reactors would bring national nuclear capacity to either 7,120 MW or 9,360 MW. Nuclear facilities would then generate between 20 and 25 percent of the indigenously produced electricity.

In fact, between 1981 and 1985, no new nuclear capacities were commissioned, and the percentage of electricity generated by nuclear power actually declined. In 1985, nuclear power accounted for only 10 percent of indigenously produced electricity and just 3 percent of primary energy consumption.[53] The 1986–1990 state plan now envisions that the Nord facility will be "made ready" by 1990. Presumably this entails bringing on line the four reactors originally scheduled to become operative between 1981 and 1985. The Stendal plant, now to be equipped with four

1,000 MW reactors, will be "put into operation" in the 1990s. A Western source, reports that the first reactor at Stendal will become operational in 1991, but a Czechoslovak source gives a date of 1995. By 1990, the plan projects, nuclear power will account for 15 percent of indigenously produced electricity. The plan adds that "preconditions for building and putting into service further nuclear power plant units in the years after 1990 are to be created."[54]

Thus, at best, East Germany will have 5,600 MW of installed nuclear capacity by the early 1990s. This is substantially less than it had originally projected for that period and only slightly more than its plan target for 1985. Additionally, in 1990 nuclear power will account for a significantly lower share of electricity than the respective figures envisioned by Bulgaria, Czechoslovakia, and Hungary.

Hungary. Hungary has been ambivalent about nuclear power. Its first (and only) NPS, located at Paks on the Danube River south of Budapest, had its genesis in a 1966 agreement with the Soviet Union to supply two reactors to be operational in 1975 and 1976, respectively. This agreement was never implemented. The government announced in 1970 that the project had been "delayed" for five years, reportedly because low prices for Soviet oil had prompted Hungarian officials to have "second thoughts" about the necessity of nuclear power. Then, in 1974, shortly after the Arab oil embargo sent WMPs for that commodity soaring, the project was officially resurrected. The 1966 agreement was now "modified": Czechoslovakia, not the Soviet Union, would supply the reactors; the capacity of the plant would be doubled, with the installation of four reactors, two each to be made operational in 1980 and 1985, respectively; and the plant might eventually be expanded to a total capacity of 4,000 MW. Other projections contemplated bringing on line one reactor of 1,000 MW capacity annually during the 1990s for a total installed nuclear capacity of between 15,000 and 20,000 MW by the year 2000. In that year, nuclear power would generate approximately one-half of indigenously produced electricity.[55]

Such optimistic projections are rare these days. The experience with making the NPS at Paks operational—a project plagued by extended delays, enormous cost overruns, and myriad administrative, organizational, and labor problems—presumably tempered optimism. The cost of the project, projected in 1976 at approximately 40 billion forints, exceeded 100 billion forints. One fifth of these expenditures were spent on measures to ensure safety in operations.[56] It was not until 1988 that all four reactors became operational. Paks now generates one-third of indigenously produced electricity.[57]

Government agencies "negotiated a long time" over the future status of Paks. Debate involved whether there should be expansion and, if so, with what capacity of reactor. Debate seemingly ended with the announcement in February 1986 that the Soviet Union would help install four more 440 MW reactors during the 1990s. The reputed advantages of this size reactor over its 1,000 MW counterpart included lower cost, shorter construction time, and more limited impact on the national power grid if a reactor ceased operating.[58]

These plans again changed with the announcement in August 1986 that the Soviet Union would render Hungary "technical assistance in the design and installation of two power units with 1,000 MW reactors." The first of these reactors was to become operational in 1996, but it now will not start producing electricity before 1998. Hungary plans to have 7,760 MW of installed nuclear capacity by 2015. This capacity includes the two additional reactors at Paks plus four 1,000 MW reactors at another NPS probably located on the upper reaches of the Tisza River. Nuclear power would then generate approximately 50 percent of indigenously produced electricity.[59]

Hungary has pursued several initiatives that if realized would represent a small but significant departure from Eastern Europe's hitherto almost complete dependence on nuclear technology from the Soviet Union. Recently, Hungary initiated negotiations with Canada to build a Canadian-designed "mini" 10 MW nuclear heating plant. Hungary also would export components for this plant to other Comecon states. In August 1988, a delegation of nuclear experts from France, including representatives of major enterprises constructing NPS's and manufacturing nuclear equipment, visited Hungary. The delegation sought to develop "Hungarian–French technical and scientific cooperation in the peaceful uses of nuclear energy" and explore "the possibilities of industrial cooperation." At the conclusion of the visit, representatives of the Hungarian National Atomic Energy Commission and the French Government Commission for Nuclear Research signed a three-year "joint work program." Substantive details of this program have not been made public.[60]

Poland. The history of nuclear power in Poland resembles the fate of the greedy King Sisyphus of Greek mythology who was condemned forever to roll uphill a heavy stone that always rolled down again. In 1971, the government first indicated its intention to build an NPS located at Zarnowiec near Gdansk, but not until 1974 did the Soviet Union announce that it would supply Poland with four reactors and other requisite equipment for the project. The first reactor would become operational in 1984, and the entire complex would be completed by 1987. Other NPS's, all built with extensive Soviet assistance, would follow. By the year 2000, Poland planned to have an installed nuclear capacity approaching 23,000 MW and derive approximately 40 percent of its electricity from the atom.

These plans never materialized, and Poland remains without a commercially operative NPS. Undoubtedly, reserves of hard coal made the rationale for nuclear power less compelling. In addition, estimates of the cost of completing the Zarnowiec complex were between two and three times greater in the early 1980s than were similar estimates in the 1970s.[61] Finally, there are intriguing but unverified reports that the Soviet Union sought to exclude Poland from nuclear cooperation in Comecon and limited aid to its nuclear program. A Western source asserts that when Poland "tried to launch a large nuclear program in the 1970s, the Soviets effectively blocked it."[62]

Consequently, for many years Poland was "merely going through the motions" in construction at Zarnowiec. Then, in 1982, the government suddenly announced (perhaps for political reasons) its commitment "to build the first Polish nuclear plant" at Zarnowiec.[63] This statement effectively ignored the previous decade-long effort to this end. Present plans call for four reactor blocks at Zarnowiec with a total capacity of 1,860 MW. The first block is supposed to be made operational in 1991, the second and third blocks in 1993 and 1994, respectively, and the final block in the late 1990s. Czechoslovakia will supply the reactors, and other socialist states, including the Soviet Union, will extend aid, but Poland is producing much of the requisite equipment domestically, with some assistance from Western firms. Domestic manufacture will entail numerous projects "never attempted" by Polish industry, including construction of a 500 MW turbogenerator designed by Polish industry under license from a Swiss firm. The turbogenerator will be the largest electrical machine ever built in Poland.[64]

In fact, the Zarnowiec project is far behind schedule, and it remains unclear if it will ever be completed. Many workers associated with the project share this assessment: "If I had to describe their mood in a single word, it would be disbelief! Disbelief in having the station built on schedule and disbelief in a radical improvement in the situation on the site."[65]

Between 1982 and 1986, the plan for capital investment at Zarnowiec was underfulfilled by more than 50 percent. This derived in part from the inability of Polish industry to deliver requisite equipment and machinery. The failure to provide high-quality cement needed to reinforce the foundations of reactors halted work at the site for five months beginning in September 1986. Acute shortages of forged and sheet metal, pipes, and electrical cables also exist.[66]

In the assessment of the minister of mining and energy, Polish industrialists treated Zarnowiec as "simply another investment" project and attached "no particular priority" to it. This same official contends that manufacturers "find it difficult to understand" that equipment for NPS's must be of a qualitatively higher standard than that intended for conventional energy projects. The principal organization coordinating the work of participating contractors at Zarnowiec only recently instituted a program to verify the quality of their deliveries.[67]

Despite its experience at Zarnowiec, Poland has announced plans to build two more NPS's with a total capacity of 6,000 MW by the year 2000. Installed nuclear capacity would then total 7,860 MW and account for 15 percent of indigenously produced electricity. Poland also plans to build nuclear heating plants for the Gdansk, Krakow, Silesia, and Warsaw conurbations in the next decade.[68]

These projects probably will not be implemented on schedule, if they are implemented at all. According to the director of the Institute of Mining and Metallurgy, "at best" Poland will have 5,860 MW of installed nuclear capacities by the year 2000. These capacities will then account for 13 percent of indigenously produced electricity but only 5.3 percent of primary energy consumption.[69] Polish sources themselves contend that a lack of funds has placed the nuclear program "very much in jeopardy." Investment monies in the current plan period are approximately 40 percent less than those originally projected for nuclear facilities.[70] The formation of a government led by representatives of Solidarity in August 1989 makes the future status of nuclear power more uncertain. During the "roundtable" discussions between the government and Solidarity earlier in the year, spokesmen for the trade union movement advocated the abandonment of nuclear power. They proposed solving Poland's energy problems by stopping the export of coal and reducing the consumption of energy in industry. The official Polish news agency reported that Solidarity felt the "economic situation of the entire country and its civilizational and economic backwardness do not guarantee the ability to build an NPS in such a way as to guarantee full safety."[71]

Romania. A Western source uncharitably but accurately asserts that "Romania's nuclear energy program displays more than a few features verging on the absurd."[72] These features include the supervision of the nuclear program by members of the family of Nicolae Ceausescu who possess no appropriate scientific or technical training for the task, the promulgation of unrealistic and never realized targets for the commissioning of nuclear capacities, and groundless claims regarding the capabilities of Romania to produce nuclear equipment for domestic use and export. An unusual feature of the Romanian program is that technology from capitalist countries plays a key role in its realization.

Targets for nuclear power in Romania have varied widely (one researcher identified fourteen different projections in the official press), ranging from 1,000 MW by 1975 to 2,400 MW by 1980 and up to 6,000 MW and 12,000 MW in 1990 and 1995, respectively. The latest available estimate envisions an installed nuclear capacity of 4,500 MW by 1990 and 9,600 MW by 2000. In 1990, nuclear power is to generate 17 to 18 percent of domestically produced electricity.[73] To date, however, Romania has commissioned no nuclear capacities.

Romania has concluded agreements with both the Soviet Union and Canada for the purchase of equipment for NPS's. The earliest agreement, concluded with the Soviet Union in 1970 and reaffirmed in 1974, called for the construction by 1978 of an NPS in Olt County equipped with (probably two) Soviet-supplied 440 MW reactors. The proposed site reportedly was chosen because it was the native county of General Secretary Ceausescu, who often located prestige projects there. Little information is available regarding this project, although the foundation for its first reactor apparently cracked in the 1977 earthquake, and it has probably been abandoned.[74]

Soviet–Romanian nuclear cooperation was rekindled in 1982 with the signing of an agreement whereby the former would supply three 1,000 MW reactors for an NPS (designated Moldova) to be located in Romania's northeastern province of Moldavia. Little was heard about the project until 1985, when a Soviet official indicated that a site for the nuclear plant would soon be chosen, and in 1986, when a Hungarian source informed that the plant would be built near Piatra Neamt and the builders "would like" to have the first block operational by 1990.[75] Czechoslovakia was then scheduled to supply the reactors for Moldava. As noted, however, Romania cancelled the order for these reactors and work on the prospect presumably has been suspended.

Nuclear cooperation between Romania and the Soviet Union illustrates the strained nature of their overall political relationship. Romania consistently avoids domestically publicizing the role of the Soviet Union in its nuclear program. In contrast, the Romanian population can discover this role by listening to Radio Moscow's Romanian Service, which stresses the vital aid that the socialist fatherland is extending to its less developed socialist partner to bring it into the nuclear age. Reportedly, the Soviet Union has shown its displeasure with Romania by insisting that it pay for a "substantial" portion of the Moldova project with hard goods.[76]

Romania also exhibited its independence from the Soviet Union when it concluded a 1977 agreement with Canada for the supply of reactors and other nuclear equipment, making it the first Soviet bloc state to reach such an agreement with a Western country. Canadian officials revealed that Canada would initiate negotiations with Romania for the purchase of four Canadian-built reactors (each of 660 MW capacity) that would cost "hundreds of millions of dollars—easily in excess of $300 million to start with and then depending on how far they want to go." Romania would minimize the costs of nuclear projects by constructing most of the plants—and much of the equipment therein—itself.[77]

In 1978, Canada extended to Romania a $1 billion credit for the purchase of these reactors for an NPS to be constructed near Cernavoda on the Danube River. The initial purchase was to be part of a larger deal whereby Romania would acquire by the year 2000 an additional twelve reactors, with some to be manufactured entirely by Canada and others by Romania under Canadian license. Romania also awarded an Italian–American consortium a $320 million contract (backed by a $120 million credit from the U.S. government) to provide turbine generator sets and associated equipment for the Cernavoda project. The first reactor at Cernavoda was to become operational in 1985, and the entire project was to be completed by 1990. Romania hoped to become self-sufficient in the production of reactors and to export them to Third World countries, paying Canada only for the license to do so.[78]

Romania concluded these agreements for both political and economic reasons. Politically, they are a component of its strategy to maintain some measure of independence from the Soviet Union. The type of reactor that Romania purchased from Canada fosters this end—a reactor fueled by unenriched uranium, thereby freeing Romania from reliance on the Soviet Union for enrichment facilities. It is unclear, however, where, if not from the Soviet Union, Romania will acquire the uranium needed for this reactor (its own indigenous deposits of uranium are apparently exhausted) or the heavy water that it uses as a coolant. Economically, the substantial credit offered and a willingness by Canadian manufacturers to accept payment partially in barter must have been attractive to Romania.

The Romanian–Canadian nuclear deal has not been a model for East–West trade. To date, none of the reactor blocks at Cernavoda are operational, and despite assurances by Canadian officials that they have an "interest" in "stepping up efforts" to commission these facilities, it remains unclear if or when they will become so.[79]

Fiscal considerations largely explain this circumstance. One problem is that Romania cannot make full use of its $1 billion line of credit from Canada because it possesses insufficient reserves of hard currency for repayment. Romania insists that all its purchases from Canadian manufacturers be repaid in barter, with preferential tariffs for those products otherwise not competitive on the Canadian market. Apparently, the Canadian nuclear industry is agreeable to these arrangements, but other domestic groups lobbied successfully to have approximately two-thirds of the value of the purchases repaid in hard currency.[80]

The Cernavoda project suffered a major setback in 1982 when the United States, expressing concern over the accuracy of data that Romania provided on its overall economic situation and specifically regarding the Cernavoda project, suspended the aforementioned $120 million credit and Canada did likewise with the remainder of its credit. While the credits were reactivated more than a year later, Canada still insists on repayment mostly in hard currency. Inflation has eroded much of the value of the original credit so that it now barely covers the purchase of two, rather than the originally projected four, reactors.[81]

In response, General Secretary Ceausescu has asserted that the nuclear program must be implemented at "minimum expense" by reducing the "excessive consumption" of building materials at Cernavoda. Canadian officials are "particularly concerned" that such initiatives could compromise the safety of the plant, especially since it is located in a sensitive seismic region.[82]

Despite these setbacks, Romanian officials have spoken about expanding the Cernavoda plant to five power blocks and even cooperating with Canada in building another NPS to be located somewhere in Transylvania. That officials of the Canadian nuclear power industry reportedly seek to cooperate with Romania to build NPS's "in third countries" only emphasizes the surrealistic nature of these events.[83]

Chernobyl and the Nuclear Debate

The explosion at the Chernobyl NPS on April 26, 1986, contaminated large areas of Eastern Europe's environment with radioactive waste. It also precipitated highly visible protests against the development of nuclear power in the region and the overall reticence of communist governments to provide full and prompt information about the scope and impact of the accident.[84]

The emergence of a discernible antinuclear lobby is unusual in Eastern Europe, where regimes typically are intolerant of incipient political pluralism and dissent. Critics charge that nondemocratic political practices themselves are factors that compromise nuclear safety and increase the risks of another Chernobyl. As a member of the Polish Academy of Sciences argued, the "great weakness" of nuclear safety measures in Poland "is rooted in the extensive and long-standing practice of concealing and falsifying breakdowns and accidents as well as their circumstances and results." He continued: "No public analyses, investigations, and trials take place, and no real causes and truly guilty people are disclosed. The situation is made worse by the ineffective and deceptive system of information and public warnings, a thing that has often created great trouble."[85]

Not surprisingly, the most widespread protests occurred in Poland, which suffered the highest levels of radioactive contamination among Eastern European states and where anti-Soviet sentiment is particularly strong. More than two thousand people in Krakow, organized by the dissident pacifist group Freedom and Peace, marched to the old royal castle carrying placards and chanting antinuclear slogans, including "No Iodine from the USSR," "Thou Shalt Not Kill," and "Today Chernobyl, Tomorrow Zarnowiec." Five Polish nuclear power experts published an open letter urging the government to reassess the safety features at Zarnowiec, which, they claimed, had "raised doubts" among the population because many features of the plant were based on untested Soviet prototypes.[86] Another critic asked how Poland could expect to build and run a technologically sophisticated facility like Zarnowiec when it has "technological problems in manufacturing toilet paper, not to mention the production of an average grade of automobile."[87] A petition from some 3,000 residents of Bialystok in northern Poland (one of the areas seriously polluted by emissions from Chernobyl) to the Sejm, the Polish parliament, demanded a halt in construction at Zarnowiec until the project could be placed under the supervision of the International Atomic Energy Agency (IAEA) and assurances could be provided that the plant would use only the most sophisticated safety systems.[88] The justifiable concern over nuclear safety makes the location of a nuclear plant in proximity to the Gdansk conurbation a "step bordering on suicide," another opponent of Zarnowiec asserted.[89]

Critics also have assailed other nuclear projects. The proposed site of Poland's second nuclear plant at Klempicz in northwest Poland has engendered "fierce disputes," which one official attributed to the "Hiroshima complex" that is "deeply rooted" in Polish society. Environmentalists oppose the site because it is in a national forest reserve where construction will inevitably upset the ecological balance.[90] Proponents of Poland's third nuclear plant are "rash and frivolous," according to opponents, because they provide no "verified and reliable economic calculations" to support the project.[91] Freedom and Peace has led thousands of protesters in several demonstrations against a proposed nuclear waste disposal facility at Miedzyrzec in abandoned bunkers built during World War II. The mayor of Miedzyrzec has said that he is "unaware of any advocates of the nuclear waste dump," and the town council has endorsed opposition to the project.[92]

A senior official of the Polish Academy of Sciences recently challenged both the economic and ecological rationales for nuclear power. He argued that a comprehensive comparison demonstrates the cost-effectiveness of coal-fired power plants over NPS's. Official calculations understate the cost of producing nuclear power. For example, they typically exclude the cost of closing obsolete NPS's. (This cost can amount to upward of 25 to 30 percent of the original cost of the plant.) In his judgment, Polish nuclear plants will have an operating life only half that of comparable Western facilities because of inadequate design, construction, and maintenance work. The economy and environment would benefit more if the monies now designated to develop nuclear power were invested in projects to reduce the excessive consumption of energy and equip coal-fired power plants with purification installations.[93]

On Environment Day, 1986, hundreds of East Germans—doubtless well informed about the Chernobyl events by West German television—submitted a petition to the government titled "Chernobyl' Is Everywhere." The petition asserted that Chernobyl had caused "insecurity and a feeling of being threatened." The petition condemned the government's alleged reluctance to discuss openly the magnitude and consequences of the accident as "irresponsible and socially dangerous" and urged the authorities through a referendum (constitutionally permitted, though never used) to initiate a "broad public discussion" about the future of nuclear power and, specifically, whether East Germany should completely abandon it by 1990.[94] Members of the Evangelical Church in East Germany, long active on issues of environmental protection, also addressed these problems. In one instance, Church activists sent a letter of protest to the Council of Ministers that called official claims about the safety of Soviet-designed reactors "erroneous" and demanded that all reactors be shut down immediately and research begun on alternative sources of energy. The subject figured prominently in the deliberations of the May 1986 synod of the Church's leadership conference. One participant remarked that the "crust of taboos" surrounding public discussion of this hitherto unmentioned subject had been broken and a "nuclear debate" had ensued among the people. The hierarchy of the Church was more circumspect. Although it acknowledged that Chernobyl had raised questions about whether nuclear power was "socially responsible," it predicted that East Germany "would probably have to live with nuclear energy for some time."[95]

In Czechoslovakia, a Western source reported "marked fear" and "panic" after Chernobyl among citizens residing near Czechoslovakia's two NPS's. *Rude pravo* implicitly confirmed this when it reported that after Chernobyl, "many people" in Czechoslovakia asked whether the development of nuclear power "cannot be slowed down or even stopped."[96] A new dissident group called Antiatom has emerged with the self-proclaimed goal of stopping the "atomic threat" in Czechoslovakia. It has distributed postcards with a picture of the Temelin NPS and a message warning about the costs and dangers (including the potential to divert fissionable materials to build nuclear weapons) of the Czechoslovak nuclear power industry.[97] The prominent dissident group Charter 77 also has criticized the Temelin project. The group points out that the site chosen for the project is situated in a region with high seismicity and population density. It also questions the safeguards against seismic movements of the Soviet-designed reactors at Temelin.[98]

Nahlas, a group of environmental activists in Slovakia, circulated a petition with fourteen hundred signatories (among them many prominent scientists and cultural figures) that demanded a "public discussion" of environmental problems, including the threat that nuclear power poses to the environment. Nahlas has criticized plans to locate an experimental nuclear reactor within the city limits of Bratislava. Ninety concerned scientists similarly opposed this project. The scientists especially criticized the transport of hazardous wastes along city streets, asserting that "it is inconceivable what would happen if there was a traffic accident."[99]

In Hungary, protests have been limited primarily to the issue of disposal of nuclear wastes.[100] Each year Hungary must dispose of upward of twenty-five hundred 200-liter barrels of liquid wastes from the Paks NPS and sundry "mildly and moderately radioactive secondary wastes" (such as contaminated instruments, tools, and protective clothing). Other nuclear wastes, including spent fuel rods from Paks, are shipped to the Soviet Union.[101] Without prior public debate on the decision, the government began construction of a nuclear waste facility at Ofalu in southern Hungary. According to an Austrian publication, opposition to this initiative has assumed "hurricane proportions."[102] Public protests, including critical commentaries in the official media, led to the appointment of an independent commission of experts to study the matter. The commission found that geological, soil-related, chemical, and hydrological factors made the proposed site "unsuitable for a nuclear waste dump." Reportedly, officials are seeking alternative locations for the facility, although construction work at the Ofalu site continues.

Antinuclear protesters in Eastern Europe are unlikely to compel authorities to abandon nuclear power. First, they operate in nondemocratic political systems that can severely restrict their activities. Second, most regimes have devoted so many resources to nuclear power that they are unlikely (except perhaps in Poland and Romania) to abandon these efforts. Third, just as in democratic societies, there are ardent proponents of nuclear power who believe that the benefits from the atom far outweigh its costs.

Nevertheless, Chernobyl and popular opposition to nuclear power appear to have fostered or reinforced reservations about nuclear power among the political elites throughout Communist Europe. These reservations are most obvious regarding the traditionally insouciant approach to nuclear safety.

Authorities in Poland decided to halt construction temporarily at the Zarnowiec NPS, reportedly because nuclear experts have become "very meticulous" about any compromises in safety at the plant. "The issue is delicate," one source adds, "because following the Chernobyl' tragedy, specialists are inclined to be overcautious, even though in such cases you can never be too careful."[103]

Both Czechoslovakia and East Germany have announced that their NPS's at Temelin and Stendal, respectively, will be protected by containment vessels—the first such structures to be installed in these countries. Czechoslovakia also is establishing a center equipped with advanced Japanese computers to train specialists in accident prevention at NPS's. Czechoslovakia plans to increase exportation of electricity to Western Europe to earn hard currency for the purchase of nuclear safety equipment.[104]

Bulgaria reports that "security systems" at the Kozloduy NPS "have been tripled" since the accident at Chernobyl. One-third of all investments to be spent in the expansion of Kozloduy are "earmarked for security measures."[105] Chernobyl even appears to have affected the nuclear program in Romania. Prime Minister Constantin Dascalescu was the only official speaker at the 1986 session of the Comecon Council who publicly indicated reservations about the development of nuclear power. "We have reached the conclusion that we have to review our nuclear energy program, proceeding from the need to increase security levels," he informed the session. Dascalescu also stated that Romania would take "firmer steps" to develop alternative sources of energy.[106]

Since Chernobyl, Communist states also have become much more active in international efforts to enhance nuclear safety. In May 1988, representatives from Comecon and the IAEA met in Moscow to examine problems relating to the safe operation of nuclear facilities and prospects for "broadening of cooperation" between the two organizations. Such cooperation would include a three-year joint program of studies in the "probability modelling of accidents for reactors of various types."[107] Czechoslovakia, Hungary, and the Soviet Union invited teams from the IAEA to inspect selected national nuclear facilities in 1988 and ensure their adherence to international standards of safety.[108] The Soviet Union has proposed that France and the United States join the Comecon states in devising permanent joint programs to train personnel who operate NPS equipment.[109]

East Germany has been especially active in this endeavor. It recently adhered to an IAEA convention (in effect since October 1986) that obligates signatories to provide early warning in case of nuclear accidents. It has concluded bilateral agreements with Austria, Denmark, and West Germany that contain similar obligations.[110] The agreement with Austria extends the obligation to inform to "unusually high levels of radioactivity caused by third parties." East Germany also has signed bilateral agreements relating to nuclear safety with Bulgaria, the Soviet Union, and the

People's Republic of China.[111] Communiqués announcing these agreements provide few details of their substantive provisions.

Political considerations undoubtedly motivate communist states to pursue these initiatives. Certainly, the Soviet Union sees cooperation with the IAEA as a means to mitigate the damage that Chernobyl inflicted on its international reputation. East Germany typically concludes bilateral agreements with capitalist states in part to enhance its standing in the international community. Yet these motivations should not obscure the importance of these states assuming obligations in the international control of nuclear energy and permitting (albeit limited) international scrutiny of their national nuclear facilities.

Prospects

Nuclear power is now entering a third stage of development in Eastern Europe that will determine its status well into the next century. The first stage of development, dating from 1955 to roughly 1970, began with grandiose dreams about the potential to exploit the atom for peaceful purposes and ended in disappointment, frustration, and recriminations as almost none of these dreams materialized. The second stage of development, spanning the decade of the 1970s and extending into the early 1980s, saw most countries place NP'S in commercial operation and all of them make plans for a substantial augmentation of nuclear capacities. The difficulties encountered therein—difficulties not unique to Eastern Europe—have clearly swept away the "excessive optimism" of earlier years and created a "more realistic" attitude as Eastern Europe enters the current stage of nuclear development.[112] Decision makers must now make hard choices regarding the status of the almost 42,000 MW of nuclear capacity either under construction or contemplated in the region. To be sure, the targets for nuclear power announced at the 1986 session of the Comecon Council in Bucharest seemingly indicate that these choices have been finalized, but the history of nuclear power in Eastern Europe is replete with prognostications never realized. The decision by Romania to cancel the order for reactors at the Moldava NPS could prove a harbinger of similar actions by other Eastern European states.

Economic considerations will be of primary importance in these deliberations. Expenditures on nuclear facilities (almost invariably far higher than initially estimated) have consumed huge amounts of investment resources in all countries of the region. The inefficiencies typical of Eastern European economies help drive up costs. For example, a Czechoslovak source estimates that France needs 30 to 35 percent less cement and metal and 50 percent less labor than does Czechoslovakia to construct nuclear facilities of similar capacity.[113] Expenditures of such magnitude severely constrain the capacity of regimes to invest in nonnuclear projects, including those designed to increase the production of other forms of energy: "A very detrimental effect on the entire economy is recorded by the constantly growing volume of investment costs per unit of output in nuclear power plants which currently limits the possibilities to make investment in other areas, even in the fuels and energy industry itself.[114]

Expenditures on nuclear power will increase as funds are allocated to dispose of ever greater amounts of nuclear wastes, to purchase nuclear fuels as indigenous reserves of uranium become depleted, to acquire the equipment and materials necessary to enhance the safe operation of nuclear facilities, and to decommission the first generation of reactors, which are now approaching obsolescence. Fiscal concerns have made the future of nuclear power in Czechoslovakia "an open question for some time yet" and have led East Germany and Hungary to a "certain adjustment" of their nuclear programs.[115] If world energy prices do not rise appreciably above existing levels, arguments challenging the cost-effectiveness of nuclear power will become even more compelling. However, the enormous material resources devoted to date to exploiting nuclear power seemingly ensure that no national nuclear program will be abandoned completely, although such a circumstance is at least conceivable in Poland and Romania.

Enhanced concern for safety also will affect the deliberations of decision makers. Such concern was evident even before the accident at the Chernobyl NPS. For example, in 1979, two scientists were permitted to publish an article in the authoritative Soviet journal *Kommunist* questioning the wisdom of locating nuclear facilities near densely populated areas.[116] Chernobyl clearly has accelerated these concerns and prompted regimes to undertake well-publicized steps to prevent future nuclear mishaps.

Yet doubts about safety persist. The nondemocratic nature of Eastern European polities represents one aspect of the problem. Elites have traditionally formulated nuclear policies with little regard for public reservations about the wisdom of their actions. The location of huge nuclear complexes within conurbations where an accident could endanger the lives of literally millions of people provides a relevant example. The emergence of antinuclear lobbies in several Eastern European states has mitigated, but not fundamentally altered, the insulation of nuclear policy from comprehensive public debate. The absence of independent institutions to monitor nuclear personnel exacerbates the seemingly universal tendency to cover up mishaps and impedes the pursuit of requisite prophylactic policies.

The economic system in communist Europe, with its emphasis on production to the detriment of other objectives, also can compromise nuclear safety. Thus, the chief inspector for nuclear safety of the Czechoslovak Commission for Atomic Energy has asserted that nuclear personnel circumvent safety procedures "to ensure production tasks": "Certain tendencies actually do exist. In operations this mainly applies to shortening the shut downs of blocks. Attempts are made to accumulate or leave out some controls as a result."[117] Similarly, Valerii Legasov, the Soviet academician who headed the initial official investigation into the causes of the Chernobyl disaster, rejected official claims that the accident was sui generis: "After being at Chernobyl, I drew the unequivocal conclusion that the Chernobyl accident was the apotheosis, the summit of all the incorrect handling of the economy that had been going on in our country for many decades."[118]

Finally, regimes already severely strained by the fiscal demands of nuclear programs may be unwilling or unable to muster the huge additional sums for requisite (at least by Western standards) safety measures.

Ironically, even after Chernobyl, concern for environmental quality may remain one of the strongest rationales for nuclear power in Eastern Europe. Admittedly, the statement by a ranking nuclear official in Czechoslovakia that nuclear power "unavoidably" necessitates that "some parts of the country will have to be more or less devastated" is hardly reassuring to environmentalists.[119] Yet the exploitation of all forms of energy, especially the brown coal and lignite prevalent throughout Eastern Europe, entails varying disruptions to the environment. On balance, while nuclear power may not be the panacea of environmental degradation in Eastern Europe, it may prove less harmful to the environment than alternative sources of energy.

However these issues are resolved, nuclear power probably will remain an important, albeit far from decisive, component of future energy balances in the region. This assessment applies especially to Bulgaria and Czechoslovakia and, to a lesser extent, to East Germany and Hungary. In contrast, the future of nuclear power seems much less certain in Poland and Romania. Events exogenous to the region—in particular, another world oil crisis that drives up the price of alternative sources of energy—could alter this somewhat pessimistic prognostication and again make the atom the key to the region's energy future.

Coal

The fate of coal in Eastern Europe bears striking parallels to the phoenix, the beautiful bird of Egyptian mythology that experienced a cycle of long life, seeming death, and subsequent rebirth. The long life of coal as the backbone of the energy balance in Eastern Europe extended through the mid-1960s. In 1965, coal still constituted more than 60 percent of the primary energy consumed in all Eastern European states except Romania, where liquid and gaseous fuels predominated in consumption. In Czechoslovakia, East Germany, and Poland the percentage of coal in primary energy consumption (more than 80 percent in each state) was among the highest in the world. East Germany was (and remains) the largest producer of brown coal and lignite (soft coal) in the world.

In the post-1965 period, coal experienced a substantial decline in energy balances throughout the region. The exception was in Romania, where its status remained essentially unchanged. As table 3–4 indicates, this decline was particularly pronounced in Bulgaria and Hungary and somewhat less manifest in Czechoslovakia, East Germany, and Poland. The rebirth of coal occurred in the 1980s, when all Eastern European states sought to close their energy gaps in part through expanded production of solid fuels. Parallels with the phoenix may end here. Unlike that creature, whose rebirth led to a subsequent long and vigorous life, efforts to revitalize domestic coal industries have encountered considerable difficulties. It remains unlikely that coal will reclaim its pre-1965 position of preeminence in primary energy consumption.

When expressed in gross tons, output of coal presents a misleading picture of the role that coal plays in closing the energy gap.[120] First, gross output figures usually are compiled before coal is cleaned of sundry impurities and noncombustible substances (ash, stones, sulfur, and water) that inflate its true weight.[121]

Second, these figures do not reflect the caloric content (the actual amount of energy) of different types of coal. Thus, five tons of low-quality soft coal may yield the equivalent energy of one ton of hard coal. This circumstance assumes special significance in Eastern Europe, where soft coal increasingly predominates in overall production. Expressing output of coal in oil equivalent rather than gross tonnage, provides a realistic indication of the total amount of energy derived from mined coal. Thus, in 1986 compared with 1970, production of coal in Eastern Europe increased by 29.1 percent when measured in gross tonnage but by 19.5 percent when measured in oil equivalent. The respective figures are 15.7 percent and 6.1 percent when Poland and Romania are excluded from the computation (table 3–5).

Third, the process of converting coal into usable energy itself consumes substantial amounts of energy and thereby constitutes an important factor exacerbating the energy gap.[122] Finally, personnel may falsify gross production figures to receive bonuses and other perquisites contingent upon fulfillment of planned targets for production. As noted, Polish offi-

Table 3–4
Eastern Europe: Role of Coal in Primary Energy Consumption
(percent of total primary energy consumption)

	1965	1977
Bulgaria	65	32
Czechoslovakia	83	62
East Germany	93	71
Hungary	70	34
Poland	90	77
Romania	18	18
Eastern Europe	79	57

Source: Calculated from data in National Foreign Assessment Center, *Energy Supplies in Eastern Europe: A Statistical Compilation*, figures 1 through 7.

cials acknowledge that they inflated output figures for coal by upward of 20 percent over actual production during the 1970s.[123]

Coal: 1960–1985

Two interrelated factors prompted the reduced reliance on coal that began in the 1960s. Mining conditions worsened as higher quality and easily exploitable deposits were depleted. The caloric content per ton of mined coal decreased in all Eastern European states between 1960 and 1977. Bulgaria and Romania experienced the sharpest declines (table 3–6). West German calculations graphically illustrate the relative inefficiency of coal

Table 3–5
Eastern Europe: Production of Coal
(percent change between 1970 and 1986)

	Oil Equivalent	Millions of Metric Tons
Bulgaria	0	20.3
Czechoslovakia	2.8	14.8
East Germany	15.6	18.4
Hungary	− 34.0	− 16.9
Poland	33.4	50.0
Romania	68.0	132.3
Eastern Europe	19.5	29.1

Source: Computed from data in appendix.

Table 3–6
Eastern Europe: Decrease in Caloric Content
per Ton of Mined Coal between 1960 and
1977
(percent)

Bulgaria	33.1
Czechoslovakia	12.4
East Germany	5.3
Hungary	16.7
Poland	6.9
Romania	29.0

Source: Calculated from data in National Foreign
Assessment Center, *Energy Supplies in Eastern Europe: A
Statistical Compilation*, table 11.

as a source of energy. In 1973, one ton of oil yielded the equivalent
energy on 17 tons of mined coal in East Germany.[124] Overall, a Soviet
source calculates that between 1971 and 1978, the cost of extracting one
ton of coal, on average, doubled in the region.[125] In contrast, liquid and
gaseous fuel exports from the Soviet Union seemingly provided Eastern
Europe with an abundant and relatively inexpensive alternative to coal.

Prospects for coal revived somewhat after the twin oil shocks of 1973
and, especially, 1979. Economic planners now viewed coal more favorably
as the price of oil on the capitalist and Soviet markets increased substantially. In the 1976–1980 period, all Eastern European states except Hungary planned increases in the production of coal.[126]

The plan targets of the several states formed a pattern that would
repeat itself in the subsequent plan period. At one extreme, Romania
established the most ambitious (and unrealistic) plan target: to increase
production in 1980 versus 1975 by between 100 and 110 percent. At the
other extreme, Hungary established the least ambitious production target.
After initially deciding to reduce production by approximately 7 percent
in 1980 versus 1975, Hungary envisioned maintaining the 1975 level of
production through 1980. Escalating costs required Hungary to allocate to
coal mining 4.7 percent of total industrial investments between 1976 and
1980, versus 3.5 percent between 1971 and 1975, to realize even this
modest production target.[127]

Bulgaria and Poland established the more ambitious targets among the
remaining states. By 1980, Bulgaria sought an increase in production
(comprising exclusively brown coal and lignite) of 36 percent over the
1975 level of production. Poland planned to increase production of hard
coal by 22 percent in 1980 compared with 1975. In addition, Poland

undertook its largest energy investment project during the 1976–1980 period to exploit the 1 MT reserves of brown coal at the Belchatow field. These reserves mostly would replace hard coal in coal-fired power plants, thereby freeing more hard coal for export to international markets to earn convertible currency. Such exports have been Poland's largest earner of convertible currency. Czechoslovakia and East Germany established more modest targets that called for raising production in 1980 by 9 percent and 13 percent, respectively, over the 1975 level.

However, the long lead time needed to construct new and expand existing mines, increase the productivity of labor through greater mechanization, and halt, if not reverse, the shrinkage of the labor force militated against crash programs to expand production of coal. In particular, coal mining throughout Eastern Europe experienced a dramatic slowdown in the growth of labor productivity during these years.[128] Consequently, the performance of coal mining in the 1976–1980 period brought, at best, mixed results. On the one hand, in 1980 overall output of coal in the region was 7.6 percent higher than in 1975, and all states, including Hungary, registered increases in production. On the other hand, other developments were not as encouraging.

First, all states substantially underfulfilled their production targets for 1980. The only exceptions were Czechoslovakia, which almost realized its target, and Hungary, which exceeded its goal. Admittedly, the overly ambitious level of the targets in several states (such as Bulgaria and, especially, Romania) contributed to this circumstance.

Second, if output from Poland is excluded, production of hard coal in the region virtually stagnated between 1975 and 1980. In reality, production probably declined because of the inflated output figures that Poland reported for this commodity during these years.

Third, national coal industries, suddenly confronted in the mid-1970s with ambitious plan targets but often with insufficient material and labor resources to realize them, typically subordinated sound mining practices— shaft preparation, water and gas removal, proper maintenance of machinery—to the immediate task of plan fulfillment. This circumstance, while economically rational for mining personnel desirous of the economic perquisites attendant upon meeting production targets, impaired the capacity of coal industries to fulfill the even more ambitious production targets of the 1980s.

The enormous increase in world energy prices between 1979 and 1981 provided the next imperative to increase reliance on coal. All national economic plans for the 1981–1985 period projected increases in coal production, but the rates of increase envisioned varied considerably. The pattern of the previous plan period reemerged: Romania and Hungary, respectively, established the largest and smallest rates of increase in production; Bulgaria and Poland projected substantial, albeit lower, rates of increase; and Czechoslovakia and East Germany sought more modest expansions in output (table 3–7).

How challenging were these targets is, like beauty, in the eye of the beholder. Both Hungary and Poland may have established the most challenging targets by seeking *any* increase in production—the former because of the enormous problems besetting the coal industry itself; the latter because of the enormous political turmoil besetting the entire country. Or East Germany might have set the most challenging target by projecting an annual increase in production of almost 2.5 percent when it already was the world's largest producer of soft coal. That Romania again established the most unrealistic target was undeniable. A Hungarian source noted that the Romanian coal program contained "strenuous" targets that would encounter "extraordinary problems" in fulfillment.[129]

The performance of all the coal industries in the region between 1981 and 1985, except in East Germany and Romania, was disappointing. To be sure, overall production of coal was almost 13 percent greater in 1985 than in 1980, and the respective figure for brown coal and lignite was almost 20 percent greater. Further, production of brown coal and lignite in East Germany grew from 258 MT in 1980 to 312 MT in 1985; the latter figure exceeded the plan target by 22 MT. Romania also experienced a substantial increase in production from 27 MT in 1980 to 46 MT in 1985, although output in 1985 was far below the plan target of 87 MT.

Negative developments were more numerous. Four countries—Bulgaria, Czechoslovakia, Hungary, and Poland—produced less hard coal in 1985 than in 1980 and less brown coal and lignite in 1985 than in 1984. Production of hard coal in the region declined in 1985 compared with 1980. This circumstance surely owed much to the political turmoil in Poland, which had a dramatically adverse effect on the performance of collieries in that country. Yet the long-run prospects for hard coal in the region clearly are bleak. The decreasing share of hard coal in total output adversely affects the amount of energy yielded in mined coal. Thus, in 1986 compared with 1980, production of coal increased by 14.2 percent in gross tonnage but by only 5.7 percent in oil equivalent. Finally, the status of coal mining in Hungary is especially worrisome. The mining sector there has experienced a "constantly deepening crisis" that "appears unavoidable."[130] Hungary possessed the dubious distinction of being the only Eastern European state to mine less coal in 1985 than in 1980. Further, it met none of its annual production targets for this commodity between 1983 and 1985.[131]

Table 3–7
Eastern Europe: Coal Production Plans versus Actual,
1985

	1985 Production (MT)		1985 Production vs. 1980 Production (percent)	
	Plan	Actual	Plan	Actual
Bulgaria	37	32.4	22.5	7.2
Czechoslovakia	132	126.6	7.0	2.1
East Germany	290	312.0	12.3	20.8
Hungary	26	24.5	1.1	−4.6
Poland	320	249.3	39.1	8.3
Romania	87	46.0	148.0	31.0

Sources: Data on production from appendix. Plan targets from national
economic plans of the respective countries.

Coal: 1986–1990

The status of coal in the national economic plans for the 1986–1990
period suggests that coal, unlike the phoenix, is not destined for another
long and vigorous life in Eastern Europe after its modest rebirth in the
early 1980s. Most states plan minimal or no increases, and one state,
Czechoslovakia, actually plans an overall decrease in production of coal
by 1990 (table 3–8). As usual, Romania constitutes the exception to these
remarks. However, Romania's projected increase in production cannot be

Table 3–8
Eastern Europe: Coal Production Plans, 1990

	1990 Plan (MT)	Growth Rate, 1986–1990 (percent)
Bulgaria	43.5	6.0
Czechoslovakia	119.0	−1.2
East Germany	335.0	1.4
Hungary	24.0	—
Poland	265.6	1.3
Romania	117.3	20.3
Eastern Europe	904.4	1.8

Source: United Nations Economic Commission for Europe,
Economic Survey of Europe in 1986–1987, 204. Based on
national statistics of the respective countries.

taken seriously and reflects only the surrealistic nature of the Romanian coal program.

Bulgaria. Bulgaria plans to increase overall production of coal in 1990 to 43.5 MT, including 32 to 33 MT of lignite. Bulgarian sources themselves admit that this is an "exceptionally difficult and responsible assignment."[132] That production of coal in 1985 compared with 1984 actually declined by 4.5 percent affirms this assessment. In 1986, however, output increased by 13.9 percent over 1985 and by 8.7 percent over 1984.[133] Typically, Bulgarian authorities provide few details publicly on specific problems besetting coal mining. They did, however implicitly confirm reservations with this industry by promulgating an official production target for 1990 that is substantially lower than the well-publicized target originally projected for that date.[134]

Czechoslovakia. Czechoslovakia has become the first state in Eastern Europe to plan an absolute decrease in production. Czechoslovakia now plans to reduce extraction of soft and hard coal in 1990 by 6.6 percent and 4.1 percent, respectively, compared with the 1985 levels of extraction. Respective reductions of 20 percent and 11.4 percent are planned for the year 2000. Production of lignite in 2005 should be approximately 75 percent of the present level of production. Projected nuclear power facilities and a decline in the energy intensity of the national economy are to compensate for less coal.[135]

These assumptions probably are unrealistic. For example, in both 1986 and 1987, Czechoslovakia failed to meet its target for reducing the consumption of energy. In response, in 1987 Czechoslovakia mined 3 more MT of coal than planned.[136] The factors that prompted the planned reduction merit elaboration, as they exist to varying degrees in all Eastern European states.

Increasing exhaustion and deterioration in the quality of reserves, escalating costs encountered in the exploitation of deposits under steadily worsening mining conditions, and the declining quality of the physical environment from using highly polluting solid fuels are among the primary factors prompting the projected decline in production.

Czechoslovakia, at current levels of extraction, is depleting its extractable reserves of hard and soft coals by 2.4 percent and 4.0 percent annually. In the North Bohemian coal basin, the comparable figure for all types of coal is 3.5 percent annually.[137] Further, the quality of the coal now being mined—as measured by its caloric value and ash, cinder, and sulfur content—is declining sharply.[138]

The cost of extraction is escalating. This is due in part to the aforementioned decline in the caloric value of coal. This circumstance increases overall costs for manpower, machinery, and transportation by requiring that more coal be mined to yield equivalent amounts of usable energy.

Steadily worsening mining conditions have driven up the per ton cost of mined coal since the late 1970s by anywhere from 33 to 60 percent, depending on conditions at individual mines.[139] Coal in the North Bohemian region increasingly is mined at depths of 300 to 400 meters versus the previous norm of 100 to 150 meters.[140] The ratio of overburden to crude coal (that is, cubic meters of waste per ton of mined coal that must be removed) at strip mines in the region is expected to double in the current decade. More than 250 million M3 of overburden are now removed annually.[141] By one estimate, labor productivity at strip mines in Czechoslovakia is one-third lower than at similar mines in East Germany, in "large part" because of more difficult mining conditions.[142] Considerable costs are incurred by the need to relocate towns, factories, rail lines, and waterways to exploit new coal deposits that will replace once accessible but now depleted reserves.[143] Finally, collieries typically concentrate on the immediate task of fulfilling production plans to the detriment of sound mining practices and the safety of miners. An account in *Rude pravo* assailed mining personnel for their "antiquated view" that the "main thing is to get the coal out at any cost," but this criticism ignores the imperatives of the production plan that foster such behavior.[144]

Reliance on coal has contributed to extensive degradation of the physical environment. From the so-called lunar landscapes created by the strip mining of soft coal to emissions of sulfur dioxide emanating primarily from coal-based combustion, coal has contributed more to the degradation of the environment in Czechoslovakia than all other forms of primary energy combined. The government has promulgated a comprehensive program to reduce environmental pollution by the year 2000 to the level found in 1970. Officials correctly assert that this goal is unrealizable without a substantial diminution in the use of coal throughout the national economy.[145]

East Germany. This country seemingly is approaching a ceiling on increases in production of soft coal. As one energy expert asserted, East Germany either "cannot increase the production of this fuel" or can do so "only to an insignificant degree."[146] The plan target for coal in the 1986–1990 period reflects this assessment: to increase production in 1990 to 330 to 335 MT, or by 5.8 to 7.4 percent, over the level of production attained in 1985. This target represents an increase in the rate of production growth that is less than one-half the rate achieved between 1980 and 1985. That production decreased in both 1986 and 1987 indicates that even this target may prove overly ambitious.

Official sources cite mining costs that are "enormous" and "continue to rise" as the principal impediment to increased production. These costs rose, on average, by approximately 50 percent per ton of mined coal in 1985 compared with 1975.[147] Deteriorating mining conditions largely account for this circumstance. Strip mining now occurs at depths of 40 to 80 meters but is soon expected to increase to depths of 80 to 120 meters.[148] The average ratio of overburden to crude coal in strip mines increased from 3.9:1 in 1980 to 4.5:1 in 1985. It will reach 7:1 in several of the mines currently under development. To achieve the plan target of 335 MT in 1990 will require the removal and disposal of upward of 1.7 billion tons of overburden. The same level of production in the year 2000 will require the removal of more than 2 billion tons of overburden.[149] Another costly problem—reportedly one of almost "astronomical scale"—is keeping strip mines free of water. For this purpose, more than 2.6 billion M^3 of water (an amount equivalent to approximately 7 percent of total annual precipitation in East Germany) must be pumped annually from the mines.[150] The relocation of housing stock, industrial facilities, and transportation infrastructure to make new deposits accessible for exploitation also demands considerable expenditures.[151]

East Germany will continue to be the largest producer of soft coal in the world, but the formidable obstacles to any substantial increase in production make it unlikely that coal will fulfill the dream of its optimistic proponents as the long-term panacea to resolve the energy gap.

Hungary. *Nepszava*, the daily newspaper of the trade unions, published a series titled, "Whither Coal Mining?," reflecting the uncertain state of that sector in Hungary.[152] As noted earlier, Hungary extracted less coal in 1985 than in 1980 and fulfilled none of its annual production targets between 1983 and 1985. In 1986, Hungary mined approximately 16.9 percent less coal (including 44 percent less hard coal) than it did in 1970. In these years, output of coal expressed in oil equivalent declined by 34 percent. To achieve these declining results, coal mining has consumed a steadily increasing share of investments in industry: In the three economic plan periods between 1971 and 1985, coal mining received 3.5 percent, 4.7 percent, and 7.5 percent of the total industrial investments.[153] These circumstances prompted one critic to liken coal mining "to the bottomless pit that swallows all the money."[154]

Hungary now hopes to maintain annual production through 1990 at least at the 24.5 MT level attained in 1985. This target appears unrealistic, since production in 1986 declined by 3.8 percent compared with 1985. Moreover, the overall amount of usable energy yielded by this coal will decrease, since the share of lignite in total production is scheduled to increase from approximately 27 percent in 1985 to more than 36 percent in 1990.[155] To compensate for costs of extraction that more than doubled between 1981 and 1985, coal mining sought investments in the present plan period equivalent to approximately 85 percent of the respective monies allocated between 1976 and 1984.[156] The monies actually allocated are approximately one-third less than those requested. Several analysts reject the official estimate that these monies are sufficient to meet production targets.[157]

Coal mining will continue to confront serious challenges in meeting production targets. This circumstance owes much to previous policies that emphasized the immediate objective of plan fulfillment to the long-term detriment of coal mining:

> If we are to understand the problems of coal mining, we have to look back over 15 years, when the idea was that the only coal mines to be developed were ones with better quality coal. This is understandable. But in the meantime the coal was needed. Therefore, there was a decrease in exploration, there was a drop in the money supply for the purchase of new mine working machines, and the manpower shortage rapidly increased.[158]

The preoccupation with plan fulfillment continues in the current decade. Laszlo Kovacs, secretary general of the Trade Union of Mining Industry Workers, characterized the 1980–1986 period as one of "enforced exploitive mining." Another source bluntly asserted that the requisite program to prepare mines for future exploitation has now "practically broken down."[159]

The combination of severe shortages in both personnel and modern mining equipment presents a formidable obstacle to fulfillment of plan targets. The number of workers directly engaged in mining operations decreased by approximately 50 percent between 1960 and 1985. This trend likely will continue. By 1990, the overall work force engaged in mining may decline by another 11 percent. Those workers engaged directly in underground mining operations could decrease by as much as 45 percent.[160] Dangerous working conditions exacerbate the labor shortage. The number of miners "crippled" at work is "increasing rapidly" and now reaches the equivalent of 11 percent of the labor force in the coal sector.[161]

The authorities have sought unsuccessfully to mitigate labor shortages. First, they have attempted to reduce labor turnover among miners by increasing their already higher than average industrial salaries and other financial benefits. While increased emoluments have generally failed to reduce turnover, they have unintentionally fostered resentment and envy among the citizenry. Many citizens view miners as "moles" who are unconcerned with the public weal and want only "to become millionaires."[162]

Second, authorities have increased overtime work among miners, approximately one-third of whom now regularly work a six-day week. In 1985, such work accounted for approximately 5 percent of national production of coal, and the respective figure at several mines exceeded 10 percent. However, this work also exacerbates the already high rate of labor turnover in the coal industry and exerts a "physical burden" on miners that endangers their health and lowers their productivity.[163]

Finally, authorities have augmented the labor force in mining with "guest workers" from other socialist states (principally Poland) and "work shirkers endangering public safety" whom courts have sentenced to mandatory work in industry.[164] These initiatives represent no panacea for the labor shortage. First, the guest workers have proven costly. By one estimate, payments to such workers have increased the costs of production in mining by approximately 10 percent. Second, work shirkers—individuals who are shunned by all industries except those desperate for workers—typically have not proven to be paragons of labor in the workplace. Professional miners indict them for a careless and indifferent attitude toward their work that lowers morale, endangers the safety of other miners, and results in damage to valuable machinery.[165]

Higher labor productivity in coal mining becomes imperative to compensate for declining manpower. One forecaster calculates that Hungary will mine barely 20 MT of coal in 1990 if labor productivity remains at the level attained in 1985 and the projected decline in the work force materializes.[166]

Considerable opportunities exist to modernize mining operations. Laszlo Kovacs notes that in 1985 almost 40 percent of all machinery used in coal mining was considered obsolete. Mechanical breakdowns of machinery idled miners for upward of 50 percent of their shift.[167] Many mining operations are not mechanized. For instance, at the Mecsek coal mines, the only hard coal mines in Hungary, manual labor performs almost all shaft cutting and associated production activities.[168]

These problems provoke considerable debate among analysts regarding the future status of coal mining. Critics contend that an inevitable decline in production justifies a substantial diminution in resources allocated to mining. To compensate for less coal, they advocate using existing energy resources more efficiently and increasing importation of energy. They would increase national wealth to pay for imports by redirecting investment monies from coal mining to modern, especially export-oriented, production sectors.[169] The opposing viewpoint typically accepts this diagnosis of the ills of the coal industry, but rejects the prescription for curing them. It argues that measures to enhance efficient use of energy and modernize production can be realized only in the long run and that no immediate alternative to reliance on coal exists.[170]

This debate is intertwined with the broader issue of economic reform in Hungary. The imperatives of reform argue for exploiting only profitable reserves of coal. The imperatives of the production plan dictate the opposite strategy. One source predicted that no more than 17 MT of coal will be mined in 1990 if profitability alone determines exploitation.[171] These conflicting imperatives create "insoluble dilemmas" for coal mining: "It is impossible to decide whether the primary goal of the enterprise is production, satisfying the needs of the economy and the population, or increasing efficiency and profitability. The two goals cannot be met at the same time, so they must decide which is primary for coal mining."[172]

The strike by hundreds of miners at the Mecsek coal combine in August 1988 illustrates the political explosiveness of these issues.[173] The strikers set forth their "major concerns" in an open letter to Prime Minister Grosz. The letter demanded, inter alia, that efforts to make coal mining profitable not threaten either job security or the standard of living of miners. Secretary General Kovacs, speaking in support of the strikers, stated that miners "demanded a more definite protection of their interests" than hitherto provided and specifically considered unemployment "unacceptable." Kovacs added that "despair . . . about the general problems of coal mining" also motivated the strikers.[174] The strike itself has now ended, but the issues that prompted it remain unresolved.

Poland. The steadily increasing share of soft coal in national production and escalating costs incurred in exploitation characterize the Polish coal industry. Between 1980 and 1985, the share of soft coal in national production increased from 16 percent to 23 percent. This trend should continue. Present plans envision the extraction of 70 MT and 81 MT of these coals in 1990 and 2000, respectively.[175] If output in 1986—which increased by upward of 16 percent over the 1985 level of production and exceeded the plan target by 4 MT—proves to be a harbinger, then the 1990 plan target will be realized. Unfortunately, soft coal has an energy yield typically one-half to two-thirds less than the hard coal traditionally mined in Upper Silesia.[176]

The future status of hard coal is more problematic. Wladyslaw Gwiazda, deputy chairman of the Council of Ministers, asserts that deteriorating mining conditions create a "practically insurmountable barrier" to achieving the 1990 plan target of 195 MT of hard coal.[177] Even if this target is met, brown coal and lignite will still make up more than 26 percent of national production in 1990. This figure could be greater if, as several analysts predict, insufficient investments drive the 1990 level of hard coal production below that attained in 1985.[178]

Whether this pessimistic prognostication will materialize remains to be seen. Most analysts argue that Poland must expand mining to compensate for the depletion of reserves and the closure of obsolete collieries. By one estimate, more than one-third of existing collieries will cease operating as early as the first decade of the next century.[179] Failure to expand mining capacities could result in a gradual decline after 1995 in output of hard coal from mines in Upper Silesia, with cost-effective mining operations ending there by the latter part of the next century. Similarly, without new investments, exploitation of brown coal and lignite deposits could cease within fifty years.[180]

Other analysts challenge this prescription. They argue that expanding mining capacities "devour with growing appetite" scarce investment monies that could be better spent on technological modernization of industry, including mining operations themselves. In this view, Poland can be saved from an "energy collapse" only if it effects a "fundamental economic turnabout" that reduces the excessive consumption of energy.[181] The director of the Institute of Energy Carriers of the Polish Academy of Mining and Metallurgy asserts that collieries can extract an additional 900 MT of coal by increasing the degree of use of mined deposits to 50 percent from the present figure of 43 percent. Collieries now "abandon" approximately 60 percent of the coal in mined deposits by exploiting only the thickest and most easily accessible reserves.[182] Given the requisite lead time to open a new mine, even a crash program to build new collieries will have little effect on production before the late 1990s.

That coal deposits are increasingly exploited at greater depths under complex geologic and hydrologic conditions is one factor increasing costs. The average depth of Polish mines has increased from approximately 360 meters to more than 500 meters in just two decades. By the year 2000, this figure may approach 900 meters.[183] In Upper Silesia, deposits traditionally were exploited at depths of 100 to 300 meters, whereas today some mines are deeper than 1,000 meters. The costs of production in these newer mines can be eight times greater than comparable costs in the older mines.[184] A similar situation exists at the newly exploited Lublin hard coal basin, where extraction is beginning at depths greater than 800 meters. The costs of production there—more than double comparable costs at selected mines in Upper Silesia—prompted critics to label the project "unsound" and a "highly ineffective" venture. Poland has sought unsuccessfully to obtain the fiscal and material participation of other Comecon states in the development of the project.[185]

Investment monies in new equipment and technologies are desperately needed in mining operations. The entire infrastructure, including equipment, at many mines is in "disastrous condition."[186] To compensate for low labor productivity, a six-day workweek (with considerable overtime) is standard in coal mining. The prevailing official attitude toward mining is that the mines must work "at full tilt . . . because coal is what counts." The debilitating physical and mental pressures of this workload promote substantial labor turnover, accidents, and chronic shortages of personnel, especially in underground mining operations.[187] The retirement each year of an "army of people" from mining due to silicosis, black lung, and other occupational diseases exacerbates the labor shortage.[188]

What monies the crisis-ridden national economy provides for investments in hard coal mining represent a key variable in the future status of the industry. If investment monies only maintain current levels of hard coal production through the 1990s, the absolute amount of usable energy from mined coal will decline as soft coal increasingly predominates in production. The revival of exports of hard coal to the international market will further increase the share of soft coal in domestic consumption. Depressed prices on this market in the late 1980s have led Poland to reduce these exports substantially.[189] As noted earlier, representatives of Solidarity advocate the cessation of these exports to mitigate domestic energy shortages.

Romania. The Romanian coal program continues its surrealistic course. The least bizarre—although still unrealizable—of several published plan targets envisions the extraction of 95 to 100 MT of coal in 1990, an increase of 105 to 116 percent over the 1985 level of production.[190] An even more unrealistic target projects pushing extraction of brown coal and lignite production "past the 100 MT mark" before 1990.[191] The most unrealistic target (contained in an official publication of the United Nations) foresees that in 1990 Romania will extract 153 percent more coal than it did in 1985. To realize this target, Romania planned to increase extraction by upward of 20 percent annually between 1986 and 1990.[192]

These targets will not be achieved. Already Romania has underfulfilled the 1986 production target by approximately 33 percent.[193] Production in that year increased by only 3.2 percent over the comparable level in 1985. Production of hard coal especially may have encountered difficulties. In the 1987 Comecon statistical yearbook, Romania for the first time did not report a production figure for hard coal.[194] Measures "to improve the organization of management, production, and labor" are expected to generate much of the planned increase in production.[195] In other words, the coal industry will receive little new equipment and technology and must squeeze greater production from existing resources. Romanian sources admit that higher labor productivity remains a "requirement of the first order" but are typically reticent about specific measures to realize this end.[196] Officials have pursued higher production targets by transferring thousands of workers from other sectors (including the armed forces) to work directly in mining and by instituting strict measures to reduce rampant absenteeism and turnover among mining personnel.[197] The poor quality of much of the coal now being mined hardly merits these efforts. Secretary General Ceausescu at one point even advocated using sunflower stalks for energy because they yielded double the energy of lignite being extracted at several collieries.[198]

Prospects

Prospects for coal likely will dissatisfy both its proponents and opponents. Proponents, particularly prominent after the oil shocks of 1973 and 1979, envisioned coal replacing prohibitively expensive liquid fuels as the panacea for the energy gap. Opponents viewed coal as a backward, highly inefficient fuel whose role should be limited in a modern highly industrialized society. "Whither Coal Mining?" has now become a prominent subject of public debate among analysts, especially in Czechoslovakia, Hungary, and Poland.

The disappointing performance of coal mining since the 1970s—despite strenuous material and physical efforts to revitalize the industry—prompted the debate. In 1985, production of hard and soft coals was, only 8.5 percent and 27 percent, respectively, greater than comparable output in 1975. The production of hard coal actually declined (by approximately 5.1 percent) during this period if output from Poland is not included. The share of soft coal in total production increased from 68 percent in 1975 to 71 percent in 1985. The concomitant decline in caloric content of mined coal yields increasingly less usable energy per unit of output. Even these meager results were obtained only through crash programs that subordinated the optimal exploitation of deposits to the immediate task of plan fulfillment. These ill-conceived programs increase costs and deplete exploitable reserves in mining.

The fate of coal will depend largely on the status of economic reform in Eastern Europe. The plethora of problems besetting coal mining—escalating costs, deteriorating mining conditions, declining quality of reserves—conflict with an intensive strategy of economic development that emphasizes efficiency and profitability. A comprehensive calculation of costs must include both direct and indirect costs incurred in the exploitation of coal. Degradation of the physical environment throughout Eastern Europe provides a relevant example of these costs.[199] That Czechoslovakia proposes to reduce reliance on coal to mitigate massive deterioration in the quality of its environment provides one example of what occurs when states consider the total costs of exploiting coal.

Czechoslovakia also illustrates the difficulty of substantially reducing reliance on coal. As noted earlier, underfulfillment of planned targets for

Table 3–9
Eastern Europe: Production of Hydroelectricity, 1986

	Production (millions of Kwh)	Percent of Total Production	Percent of Domestically Produced Electricity	Percent of Exploited Reserves[1]
Bulgaria	2,326	9.7	5.5	26.9
Czechoslovakia	3,990	16.7	4.7	42.2
East Germany	1,767	7.3	1.5	75.0
Hungary	154	0.5	0.5	5.5
Poland	3,784	15.9	2.7	27.2
Romania	11,896[1]	50.0	16.6[1]	35.0[2]
Eastern Europe	23,917			

Sources: *Statisticheskii ezhegodnik stran-chlenov Soveta Ekonomicheskoi Vzaimopomoshchi*, 77; *Hospodarske noviny*, no. 40 (1985), in JPRS-*EEI*, no. 92 (9 December 1985): 6; Agerpres, 10 October 1988, in FBIS-*EEU*, 2 November 1988, 36.
[1]1985 data.
[2]1988 data.

nuclear power and energy conservation likely will prevent Czechoslovakia from realizing this end. As long as Czechoslovakia and other Eastern European states remain inordinate consumers of energy, coal will remain an important component of energy balances throughout the region.

Other Energy Resources

Hydroelectric Power

The role of hydroelectric power is and will remain limited in Eastern Europe. Only in Romania does hydroelectric power generate more than 5.5 percent of domestically produced electricity (table 3–9). And primary electricity itself—that generated by hydropower and nuclear power—composed only a minuscule share of primary energy production throughout the region, except in Bulgaria.

Several factors account for the limited use of hydropower. In the region, only Romania is endowed with substantial water resources suitable for exploitation. Conversely, readily available reserves of indigenous coal and imported liquid and gaseous fuels provided little economic incentive for states to develop existing water resources. In addition, economic planners, imbued with the Stalinist fixation for giant projects, usually ignored the exploitation of local water resources suitable for small-scale hydropower facilities. The 1988 session of the Comecon Council, calling for the use of "literally all resources" to generate power, explicitly endorsed the development of small-scale hydropower projects: "The declared objective is this: in addition to the traditional construction of major hydroelectric power stations to create a network of lesser stations on small rivers."[200]

Romania has announced the most ambitious plans to develop hydropower. Typically, Romanian sources issue contradictory reports regarding these plans. Thus, in one three-month period, the official news agency provided figures of 18 percent and 25 percent as the share of electricity to be generated by hydropower in 1990.[201] In 1990 and 2000, Romania plans to use, 65 percent and 100 percent, respectively, of its exploitable water resources.[202] That Romania used only 30 percent of these resources in 1983 indicates either the ambitious or unrealistic nature of these targets.

Czechoslovakia has promulgated a Comprehensive Program to Develop Hydroelectric Power up to the Year 2000.[203] The program envisions that by the next century, Czechoslovakia will use 63 percent of its exploitable water resources and have an installed hydroelectric power capacity of 10,000 MW. Many of the planned projects will be small-scale facilities solely for local use.[204] Minister of Fuels and Power V. Ehrenberger defended the cost-effectiveness of hydroelectric power, although he admitted that "many doubters" dispute this assessment.[205] Requisite resources to maintain rapidly aging facilities (many hydroelectric plants are "even older" than fifty years) represent a key factor increasing the unit cost of producing hydropower.[206] Even if all planned targets are met, hydropower will generate only 6.8 percent of domestically produced electricity in 2000.

The Gabcikovo-Nagymaros power plant and barrage system on the Danube River, which is being jointly developed by Czechoslovakia and Hungary, represents one of the largest hydroelectric projects ever undertaken in Eastern Europe. The project envisions the construction of hydroelectric power plants (totaling 878 MW of installed capacity) and dams at Gabcikovo in Czechoslovakia and Nagymaros in Hungary. The project has encountered substantial delays and been embroiled in controversy almost since its inception in 1977.[207]

The initial agreement projected that the entire facility would be completed by 1991. However, in October 1981, Hungary, citing limited fiscal resources, discontinued construction at Nagymaros and proposed an overall suspension of work on the project until 1990.[208] In ensuing negotiations, Hungary, reportedly under intense pressure from Czechoslovakia, agreed to resume the project, which is now scheduled to be completed in 1995. Subsequent work has been plagued by shortages of equipment, materials, spare parts, and, especially, personnel.[209] In 1986, Hungary was forced to contract with Austrian firms to finance and build many of the remaining facilities at Nagymaros. Hungary will repay this assistance by supplying Austria with two-thirds of its annual share of electricity from the project (or 1.2 billion kwh) for a twenty-year period beginning in 1996.[210]

The project also has engendered widespread protests, primarily in Hungary, against its potentially adverse impact on the environment. In numerous public forums, including demonstrations involving thousands of individuals, environmentalists have protested that the project will flood huge areas of fertile agricultural and forest lands, reduce the water table and endanger the water supply for millions of residents of nearby localities, and increase pollution in the already heavily contaminated Danube River. Environmentalists also question allocating such large resources to Nagymaros when the Paks NPS is supposed to provide a surplus of electricity by the year 2000.[211]

Critics of the project received assistance from an unexpected source when the Soviet House of Culture in Budapest invited the public to view a Soviet film on why barrage systems should not be built on flat land (as is Nagymaros). The letter accompanying the invitation asserted: "No single other enemy out to destroy our planet earth has ever done so much damage as the constructors of (these) barrage systems. The barrage systems are the product of shortsighted, tunnel-visioned technocrats out to overpower everything; they stand in opposition to . . . environmental protection."[212]

The controversy culminated in an unprecedented debate in the Hungarian National Assembly on the future status of the project. The final vote—317 deputies voted in favor of the project, 190 opposed it, and 31 abstained—reflected neither the acrimonious nature of, nor the depth of opposition expressed in, the debate that ensued. Opponents criticized the project as both economically and environmentally unsound. One deputy asserted that "if there had been democracy in Hungary in 1977, then we would not be here debating the barrage system today." This official accused the government of deliberately underestimating the total cost of the project (which could now total upward of 150 billion forints versus official estimates of 55 billion forints in 1986 and 20 billion to 25 billion forints in 1977). Opponents of the project included Rezso Nyers, member of the ruling Politburo and founder of Hungary's economic reform, who cited both ecological and economic reasons for his abstention on the vote.[213] Both the National Assembly and the Ministry of Environmental Protection and Water Management will now establish special commissions to ensure that construction at Nagymaros meets requisite standards for environmental protection. The minister of the latter agency responded "unequivocally yes" when asked if critics of Nagymaros would be represented on the ministry's special commission.[214]

The latest development in this saga occurred on May 14, 1989 when the Hungarian government, citing both ecological and economic considerations, suspended most construction work on the project. A joint Czechoslovak-Hungarian commission of experts was appointed in an unsuccessful attempt to resolve outstanding issues between the two sides. The Hungarian government has promised to issue a final decision on the status of the project (which must be approved by the Parliament) by October 31, 1989. Czechoslovakia has announced that it will demand compensation if Hungary fails to fulfill its obligation to complete the project. Austria insists that Hungary honor its agreement to repay Austrian financial assistance for the project with electricity beginning in 1996, although the electricity could come from a source other than Nagymaros. This latter circumstance would permit Hungary to cancel the Nagymaros project and fulfill its obligations to Austria (perhaps with electricity from the Paks NPS).[215]

Liquid and Gaseous Fuels

Indigenous production of these fuels, except in Hungary and Romania, can make only a modest contribution to closing the energy gap in Eastern Europe. Further, Hungary and Romania—the only states in the region where these fuels constitute a significant share of primary energy production—will experience through the rest of this century considerable difficulties in maintaining even current levels of production.

Hungary produces around 2 MT of crude oil and 7 billion m³ of natural gas annually. In 1986, Hungary met 23 percent and 64 percent, respectively, of its consumption of these fuels through domestic production. Rates of exploitation exceed rates of discovered new reserves for both fuels. Many newly discovered reserves are of diminishing caloric content and are located in small deposits that increase the cost of exploitation.[216] Some analysts predict that production of both fuels will decline as early as 1990, while others see this occurring only in the next decade.[217]

Romania, traditionally the largest producer of crude oil and natural gas in Eastern Europe, has experienced sharp declines in production of both fuels since 1975. In 1985, Romania produced 26.5 percent and 13.9 percent less crude oil and natural gas than it did in 1975. Prospects for reversing these declines in the near future are not propitious. Extensive efforts to discover new reserves of either fuel have yielded limited results. Since the late 1970s, Romania has announced the discovery of large reserves of oil and natural gas on the continental shelf of the Black Sea. A huge infrastructure to transport and refine these reserves has been built in anticipation of their commercial exploitation. Only in 1987 did Romania report that it had extracted the "first amounts" of oil and natural gas from the continental shelf. Western analysts express considerable skepticism regarding both the size and commercial viability of these reserves.[218] Increasing the rates of recovery from existing reserves is the most likely source of any increase in output. Romania announced in 1981 that by 1985 it would raise this rate for crude oil to 40 percent from the then current rate of 32 percent.[219] However, the rate of recovery for oil remained essentially unchanged between 1981 and 1986. Romania now hopes to attain the 1985 target for recovery by 1990.[220]

Production of oil and natural gas combined does not exceed 5 percent of primary energy production in any other state. Bulgaria and East Germany produce negligible amounts of oil, and the former produces negligible amounts of natural gas. East Germany did significantly increase its known reserves of natural gas between 1983 and 1988, but these reserves would still be exhausted in 14 years at the 1987 rate of extraction.[221] In Czechoslovakia, newly discovered reserves may permit output of both oil and natural gas to double by 1990 (although the absolute level of output will remain small).[222] Poland recently announced the discovery of "rich deposits" of natural gas at depths of almost 4,000 meters in the districts of Kozalin and Pila.[223] The overall rate of discovered new reserves for both oil and natural gas, however, lags far behind current rates of exploitation.[224] The powerful coal lobby reportedly has opposed efforts to intensify the search for new deposits of both fuels.[225] Finally, prospects are limited for the exploitation of oil and natural gas in coastal waters of the Baltic Sea. Petrobaltic, a joint company established by East Germany, Poland, and the Soviet Union, has discovered few commercially exploitable reserves of either fuel in these waters.[226]

Nontraditional Energy

In Eastern Europe, as elsewhere, imposing technological, economic, and geographic factors have impeded the widespread exploitation of nontraditional sources of energy.[227] Geothermal waters are used in Hungary to provide heat and hot water for six thousand apartments and two industrial plants. Between 1986 and 1988, Romania produced almost 450,000 tons of conventional fuel from nontraditional souces of energy. Bio-gas production accounted for over 80 percent of this energy. By 1995, Romania plans to use approximately 50 percent of the bio-gas and 60 percent of the geothermal waters that are commercially exploitable.[228] East Germany appears to be the leader in using animal and human wastes to produce biogas for energy purposes. Romania envisions the most ambitious use of these nontraditional sources of energy. It has promulgated a comprehensive program to exploit the energy potential of waves, wind, and sun of the sea and its environs.[229]

Overall, in 1985 Comecon states produced only 0.2 percent of their primary energy from these sources.[230] All the states have announced plans to increase the use of nontraditional energies, but their contribution to the energy balance will remain minuscule.

Summary

Eastern Europe is finding it increasingly difficult to close the energy gap through increases in primary energy production. The average annual increase in primary energy production in the 1981–1985 period compared with the 1976–1980 period slowed considerably in Bulgaria, Czechoslovakia, Hungary, and Poland. East Germany and Romania were exceptions to this trend. Overall, the average annual increase in primary energy production in the region remained essentially unchanged between 1976 and 1985 (table 3–10).

One cannot be optimistic about any substantial change in this situation. The diminishing caloric content of mined coal will continue to yield less usable energy per unit of output. No Eastern European state possesses

Table 3–10
Eastern Europe: Primary Energy Production*
(average annual percentage change)

	1976–1980	*1981–1985*
Bulgaria	2.1	0.9
Czechoslovakia	1.3	0.5
East Germany	1.2	4.0
Hungary	2.1	1.4
Poland	2.0	0.6
Romania	0.4	1.9
Eastern Europe	1.4	1.5

Source: United Nations Economic Commission for Europe, *Economic Survey of Europe in 1986–1987*, 197.

*Calculated from data on primary energy production converted into standard coal equivalent (coefficients vary across countries). Due to the methodology applied, the figures in this table may differ from national or other sources.

the potential to expand substantially the production of gaseous, liquid, and hydropower resources. Nontraditional sources of energy will compose for the foreseeable future a minuscule share of primary energy production.

Nuclear power represents the only source of energy whose potential remains largely unexploited. Increasing the efficiency of mining operations represents another potential source of energy. Losses of extractable reserves in mining operations in Eastern Europe now average between 30 and 40 percent for coal, 50 percent for natural gas, and 70 percent for crude oil.[231] Reducing these losses will be expensive, requiring the purchase of modern mining equipment and technologies. Western states are the exclusive manufacturers of much of this equipment.

These generalizations inevitably require modification when assessing the future status of primary energy production in individual Eastern European states. However, all the states must consider the opportunity costs of depending so heavily on supply-side initiatives to expand the production of energy. These costs include economic opportunities that are overshadowed by the necessity to devote huge investments to maintain this expansion. They also include less obvious costs, such as the enormous deterioration of the physical environment and health of the people, which are attendant upon the widespread exploitation of brown coal and lignite.

4

The Supply Side:
The International Energy Market

> No doubt it would be a mistake if the Comecon countries were to judge the long term possibilities of raw material and energy imports from the developing countries on the basis of their temporarily rather disadvantageous solvency experience at the beginning of the 1980's.
>
> —*Nepszabadsag*, 13 November, 1984

Eastern Europe has traditionally played a limited role in the international (world) energy market. Individual states—Poland as an exporter of hard coal and Romania as an importer of crude oil and an exporter of refined products—are exceptions to this generalization. Importation from the international market continues to make up a modest, though expanding, share of total importation of fuels and energy in Eastern Europe. Much of this imported energy is crude oil, which is not consumed domestically but is reexported either directly or in refined form. Eastern Europe consistently has remained a net exporter of energy, although not necessarily of oil (combined crude oil and refined products), to the international market.[1]

Several factors explain these circumstances. First, Eastern Europe imported little energy from any source when primary energy consumption consisted overwhelmingly of indigenously produced solid fuels. Only when Eastern Europe began consuming significant quantities of liquid and gaseous fuels did this circumstance change. Second, until the late 1970s, the Soviet Union supplied Eastern Europe with most of its requisite importation of energy. Third, in contrast to the Soviet Union, suppliers on the world market usually demanded payment from Eastern Europe in hard goods or currencies. Fourth, Eastern Europe probably has seen the Soviet Union as a more reliable source than the international market, where political developments can disrupt supply. Relevant examples include the overthrow of the shah of Iran, a leader willing to export energy to socialist states on favorable terms of trade, and OPEC producers playing their oil card to pressure Romania to alter its policy toward Israel. To be sure, the issue is one of relative reliability. After all, the Soviet Union has not refrained completely from playing its own oil card in Eastern Europe, nor did it honor its contractual obligations for oil to the region during the 1981–1985 period. Finally, states may lack requisite refining capacity to process large amounts of imported crude oil. In Czechoslovakia, analysts claim that substantial investments would be required to make refineries capable of processing crude oil with a chemical composition different from that of the Soviet crude for which they are designed. These expenditures could be justified only in the unlikely event that large and stable deliveries of crude from the world market were guaranteed.[2] In Poland, considerable quantities of additional crude could be processed only if the country's neglected refinery capacity were substantially expanded and modernized. "It is just not a question of hard currency" to purchase crude, the director of one refinery explained. "Poland's refining capacity is depreciating rapidly and is insufficient to meet increased demand."[3]

Importation

The twin oil price shocks of 1973 and, especially, 1979, which dramatically increased WMPs for energy, and the overthrow of the shah of Iran represent seminal developments in Eastern Europe's importation from the international energy market.

In the late 1960s, the Soviet Union began urging its allies to meet part of their requirements for energy by importing from the international market.[4] Consequently, by 1973, all Eastern European states imported oil from this source. Most of the crude oil was supplied under barter agreements concluded with Iran, Iraq, and Libya (table 4–1). East Germany also imported substantial quantities of oil from West Germany. The Soviet Union itself appears to have reexported to Eastern Europe some of the crude that it obtained from the international market, partly as payment for military equipment that it supplied to countries such as Libya.[5]

Eastern Europe, excluding Romania, derived 13 percent of its total imports of crude oil from the international market in 1973 versus 8 percent in 1970. The respective figures including Romania were 19 percent and 13 percent. Romania, Bulgaria, and East Germany, in that order, derived the largest share of their imported crude from the international market.[6] The refusal of the Soviet Union to export crude to Romania and the inability of domestic production to satisfy the requirements of its burgeoning petrochemical industry for this fuel led Romania to expand importation of crude from the international market after 1970. Bulgaria and East Germany were net importers, and the remaining states typically net exporters, of oil to the international market between 1970 and 1973.

Eastern European analysts, while never viewing the international market as the panacea to close the energy gap, did expect it to play an

Table 4–1
Eastern Europe: Importation of Crude Oil from the Middle East*
(thousands of tons)

	Algeria	Iran	Iraq	Libya	Kuwait	United Arab Emirates	Total
1970	740	1,200	425	6	—	—	2,371
1971	1,055	3,395	675	550	—	—	5,675
1972	1,185	5,145	5,265	3,295	—	—	14,890
1973	410	6,630	10,380	3,890	160	—	21,470
1974	890	4,620	7,070	465	—	—	13,045
1975	935	2,425	8,320	1,225	1,640	705	15,250
1976	435	3,955	11,145	2,710	1,575	1,040	20,860
1977	180	5,870	10,285	1,365	1,300	1,040	20,040
1978	1,045	3,635	10,565	2,515	1,140	835	19,735
1979	640	3,185	15,540	3,290	5	995	23,655
1980	450	485	12,150	2,500	560	855	17,000

Source: OPEC Yearbook, 1980, pp. 34–44, reprinted in Stern, "CMEA Oil Acquisition Policy in the Middle East and the Gulf," 1, 419.
*These figures probably include Yugoslavia.

increasingly important role to this end. In 1974, a Hungarian source predicted that by 1980 the Comecon states might import upward of 150 to 170 MT of crude oil from the international market, a tenfold increase over the amount imported in 1972.[7] Another Hungarian source predicted that by the late 1980s, Eastern Europe alone would import 60 to 90 MT of crude oil and 40 billion to 50 billion m^3 of natural gas annually from developing countries.[8]

The Adria pipeline project, initially discussed in 1965 among Czechoslovakia, Hungary, and Yugoslavia, represented the first major attempt to realize these goals.[9] The project originally envisioned the joint construction of a pipeline from Yugoslavia to Hungary and Czechoslovakia to carry more than 30 MT of crude oil annually from Middle Eastern states. As part of the project, Czechoslovakia concluded an agreement with Iran in 1969 to purchase 20 MT of crude over a ten-year period in return for Czechoslovak industrial goods worth an estimated $200 million.[10]

Controversy plagued the project from its inception. Not only could the participating states not agree on its route, but public protests in Yugoslavia questioned its potentially adverse impact on the environment. The parties finally reached an agreement in 1973 to construct Adria by 1975 with an annual capacity of 34 MT of crude oil. Yugoslavia would receive 24 MT of this capacity, and Czechoslovakia and Hungary would each receive 5 MT. Poland and Romania also expressed interest in the

Table 4–2
Eastern Europe: Comparison of Planned
Importation of Crude Oil from the
Middle East, 1980, and Actual Importation,
1975
(*millions of metric tons*)

		1980	
	1975	Early Plans*	Revised Plans
Bulgaria	0.4	6	2
Czechoslovakia	0.3	5	1
East Germany	1.9	6	3
Hungary	1.5	6	3
Poland	2.4	18	4
Romania	5.0	—	11
Eastern Europe	11.5	41	24

Source: Haberstroh, "Eastern Europe: Growing Energy
Problems," 387.
*Estimated.

project. Poland indicated it might provide credits and equipment for the
pipeline in return for between 4 and 11 MT of crude oil annually.[11]

Kuwait, Libya, the World Bank, and the participating states provided
financing for the estimated $450 million cost of the project. Kuwait and
Libya extended credits of $150 million and $70 million, respectively, to
this end. The pipeline actually was completed in 1979 at a cost of $620
million. Czechoslovakia and Hungary each contributed $25 million of this
amount.[12]

Unfortunately, the pipeline never fulfilled its intended purpose. Escalating WMPs for oil after 1973 and the replacement of the shah of Iran
with a regime initially determined to export crude oil only for hard currency made importation of requisite quantities of Middle Eastern crude
economically unfeasible. Use of the pipeline finally began in 1987, when
the Soviet Union shipped 400,000 to 450,000 tons of crude to Yugoslavia
via Adria. Hungary receives a transit fee for the use of Adria on its
territory.[13]

The fate of Adria illustrates sundry difficulties Eastern Europe has
experienced on the international energy market. The substantial increase
in WMPs for oil that ensued after the Arab–Israeli War of 1973 led
Eastern Europe to revise its projected plans for importation from the
Middle East (table 4–2). If Eastern European states (excluding Romania)
had actually imported the 41 MT they originally planned from the Middle
East, it would have cost them upward of $3.5 billion at 1977 prices—a

prohibitively high sum if paid entirely in hard currency.[14] By 1975, Bulgaria, Czechoslovakia, and East Germany (exclusive of oil it imported from West Germany) had reduced their crude oil imports from the international market by more than two-thirds of the comparable level in 1973. In contrast, Hungary, Poland, and Romania continued to increase substantially their importation of crude from this source. This trend persisted in Poland and Romania through the late 1970s as both states increasingly relied on the international market to satisfy part of their domestic demand for oil (table 4–3).

The price paid for crude at the Libyan oil auction in December 1973 illustrates the impact of the post–October 1973 price increases on Eastern Europe. There, Poland purchased 1 MT of crude and Bulgaria and Hungary each 500,000 tons at $160 per ton—a price approximately 2.5 times more than that paid in October 1973.[15] Further, OPEC producers, able to purchase high-quality Western goods with their now abundant "petrodollars," were less willing to accept inferior goods in barter trade with Eastern Europe.[16] Eastern Europe recovered a small portion of its expenditures for imported oil through low-interest loans and grants from OPEC states funded with petrodollars.[17]

Oil exporters imposed more stringent financial terms on Eastern Europe despite unwavering (except from Romania) Soviet bloc support for the Arab cause against Israel. The exporters probably reasoned that their policy would not alter the political rationale that determined this support. Arab oil exporters had even less political incentive to extend favorable terms to Romania, the only Soviet bloc state that continued to maintain

Table 4–3
Eastern Europe: Importation of Crude Oil from Noncommunist Countries
(barrels per day)

	1970	1971	1972	1973	1974	1975	1976	1977	1978*
Bulgaria	18,740	34,940	38,280	42,780	32,400	11,960	16,340	18,280	26,840
Czechoslovakia	7,920	16,740	13,280	22,600	7,280	6,720	15,320	27,000	17,300
East Germany	22,020	23,300	72,900	60,400	45,980	38,000	40,480	40,700	44,000
Hungary	7,940	9,800	17,540	15,840	13,820	29,480	21,200	16,440	29,260
Poland	0	0	0	11,400	16,540	48,480	69,000	72,540	76,300
Romania	45,820	57,160	57,460	82,860	90,760	101,700	169,500	176,880	258,740
Eastern Europe	102,440	141,940	199,460	235,880	206,780	236,340	331,840	351,840	452,440

Source: National Foreign Assessment Center, *Energy Supplies in Eastern Europe: A Statistical Compilation*, table 19.
*Estimated.

diplomatic relations with Israel after the Arab–Israeli War of June 1967. Indeed, Arab states now began playing their oil card against Romania. In November 1975, Kuwait delayed a new trade agreement with Romania because of the latter's "close ties with Israel."[18] The Arab Boycott Office similarly blacklisted Romanian firms for trading with Israel.[19] This pressure may have contributed to Romania's 1976 decision to cancel a pipeline contract with Israel for transshipment of Iranian oil to the Gulf of Aqaba. Romania insisted it based its decision on "purely commercial grounds," although an Israeli radio broadcast accused Romania of having "surrendered to the Arab boycott." Shortly after the Romanian action, the Arab Boycott Office removed all Romanian firms from its blacklist.[20]

The oil price shock of 1973–74 adversely affected, but did not end, Eastern Europe's involvement in the international energy market (table 4–3). Eastern Europe actually imported upward of 80 percent more crude oil from the international market in 1979 than in 1973. However, Poland and Romania were responsible for most of this increase. By 1978, these two states accounted for approximately 75 percent of the estimated crude oil Eastern Europe imported from nonsocialist states. Romania alone accounted for almost 60 percent of this amount. After 1974, Hungary also increased importation, although the absolute amount of crude oil involved remained relatively small. In contrast, both Bulgaria and Czechoslovakia sharply curtailed importation after 1973. Between 1974 and 1978, Bulgaria never exceeded its 1973 level of importation from the international market, and Czechoslovakia did so only in 1977. In 1979, these two states accounted for less than 10 percent of the estimated crude oil imported by Eastern Europe from the international market. East Germany exhibited two distinct patterns of importation during these years. Between 1973 and 1975, it pursued a policy of substantially reducing importation similar to that of Bulgaria and Czechoslovakia. East Germany imported approximately 35 percent less crude oil from the international market in 1975 than in 1973. Most of this reduction involved importation from the Middle East. Between 1976 and 1978, East Germany maintained an almost constant level of importation slightly higher than that attained in 1975. During the 1970s, East Germany remained a substantial net importer of crude oil and a small net importer of combined crude oil and products from the international market. This circumstance reflected the role of East Germany as an important exporter of refined petroleum products to this market.

Eastern Europe financed this importation with hard currency and barter. Part of the hard currency was raised through loans on Eurocurrency markets. Between December 1975 and March 1976, Eastern European states completed or were negotiating loans totaling approximately $310 million primarily for the purchase of oil from OPEC producers.[21] Eastern Europe exported mostly primary products (chiefly food, including live animals) and intermediate goods (chemicals, steel, cement, glass, textiles, and the like) in exchange for OPEC oil. Eastern Europe accounted for 58 percent of the live animals and 72 percent of the meat and sugar that Libya imported in 1976. In that same year, Iran obtained from Eastern Europe 34 percent of the live animals, 16 percent of the meat, and 24 percent of the dairy products that it imported.[22] In contrast, Eastern Europe obtained only a minuscule share of the OPEC market for imported finished manufactures. Eastern Europe, excluding Romania, consistently maintained a positive balance of trade with OPEC between 1970 and 1978. Romania, burdened with an imported oil bill that reached $1.2 billion in 1978, ran a substantial trade deficit with OPEC after 1973. In 1978, this deficit approached $600 million.[23]

The shah of Iran proved especially willing to conclude barter agreements for energy. Between 1975 and 1978, Eastern Europe increased its exports to Iran by 3.7 times to an estimated $565 million. In 1978, Iran accounted for 29 percent of total OPEC imports from Eastern Europe.[24] Czechoslovakia concluded its largest barter deal ever with a nonsocialist state when in 1976 it became a participant with Iran and the Soviet Union in the IGAT-II natural gas pipeline project. The project represented an expansion of the Soviet–Iranian energy relationship, which had begun in the late 1960s with Iran exporting around 10 billion m³ of natural gas to the Soviet Union annually. The IGAT-II project called for the Soviet Union to import 17 billion m³ of natural gas annually from Iran for use in its southern republics and then export 15 billion m³ of its own gas to Czechoslovakia and Western Europe. In 1976, Czechoslovakia signed a contract worth more than $2.5 billion to purchase 3.6 billion m³ of this gas annually between 1981 and 2003. The annual volume of gas that Czechoslovakia would receive from this project (including gas acquired for pipeline transit fees) was equivalent to almost 3 MT of oil or about 6 MT of good quality coal. This volume would cover approximately one-third of Czechoslovakia's estimated requirements for importation of natural gas in the 1980s.[25]

The overthrow of the shah in January 1979 by a Muslim fundamentalist movement headed by the Ayatollah Ruhollah Khomeini halted—at least temporarily—the export of most Iranian energy to Communist Europe. Not only did the movement's religious fervor clash with the avowedly atheistic ideology of communist polities, but the revolutionary government explicitly accused the Soviet Union of having "swindled" Iran with its purchase of natural gas during the shah's reign. "If you take delivery of Iranian natural gas at the border and then, without involving yourself in any processing, resell it then and there for three times the amount you paid for it, then this is a clear case of swindling, even if you are the Soviet Union," Iran's revolutionary radio charged.[26] Consequently, Iran halted natural gas exports to the Soviet Union in October 1978, formally canceled the IGAT-II project in the following year, and effectively terminated energy exports to Eastern Europe by demanding only hard currency in payment for energy. These initiatives, while bothersome to the Soviet Union, created serious problems for Czechoslovakia (with its anticipated imports of Iranian natural gas) and for Romania (which had been importing about 5 MT of crude annually from Iran). In a public statement that probably belied private belief, Premier Strougal initially asserted that Czechoslovakia "expected" Iran to honor the "binding" contracts between the two states.[27]

The second oil price shock, in which the average OPEC price for crude increased from $18.67 per barrel in 1979 to $30.87 per barrel in 1980, further undermined the capacity of Eastern Europe to import from the international market. This development occurred at a particularly inopportune time for Eastern Europe, when many states already were encountering difficulties in repaying substantial debts to Western creditors. A Hungarian press report labeled the 1979 OPEC price increase "irresponsible" because of its destabilizing effect on the international economy.[28] The comment is a suggestive one.

First, it is an implicit criticism of the Soviet Union, which charges the OPEC price for its petroleum exports to capitalist and, to some extent, socialist states.

Second, it is a tacit indication of divergent interests between the Soviet Union and Eastern Europe. The Soviet Union presumably wants OPEC to charge the highest feasible market price to maximize its earnings of hard currency from the sale of energy. Eastern Europe, in its capacity as an importer from the international market, has a vested economic interest in OPEC's charging the lowest possible price for oil. Of course, this statement is less applicable to Eastern European states such as Poland that are important exporters of energy to the world market.

Third, the comment represents de facto refutation of the then prevailing official contention that socialist states were largely immune to the vicissitudes of the capitalist-dominated international economy. The 1979–80 price increases not only made imported energy increasingly expensive, but, more significantly, they unleashed inflationary pressures in the capitalist world that drove up the price to Eastern Europe of borrowing money and importing goods from the West. President Nicolae Ceausescu of Romania called the interest rates on the Eurocurrency markets a "new form of exploitation" and demanded "an end to this imperialist plundering."[29]

The overthrow of the shah and the 1979 price shock led to a sharp decline in Eastern Europe's importation of crude oil from OPEC members. The 1981 level of importation was less than that in 1977. Overall, Eastern Europe imported almost one-third less crude from this market in 1981 than in 1979 (table 4–4).

These developments especially affected Romania and Poland, the Eastern European states most involved with OPEC. Romania tried several ways of finding substitute sources for oil previously imported from Iran and coping with price increases that made imported oil nearly $1.5 billion more expensive in 1980 than in 1979.

First, as a palliative measure Romania sought to finance imports by securing hard currency loans from a consortium of Arab banks (totaling $85 million) and from the International Monetary Fund (totaling $1.5 billion).[30] More substantively, it reduced crude oil imports from the OPEC market by more than one-third in 1982 compared with 1980. A shortage of crude to process in 1982 idled approximately one-third of Romania's annual petroleum-refining capacity of 30 to 33 MT.[31]

Finally, Romania initiated numerous contacts with both socialist and nonsocialist states to find new suppliers of crude and increase imports from existing ones. These efforts brought mixed results. The most notable success with socialist suppliers involved the Soviet Union, which began exporting crude to Romania—with payment in hard goods at WMPs—in 1979. The search for socialist suppliers even led to Albania, which in 1979 agreed to export an unspecified amount of crude and other raw materials in exchange for Romanian industrial goods, including oil field equipment.[32]

Table 4–4
Eastern Europe: Importation of Crude Oil from OPEC States
(millions of metric tons)

	1979	1981
Bulgaria	2.5	1.5
Czechoslovakia	0.7	Negligible
East Germany	2.3	4.1
Hungary	2.1	0.5
Poland	3.2	0.4
Romania	13.9	10.2
Eastern Europe	24.7	16.7

Source: Adapted from McMillan, "Eastern Europe's Relations with OPEC Suppliers," 370.

In 1979–80, Romania made similar contacts with many Middle East-ern states, including Iran, Iraq, Kuwait, Libya, Saudi Arabia, and the United Arab Emirates.[33] Iran agreed to supply Romania with 100,000 barrels per day of crude (a 60 percent increase over the existing level of exportation) at the prevailing WMP.[34] Negotiations with Kuwait and Libya were less successful. Romania hoped that Kuwait would play a key role as both financier and supplier of crude oil to a large petrochemical complex then under construction. Negotiations ceased, however, when Romania rejected Kuwait's demand that crude be paid for in dollars and shipped in Kuwaiti tankers. Consequently, Kuwait exported no crude to Romania in 1979.[35] Initially, negotiations with Libya were more fruitful. In 1979, Romania announced that henceforth it would import 2.5 to 3 MT of crude from Libya annually at WMPs with payment in hard goods and currency. Libya actually exported to Romania 2.3 MT of crude in 1979 and 1.7 MT in 1980, probably because of the latter's inability to meet the terms of payment. Subsequent articles in the Romanian press demanding that existing contracts with Libya be honored suggest that the 1979 agreement continued to be underfulfilled.[36]

In Poland, these developments coincided with a political and economic crisis that included the ouster of Edward Gierek in 1980 as first secretary of the Polish United Workers party, the imposition of martial law in 1981, and a seemingly irreversible decline in the economy that made the country essentially insolvent. Therefore, Poland had little choice but to reduce drastically importation from the OPEC market, slashing these im-ports from a peak of 3.6 MT of crude in 1979 to 300,000 MT in 1982. That liquid fuels accounted for a relatively small share of the energy balance in Poland mitigated the economic consequences of this step.

The international market became more attractive to Eastern Europe after 1982, when WMPs for oil began to decline. Not only were the prices themselves lower, but the soft international market predisposed exporters to conclude barter deals with Eastern Europe. Between 1982 and 1985, all Eastern European states increased the absolute level of their crude oil imports from this source. In four states—Bulgaria, Czechoslovakia, East Germany, and Hungary—the 1985 level exceeded the comparable level attained in 1979 when WMPs for oil began to escalate. In 1985, Romania imported only slightly less oil from the world market than it had in 1979. However, Poland has never again approached its level of importation in 1979. In 1985, it imported 66 percent less crude oil from the world market than in 1979. In 1985, Eastern Europe derived almost 30 percent of its total imports of crude oil from the world market. The comparable figure excluding Romania was approximately 15 percent.[37]

Eastern Europe and Iran have maintained a complex energy relationship in the 1980s. Mutual economic and political interests stimulated this relationship. The soft international energy market made Iran more willing to conclude barter deals for crude oil with Eastern Europe. The Iran–Iraq War had similar consequences. Iran exported crude to Eastern Europe in return for arms to prosecute the war.[38] Iran concluded "arms for oil" deals with Bulgaria, Czechoslovakia, and the Soviet Union. Similar exchanges may have transpired with other Eastern European states, but little public information exists on this trade. The Soviet Union and Eastern Europe benefited both economically and politically from these exchanges. The economic benefit was obvious: Eastern Europe received crude on favorable terms of trade. Politically, the exchanges mitigated the bitter relations between Iran and the Soviet bloc engendered by the latter's diplomatic and military support for Iraq during the Iran–Iraq War, Iran's opposition to the Soviet invasion of Afghanistan, and the Khomeini regime's persecution of the Iranian Communist (Tudeh) party.

Iran's need for a secure trading route during its war with Iraq provided an early impetus for rapprochement, and by 1981 approximately 20 percent of Iran's imports were entering the country via the Soviet Union (compared with 6 percent before the revolution). In 1982, the Iranian minister of energy visited both Czechoslovakia and the Soviet Union. In Prague, the two sides discussed mutual trade and especially "prospects for the long-term supply of Iranian products to Czechoslovakia." The Iranian official also remarked that a resumption of natural gas exports to Czechoslovakia (and, presumably, the Soviet Union) depended on the "solution of economic and technical problems."[39] In Moscow, the Iranian official declared that an Islamic Iran and an atheistic Soviet Union can coexist because "neither country interferes in the domestic affairs of the other." He added, "Iran and the Soviet Union are to develop economic relations, notably in the energy field." Despite this assertion, the two sides could not agree on financial terms for the resumption of Iranian natural gas exports to the Soviet Union.[40]

In 1981, Iran exported more than 10.5 MT of oil to the Soviet Union and Eastern Europe compared with a minuscule amount exported in 1980.[41] In 1982, Iran agreed to export 4 MT of oil annually to Romania (approximately 80 percent of the amount that Romania received annually during the shah's last years in power). Romania would provide payment in part by reconstructing refineries and oil installations damaged in the war with Iraq and furnishing experts and spare parts for the oil and gas industry. Iran also would use Romanian refineries instead of its own war-damaged refineries to process 30,000 barrels of oil per day.[42]

Iran and Czechoslovakia also concluded barter deals for the export of Iranian crude in 1984 (900,000 MT) and 1985 (more than 1 million MT).

Official terms of trade have not been published. In 1984, Iran reportedly priced crude at $2.10 per barrel less than the official OPEC benchmark price. Czechoslovakia may have supplied military equipment to Iran as part of the agreement. A Czechoslovak commentary on the agreement noted merely that the parties would expand their cooperation "in the fields of energy, the crude oil industry, the gas industry, coal extraction, the utilization of nonferrous metals, and geological surveys."[43] These agreements were concluded despite Czechoslovakia's condemnation of Iran for "persecution" and conduct of a "court farce" in the 1984 trial of leaders of the Tudeh party.[44] Similarly, Iran's persistent criticism of the Soviet Union for extending military aid to Iraq did not prevent the two sides from agreeing to exchange Iranian crude oil for Soviet-refined petroleum products in 1987.[45]

Iran and selected Eastern European states continue to discuss the expansion of their energy relations. In 1987, Czechoslovakia and Iran held talks in Tehran on "prospects of cooperation between the two countries in the exploitation of oil and natural gas."[46] Iran and Hungary are negotiating a long-term contract in which Hungary will purchase between 700,000 and 1 million MT crude oil from Iran annually. In 1987, Hungary bought 700,000 MT of crude from Iran. To date, the two sides cannot agree on a price for crude in the long-term contract. This subject was a "key issue on the agenda" when Prime Minister Grosz visited Iran in October 1988. Hungary offered a price of $12 to $13 per barrel, while Iran insisted on a price of more than $14 per barrel. Hungary hopes to export agricultural commodities and foodstuffs, power plant equipment, building materials, and other goods to Iran in exchange for oil.[47] Iran agreed to export 1 MT of crude oil to Poland in 1989. Poland was to compensate Iran by exporting building and road building equipment, machine and hand tools, equipment for the mining industry, fishing vessels, chemicals, coking coal, and metallurgical products.[48]

In July 1989, Iran agreed to export 3 billion m³ of natural gas annually to the Soviet Union. Precise terms of trade have not been published, but Sergei Kashirov, Soviet deputy minister of the gas industry, earlier indicated that payment would include industrial machinery and services on Iranian gas pipelines, but he made no mention of payment in hard currency.[49] This deal could become part of a larger arrangement involving Poland, Czechoslovakia, and Bulgaria. During a visit to Poland in January 1989, Mir Hoseyn Musavi, prime minister of Iran, stated without elaboration that "some decisions had been made" on the initiation of Iranian natural gas exports to Poland.[50] Reportedly, Czechoslovakia has proposed an arrangement similar to the defunct IGAT-II project wherein the Soviet Union would import natural gas from Iran on Czechoslovak account for use in its southern republics and then export an unspecified volume of its own gas via existing pipelines to Czechoslovakia. The Minister of Fuels and Energy indicated that Czechoslovakia could receive between 2 and 4 billion m³ of natural gas annually under this arrangement.[51] Beginning in 1990, Bulgaria will receive more natural gas from Iran. The Iranian Minister of Petroleum presumably referred to the Soviet Union when he stated that the gas would reach Bulgaria "through the territory of a country that is friendly to Bulgaria."[52]

Pragmatic considerations of national interest have led to a fruitful energy relationship between Communist Europe and Iran. This relationship belies fears expressed during the presidencies of Jimmy Carter and Ronald Reagan that the Soviet Union would invade Iran and other states of the Persian Gulf region to acquire energy for itself and its allies.[53] Commercial exchanges, not reckless military adventures, have sufficed for Communist Europe to acquire the limited amount of energy it imports from the international energy market.

Exportation

The role of Eastern Europe as exporter to the international energy market merits brief comment. Eastern Europe has consistently been a small net exporter to this market.[54] Exports of hard coal from Poland are a primary reason for this. Between 1974 and 1979, these exports averaged almost 25 MT annually. They dropped dramatically between 1981 and 1983—to 7.9 MT, 14.2 MT, and 17.5 MT for 1981, 1982, and 1983, respectively— when coal mining experienced rampant labor unrest and disruption in production. The subsequent revival of domestic mining permitted exportation to approach the levels attained in the 1970s, but these exports began declining in the late 1980s in response to soft WMPs for energy. In 1988, Poland exported 17.5 MT of hard coal to the international market and planned to export only 12 MT in 1989. Several officials have even called for the cessation of these exports, which they contend have become "entirely unprofitable."[55] As noted earlier, representatives of Solidarity are among those who propose this.

Eastern Europe also participates in the international oil trade by reexporting either directly or in refined form crude oil imported primarily from the Middle East. According to one Western estimate, these exports reached almost 23 MT in 1985, an increase of upward of 50 percent over 1979.[56] Refined products typically constitute between 80 and 90 percent of these exports. Eastern Europe remains a net importer of oil from the international market, however.

Romania and East Germany accounted for roughly two-thirds of these exports between 1981 and 1985. Historically, Romania had participated in a profitable trade by processing domestic crude oil for export. It remained a net exporter of oil to the international market through the mid-1970s. It subsequently became a net importer of crude oil when its refinery capacity expanded far beyond the capability of domestic production to provide for it. The economic irrationality of this expansion became apparent when escalating WMPs for crude oil forced Romania to reduce importation and thereby idled much of the refinery industry.

In contrast, exportation is always profitable for East Germany regardless of changes in market conditions. A "cost plus" contract in which East Germany annually exports substantial quantities of refined products (mostly heating oil and diesel fuel) to West Germany largely explains this propitious circumstance. Approximately two-thirds of the gasoline consumed annually in West Berlin comes from East Germany, which also exports oil to other Western states. The overall dimensions of this trade are unknown, since East Germany does not publish official statistics on it. Western analysts estimate that East Germany consumes between 10 and 13 MT of the 22 to 23 MT of crude oil it imports annually. This would leave between 9 and 12 MT of crude available for export.[57]

The international oil trade has provided a lucrative source of hard currency for East Germany, which receives payment in Western currencies for oil that it acquires mostly through barter. East Germany reexports to the West (probably) all of the 4 to 5 MT of crude that it imports annually on barter from Angola, Iran, Iraq, Libya, and Mexico. Western analysts differ over whether East Germany reexports this crude directly or in refined form.[58] East Germany has been reexporting in refined form about 7 MT of the 17 to 19 MT of crude that it receives annually in barter trade with the Soviet Union. Finally, West Germany sells East Germany about 1 MT of crude annually within the framework of intra-German trade. This trade is conducted in accounting units, not hard currency. East Germany has incurred considerable losses from the decline in WMPs for oil in the mid-1980s. In 1986 alone, East Germany may have suffered a net reduction in earnings of close to $1 billion from the decline in these prices.[59]

The remaining states have engaged selectively, and often imaginatively, in the oil trade. Hungary and Bulgaria provide examples. Hungary has acquired hard currency by immediately reexporting oil it has imported on credit at what may be a below-market implicit rate of interest.[60] Hungary also has acquired crude for reexport by importing oil from Libya on the account of a third country, probably the Soviet Union. This complex undertaking apparently involves the Soviet Union's reexporting to Hungary crude it received from Libya in payment for military equipment and capital goods. The Soviet Union uses the reexported crude to offset deficits in its convertible currency trade with Hungary.[61] Hungary has been uncharacteristically reticent in publishing data on this trade, providing no data in the 1988 edition of the Comecon statistical yearbook and data only on the value (expressed in rubles), but not the volume, of this trade in earlier editions of the yearbook during the 1980s.[62] Declining WMPs may have cost Hungary upward of $100 million in revenue from oil exports in 1986.[63]

Bulgaria reexports both directly and in refined form crude it acquires in barter trade with Middle Eastern states (especially Iran and Libya) and the Soviet Union. The volume of these exports can only be estimated because Bulgaria publishes no data on this subject. One Western source estimated that these exports averaged 2.75 MT annually between 1978 and 1984. In 1985, when Bulgaria was a net importer of oil, exports may have declined to 2 MT. Cutbacks in Soviet oil deliveries to Bulgaria could partly explain this reduction.[64] Bulgaria also may have had less incentive to export oil when WMPs for this commodity were declining rapidly.

This latter circumstance presumably lessens the financial attractiveness of oil exports to all Eastern European states except East Germany. However, these exports should remain a cost-effective means of earning hard currency as long as Eastern Europe can reexport oil acquired in barter trade for soft goods.

Eastern Europe also exports a small but growing amount of electricity to Western Europe (including Greece and Turkey). Net exports of electricity to this region increased from barely 1 million kwh in 1979 to 5 million kwh in 1985.[65] Exporters include Bulgaria (to Greece and Turkey), Czechoslovakia (to Austria, West Germany, and Switzerland), East Germany (to West Berlin), and Hungary and Poland (to Austria). The future status of the Gabcikovo-Nagymaros hydroelectric power project will affect the volume of these exports. As noted earlier, Hungary is scheduled to export electricity to Austria in the 1990s as repayment for financial assistance on the project. Austria also is scheduled to purchase electricity from the project at regular commercial rates. Czechoslovakia now plans to increase net exports of electricity to 700 gigawatt-hours annually in 1989–90. In 1988, these exports reached approximately 690 gigawatt-hours compared with an original plan target of 120 gigawatt-hours.[66] Czechoslovakia has designated the hard currency revenues from these exports to finance high-priority imports from capitalist states not originally contained in the current five-year plan. In likely response to the accident at the Chernobyl NPS, these imports will include diagnostic and communications equipment "to enhance the safety of the operation of the Czechoslovak nuclear power industry."[67] In the longer term, Czechoslovakia will substantially increase exports of electricity to West Germany when a 400 kv power transmission line between the two states becomes operational in 1993. The two states will begin joint construction of the line in 1990.[68]

Prospects

The past is not necessarily predictive of the role of Eastern Europe on the international energy market. Factors that limited this role in the past—steadily increasing and seemingly assured supplies of energy from the Soviet Union and insufficient reserves of hard currency and commodities to meet the terms of trade—clearly are subject to change.

For example, in 1982, a respected Western analyst presented a pessimistic assessment of the capacity of Eastern Europe to import crude oil from the international market in the late 1980s. His scenario assumed that the WMP for oil would then be around $30 per barrel—a price that, presumably, would largely exclude Eastern Europe from the international market.[69] Yet the actual price for oil in late 1988 was under $15 per barrel. The point assuredly is not to chastise this analyst but to demonstrate the inherently tentative nature of prospective assessments of the international energy market. At the current WMP, Hungary has offered to purchase as much as 1 MT of crude annually from Iran. This amount is equal to more than 13 percent of Hungary's total inmportation of crude in 1986. Poland, under an agreement concluded in 1989, will import 1 MT of crude oil annually from Iran. If WMPs for oil do not rise appreciably in the near future, Eastern Europe may again view the international market as a viable (albeit limited) instrument to close the energy gap.

To be sure, Eastern Europe confronts formidable obstacles to trading with developing countries, including those that export energy. That trade with developing countries is only a minuscule share of total trade turnover throughout Eastern Europe reflects this circumstance (table 4–5).

Similar impediments to trade with developing countries exist in vary-

Table 4–5
Eastern Europe: Trade with Developing Countries, 1987*

		Exports	Imports
	Percent of Total Trade	Percent of Total Exports	Percent of Total Imports
Bulgaria	7.5	10.5	4.5
Czechoslovakia	4.3	5.2	3.5
East Germany	4.0	4.6	3.3
Hungary	7.9	9.3	6.6
Poland	4.1	4.8	3.3

Source: *Statisticheskii ezhegodnik stran-chlenov Soveta Ekonomicheskoi Vzaimopomoshchi 1988*, table 155.
*This table provided no data for Romania.

ing degrees in all Eastern European states.[70] These impediments include an insufficient supply of quality goods and services for export, a lack of spare parts and maintenance facilities to provide requisite service, inflexible and antiquated modes of credit, complicated procedures for obtaining permits for export, an aversion among enterprises to participate in what they consider high-risk trading ventures, and ignorance of foreign methods of operation. Overall, such impediments reflect the stress that command economies traditionally place on autarky. Developing countries themselves may present obstacles to trade. Polish firms reportedly encounter "many difficulties" in trading with Libya, "especially" in obtaining payment for services rendered.[71]

Ironically, Eastern European states, which typically export many similar products, often compete among themselves for scarce international markets. To mitigate this circumstance, Czechoslovakia has proposed that Comecon states organize joint purchases of energy on the international market. One such proposal envisions these states jointly constructing turnkey plants in developing countries with repayment in energy. In 1983, Premier Strougal of Czechoslovakia reported that these proposals had met "without success so far."[72]

An ideal scenario for Eastern Europe's becoming more involved in the international energy market includes the persistence of depressed WMPs for oil, a concomitant willingness by OPEC producers to engage in barter trade, the refusal of the Soviet Union to increase exports of energy to the region, the revival of economic growth that stimulates indigenous demand for energy, and elimination of those features of the command economy that promote autarky. Several components of this scenario probably will materialize. Certainly, the Soviet Union appears unlikely to export appreciably more oil to Eastern Europe. The soft international energy market could persist into the early 1990s, giving oil exporters such as Iran and Libya an incentive to conclude barter deals with Eastern Europe. The revival of economic growth and the elimination of tendencies toward autarky are less certain occurrences. Their realization will depend decisively upon the fate of Mikhail Gorbachev's program of economic perestroika that most Eastern European regimes are pursuing with varying degrees of enthusiasm.

In sum, the model for Eastern Europe's participation in the international energy market in the 1990s may be the period 1970–1973, when prevailing WMPs for energy and the willingness of energy exporters to conclude barter deals permitted Eastern Europe to increase importation from this source. This assessment applies both to oil and natural gas. Importation of natural gas could involve substantial quantities if Iran and interested states in Communist Europe can conclude an arrangement similar to the IGAT-II project proposed in the 1970's.

5
The Demand Side:
The Conservation of Energy

Energy Savings Are the Only Way Out
—*Rzeczpospolita*, 19 September, 1986

Many analysts argue that Eastern Europe must effect a "revolutionary shift" to "assiduous and ruthless" conservation of energy.[1] A Polish source explains why:

On the one hand, satisfaction of the growing need for energy is a condition for economic growth; on the other, as a result of a lack of funds to develop energy, including a lack of funds for importing fuel, this condition cannot be fulfilled. In this situation, the only thing that remains is a radical reduction in the energy intensiveness of the entire economy.[2]

The European Comecon states plan to use existing resources more efficiently to meet 65 to 70 percent of their additional demand for energy in this century.[3] Studies find that it typically costs one-half to two-thirds less to conserve than to produce an equivalent amount of energy.[4] The dissident group Charter 77 estimates that the monies necessary to increase power-generating capacities by 1,000 MW yield an equivalent of 2,000 MW when spent on conservation measures.[5] In contrast, two factors can lessen the economic attractiveness of conservation measures: (1) such measures often entail substantial up-front expenditures that are recovered over an extended period of time, and (2) such measures encounter increasing marginal costs as they exhaust easily exploitable sources of saving.[6]

Considerable potential for energy conservation exists throughout Eastern Europe. As noted, Eastern European and Soviet data indicate that the Comecon countries on average consume between 30 and 50 percent (and some countries upward of 80 percent) more energy than do industrialized capitalist countries to produce similar units of national income.[7] One source estimated that these countries could increase their national incomes by approximately one-half if they consumed energy as efficiently as do members of the European Economic Community.[8] Table 5–1 demonstrates that Eastern European states, even with far smaller national economies and stocks of motor vehicles, have levels of per capita energy

Table 5–1
Selected Countries: Per Capita Energy
Consumption, 1985
(barrels of oil equivalent)

East Germany	43
Czechoslovakia	36
West Germany	32
Bulgaria	29
France	26
United Kingdom	26
Poland	24
Romania	23
Japan	23
Hungary	22

Source: Computed from data in Directorate of Intelligence, *Handbook of Economic Statistics, 1987*, tables 2 and 3.

consumption that equal, and often exceed, those of many industrialized capitalist countries.

That Eastern European states are comparatively inefficient consumers of energy seems clear, although the relevant data should not be interpreted literally. First, Western analysts warn that methodological problems associated with their computations may distort—typically, but not always, by overstating—the relative energy inefficiency of the Comecon states vis-à-vis the West.[9] Second, the concept of net material product used in Eastern Europe to report economic output includes only net output in the material sphere, although an important share of primary energy is consumed in the nonmaterial sphere and in households. This circumstance distorts calculations of the energy intensity of net material product (the ratio of gross primary energy consumption to net material product in constant prices) commonly used to measure the energy efficiency of an economy.[10] Third, enterprises may manipulate data to demonstrate paper gains in energy efficiency. For example, in Czechoslovakia,

> [t]he manner of monitoring the development of energy intensiveness has not yet been cleared up. In the first two years of the current economic plan (1986–1990), it developed twice more favorably in relation to gross output than it did in relation to adjusted net output. Enterprises are therefore reporting their energy-intensiveness in relation to gross output and the results on paper are much better than the actual efficiency in the use of fuels and energy.[11]

Several factors promote the excessive consumption of energy. Most fundamentally, this condition is inextricably related to the Stalinist "command economy" and concomitant strategy of extensive growth that the Soviet Union imposed throughout the region after 1948. That conservation of resources received little attention in this strategy is accurate but misleading. Rather, conservation was actively discouraged as antithetical to extensive growth. A Polish source correctly labels the economic model "our Achilles' heel" in the conservation of energy.[12] The post-Stalin regimes have (sometimes substantially) modified the pure Stalinist model, but its essential features persist and foster excessive consumption of energy.

The imperative to fulfill production targets is among the more important of these features. Producers may, as critics charge, exhibit "appalling," "careless," "haughty," and "literally shocking" attitudes toward conservation,[13] but their behavior is rational. Rational production personnel seek to maximize gains and minimize losses. Since fulfillment of the plan is their raison d'être and source of bonuses, promotions, and other perquisites, they naturally subordinate all other objectives (including energy conservation) to this end. Paradoxically, producers possess an economic incentive to maximize expenditures of energy and other inputs to inflate the gross output or value indicators used to measure fulfillment of the plan. As a Bulgarian source explains, the plan "encourages extravagance," and "unsound as it is," producers "receive an award instead of punishment" for wasting materials.[14]

The price system, wherein prices reflect the preferences of political elites rather than the dictates of supply and demand, represents another feature of the Stalinist model impeding conservation. For several reasons— the Marxist law of value that considers natural resources "free goods," a desire to encourage the production of commodities with a high energy content, and a concern to avoid political unrest among the population— prices for energy resources traditionally have been too low to stimulate conservation. Indeed, producers in a command economy are largely immune to any economic stimuli to use energy and other resources efficiently.[15]

Consequently, officials typically seek this end by imposing obligatory norms for consumption of energy. This approach has manifest defects. The norms frequently are inflated because producers, possessing obvious incentives to overstate requirements for energy, provide the data to determine them. Thus, production units simultaneously may remain excessive consumers of energy while proclaiming that through herculean efforts they have reduced consumption below stipulated norms.

Penalties for noncompliance with existing norms usually are minimal and unenforced. The result, a Soviet source explains, is that norms are "simply ignored" by most enterprise managers.[16] Technologically substantiated norms for energy consumption do not exist for many products and production processes. For example, in Czechoslovakia by the end of 1983, such norms existed for only one hundred of four hundred energy-intensive products and technologies. Producers presumably could expend whatever energy they desired for the remaining commodities.[17]

Finally, the Stalinist model promotes excessive energy consumption through an obsessive emphasis on developing a heavy industrial base composed of energy-intensive industries. In remarks applicable to all Eastern European economies, a Polish source noted that "the structure of our economy conjures up early capitalism rather than the end of the 20th century with its scientific-technical revolution."[18] Escalating WMPs for energy after 1973 did not alter this condition. National economic plans for the 1981–1985 period typically projected that energy-intensive industrial sectors would grow more rapidly than the economy as a whole.[19]

The Stalinist model is not entirely culpable for the excessive consumption of energy. The disproportionate share of brown coal and lignite of low caloric content in most energy balances in the region also promotes this. Such fuels incur much greater losses of energy in extraction, transportation, and conversion into usable forms of power than do other forms of primary energy. Ironically, much of what passes for energy conservation in Eastern Europe is actually the substitution of brown coal and lignite in primary energy consumption for more energy-efficient but expensive liquid hydrocarbons. Such substitution, all things being equal, actually increases the energy intensity of the national economy.

Additionally, an overall state of relative technological backwardness in the region contributes to this condition. For example, the iron and steel industries in Poland consume 1.5 to 2.2 times more energy per ton of steel than do comparable industries in Western Europe.[20] Inefficient and obsolete power equipment abounds in the region. In Hungary, almost 60 percent of coal-burning industrial furnaces were over thirty years old in 1978; in Czechoslovakia, 30 percent of all boilers had depreciated below zero by 1980; and in Poland, at current levels of production it would take between sixty and eighty years to modernize the national stock of industrial and residential power equipment.[21] Consumer goods and other commodities for mass consumption exhibit similar backwardness and obsolescence. The notoriously poorly constructed, insulated, and maintained housing stock provides an appropriate example from Poland. One source noted, "If we do not change the technique of erecting and finishing our residential units we will be forced to allocate all the energy in the country available just to heat these buildings as early as the beginning of the 21st century."[22]

Undoubtedly, limited fiscal resources, especially to import energy-saving equipment and technologies from the West, help perpetuate these conditions. Yet the imperative to fulfill the production plan also fosters them. First, research and design organizations, typically attached to the very ministries responsible for production, concentrate on developing products that contribute directly to fulfillment of the plan regardless of how energy intensive they may be. Second, the imperatives of plan fulfillment make enterprise managers uninterested in assimilating modern energy-saving technologies that provide no immediate return on investment. Projects to save energy are "always the first to be eliminated from the plan," a Czechoslovak source explained.[23] Capitalist managers may behave similarly, but the absence of realistic prices for energy resources makes the "time horizon" of socialist managers even shorter and almost preordains that they will favor production over conservation.[24]

National Conservation Programs

The first period of measures to conserve energy coincided with the twin explosions in world energy prices in 1973–74 and 1979–80. These measures entailed short-run, largely propagandistic campaigns that did not alter the fundamental factors promoting excessive consumption of energy.

This observation applies especially to measures undertaken before 1979. Typical initiatives included propaganda campaigns and national competitions to encourage energy conservation, restrictions on consumption of electricity, the extension of daylight saving time, and initiatives to reduce fuel consumption in motor vehicles. There was some discussion, but little action, on encouraging the development of less energy intensive industries and technologies.[25] All national economic plans for the 1976–1980 period projected substantial rates of growth in national income, industrial production, and consumption of energy.[26]

Only Hungary devoted more than cursory attention to the discrepancy between domestic and world market energy prices. In 1975, Janos Kadar, head of the Hungarian Socialist Workers party, argued: "We cannot speak of effective construction if our production is based not on real but on fictitious prices. . . . [W]e must take world market prices into consideration in calculating our own production costs; otherwise the price of imported raw materials, semifinished products, or our sources of energy would be completely fictitious."[27] Despite the cogency of this argument, the gap between domestic and world prices persisted.

In contrast, increases in prices for energy were integral components of conservation initiatives undertaken in 1979.[28] These revisions, enacted at the retail level by all states except East Germany, sought to reduce overall consumption of fuels and energy by approximately 20 percent.[29] East Germany did raise wholesale prices for fuel to industrial consumers by an average of 30 percent. The Romanian revisions provoked considerable controversy because they provided that Romania would accept only hard currencies from foreign tourists in payment for gasoline, thereby stranding thousands of Eastern bloc vacationers and prompting unprecedented public diplomatic protests from several "fraternal" regimes.[30]

Regimes feared that the price increases could provoke political unrest. This fear probably explains why East Germany eschewed such measures. In Czechoslovakia, highly visible and heavily reinforced police patrols accompanied announcement of the increases.[31] Regimes risked unrest in part because government subsidies—their traditional alternative to increases in retail prices—were becoming prohibitively expensive. For example, in 1979 such subsidies in Poland consumed approximately one-third of the national budget, while in 1978 Czechoslovakia extended more than $300 million in subsidies solely to maintain the price of household fuel at the 1953 level.[32] Several regimes sought to cushion the impact of higher retail prices through income supplements to various economically deprived groups.[33]

The conservation measures pursued during this period were relatively ineffective (table 5–2). In four countries—Czechoslovakia, East Germany, Hungary, and Poland—several indices of energy usage increased during the 1970s. Moreover, the slowdown in economic growth in Eastern Europe in the late 1970s appears to have had a greater impact on rates of energy consumption, than did conservation measures per se.[34] These circumstances prompted sharp criticism from Hungarian economists. One economist labeled the Comecon response to higher world energy prices after 1973 "grossly inadequate" and asserted that conservation measures "left energy use patterns in most of the Comecon countries unaffected into 1980." Another charged that "essentially nothing was done" to conserve energy in the 1970s. A third predicted that the use of "real" prices to compute national income "would further worsen the picture" of indices of energy intensity.[35]

Their indictment is accurate but perhaps overly harsh. The Eastern Europeans probably reasoned that economically and politically costly measures to conserve energy were unjustified while the Soviet Union was expanding energy exports at heavily subsidized prices and Western bankers were providing a seemingly endless stream of credits to cover deficits in the trade balance.[36] Events of the 1980s refuted this reasoning, but the Eastern Europeans had behaved as *Homo politicus* usually does when confronted with unappealing choices: They temporized and used the twin crutches of energy exportation from the Soviet Union and credits from the West to rationalize their behavior.

Several factors—the 1979 increases in world energy prices and their concomitant economic dislocations, the growing indebtedness of Eastern

Table 5–2
Eastern Europe: Trends in Primary Energy Consumption

	Per Capita Consumption (average annual rate of growth)		Energy Elasticity*	
	1965–1973	*1974–1979*	*1965–1973*	*1974–1979*
Bulgaria	6.6	3.7	0.88	0.63
Czechoslovakia	1.4	2.1	0.28	0.64
East Germany	1.5	2.0	0.28	0.37
Hungary	0.7	3.8	0.17	0.81
Poland	2.9	3.9	0.50	0.95
Romania	7.0	4.3	0.90	0.57

Source: Dobozi, "The 'Invisible' Source of 'Alternative' Energy," 212. Reprinted with permission.
*Ratio of the annual percentage change in energy consumption to the annual percentage change in national income.

European regimes that made them more leery of borrowing on hard currency markets, and the realization that the level of oil exportation from the Soviet Union probably had peaked and might even decline—made such temporizing less viable in the 1980s. If measured by the rhetoric devoted to the subject, conservation has now become one of the centerpieces of all energy management programs in the region. Of course, rhetoric and reality in Eastern Europe (as elsewhere) often diverge. As a Bulgarian source argued, "The distance between what has been said about economizing and what has been accomplished is truly striking. Day after day words become sharper, arguments in favor of conservation weightier, appeals increasingly persistent; meanwhile, the figures listed in reports of outlays do not change. This five-year plan we made virtually no progress."[37]

The conservation programs in East Germany, Hungary, and Romania present a typology of approaches to this task in the region. East Germany is the most successful practitioner of what has been labeled "conservation by decree": administrative measures promulgated and enforced from above by higher bodies upon subordinate units. Less successful emulators include Czechoslovakia and Poland. Hungary embodies the market approach wherein various economic levers seek to stimulate the conservation of energy. Romania pursues an extreme variant of the conservation by decree approach that features draconian administrative measures to coerce consumers to use less energy.

Table 5–3
East Germany: Energy Conservation Measures, 1981–1985

Category	Contribution to Planned Total Savings (percent)
Energy-related improvements in industrial heating processes (especially during the use of industrial furnaces)	36.0
Increases in efficiency of energy conversion and transmission (especially in large power plants)	33.0
Energy-related improvements in electrical motors, lighting, and electrical household appliances	11.5
Rationalization of transportation processes	11.0
Increases in the effectiveness of space heating processes	8.5

Source: *Energietechnik*, December 1983, in JPRS-*EEI*, no. 18 (9 February 1984): 38.

East Germany

In September 1980, East Germany promulgated a plan titled "Rational Use of Energy during the 1981–1985 Five-Year Plan" that established targets and specified measures to conserve energy (table 5–3). In this period, primary energy consumption would grow by only 0.7 percent per annum and specific energy consumption would be reduced by 170 MT of crude lignite equivalent in 1985 as compared with 1980. Measures to increase technological modernization would generate approximately 80 percent of the projected savings.[38]

Increased exploitation of secondary energy (waste heat, waste and flue gases, solid material heat, and by-product fuels) would account for almost 15 percent of these projected savings. Calculations indicate that expenditures to exploit such energy typically are between 70 and 80 percent less than expenditures required to produce equivalent amounts of primary energy. By 1985, East Germany hoped to exploit at least 75 percent of the potential usable sources of such energy versus a comparable figure of 50 percent in 1983. To realize this end, it established the *Secondary Energy Data Book* to disseminate information about this technology, and it extends bank credits on "favorable terms" for secondary energy projects.[39] The use of industrial waste heat for heating residential dwellings represents a promising example of such initiatives. By 1985, approximately 20 percent of the housing stock was tied to district heating networks fueled by industrial waste heat. East Germany leads Eastern Europe in use of such energy.[40]

Another prominent feature of the conservation program entails an extensive system of energy consumption norms for producers (in reality, a method for rationing the use of energy), with severe financial penalties for noncompliance. Since 1980, producers must pay ten times the regular price for energy used above the norms. Such norms now regulate approximately 70 percent of national energy consumption. While the norms seemingly are enforced more vigorously than elsewhere in Eastern Europe, press commentaries detail problems with enforcement, the tendency of producers to inflate norms, and difficulties encountered in constantly revising norms to reflect the latest technological achievements.[41]

The energy efficiency of residential dwellings and household appliances has improved. Between 1981 and 1984, 270,000 apartments were built or modernized using energy-saving planning and technologies. These initiatives include architectural designs and layouts that maximize heat retention, the installation of dual-pane windows and improved insulation materials, energy-efficient lighting and control fixtures, and so on. Technical improvements in washing machines and refrigerators (energy-saving programming devices, improved insulation, and new refrigeration compressors) have reduced specific energy consumption in these appliances by 10 to 25 percent.[42]

The transport sector consumes 15 percent of final energy and almost 70 percent of diesel fuel. Energy-saving measures in this sector involve shifting road transport to less energy intensive rail and inland waterway carriers, electrifying rail lines, optimizing transportation routes, lowering speed limits on main roads (but not autobahns) and for commercial vehicles, and instituting mandatory adjustments for carburetors. The electrification of railways produces considerable savings in energy, since electric locomotives consume upward of 70 percent less energy than diesel locomotives to haul an equivalent amount of goods. Some 20 percent of the 14,000 km of rail lines in East Germany are now electrified, and electric locomotives account for almost 50 percent of all rail transportation output.[43]

The comprehensive nature of the conservation program represents its most salient characteristic. For example, the beverage bottling and fruit and vegetable industries use more than 1.1 billion returnable bottles and jars annually (the respective figure in 1975 was 700 million) to satisfy their needs. This saves the equivalent of 160,000 tons of crude lignite that would be needed to produce new containers.[44] The armed forces initiated a "To Drive the Most Economical Kilometer" movement to reduce fuel consumption in motorized transport. Military training exercises increasingly use simulators instead of "fuel intensive battle technologies." The air force has elaborated standardized procedures for flight maneuvers to eliminate disparities in fuel consumption of more than 300 liters for different pilots performing the same maneuver.[45] A propaganda campaign under the general slogan "Economize, and Once Again Economize" disseminates information about energy conservation. Twelve hundred production units have received the certificate "For Exemplary Power Economy Work" for outstanding achievements in this field. For similar achievements, individual workers earn titles such as "Best Stoker" or "Best Furnace Operator," which are "much appreciated," one account informs.[46] Between 1980 and mid-1982 alone, more than two thousand commentaries in the local press examined the rational use of energy and two television series devoted more than one hundred segments to this subject. The Rational Energy Use Working Group, attached to the Council of Ministers, coordinates all activities at the national level relating to energy conservation, and Centers for Rational Use of Energy perform similar functions in the six largest cities.[47]

In contrast, East Germany has made only limited use of prices to promote energy conservation. For political reasons, East Germany has exempted household consumers from increases in retail prices for energy. The ensuing disincentive to conserve probably contributed to increases in household energy consumption that exceeded the national rate in both 1984 and 1985. East Germany did enact several increases in industrial wholesale prices, but these had little appreciable effect on consumption. First, these prices still do not reflect marginal cost. Second, industrialists passed on to consumers part of the price increase as a cost factor.[48]

By Eastern European standards, East Germany has achieved an impressive record in energy conservation (table 5–4). It has done so, unlike several states in Eastern Europe, while simultaneously maintaining steady rates of increase in economic growth. Yet East Germany remains far behind developed capitalist countries in overall energy efficiency.[49] Further, the annual average increase of 3 percent in primary energy consumption in 1984 and 1985 represented a substantial increase over the figures for 1981, 1982, and 1983. A Western scholar attributes these increases to the absence of "economic levers" to stimulate the conservation of energy. In his assessment, the conservation by decree approach eliminated only the most obvious sources of wasteful usage of energy.[50]

Hungary

Energy conservation in Hungary is inseparably linked to its widely known efforts to reform the economy and pursue intensive economic growth.[51] As Hungarian economists conceive it, intensive growth requires a price system responsive to the dictates of international supply and demand. A prominent proponent of this view explains its connection to energy conservation:

> Domestic energy prices should reflect marginal cost and since most countries rely on imports to satisfy some of their energy needs, the marginal

Table 5–4
East Germany: Annual Change in Intensity of Primary Energy Consumption*
(percent)

1978	1979	1980	1981	1982	1983	1984
−1.3	−2.5	−5.4	−4.3	−4.3	−4.5	−2.7

Source: Computed from data reprinted in *Wirtschaftswissenschaft*, January 1986, in JPRS-*EER*, no. 42 (21 March 1986): 6.
*Primary energy consumption per unit of national income.

cost is the world market price. Past experience has suggested that continued energy pricing below world market prices or long term replacement costs has seriously weakened the impact of pricing as a policy instrument to slow the growth of primary energy demand.[52]

"The Energy Management Program" (1980) specified targets for energy conservation during the 1981–1985 period. Hungary sought to limit the annual growth in primary energy consumption to "no more" than 2 percent and that for electricity consumption to 3.5 percent (versus 3.3 percent and 4.9 percent, respectively, in the 1976–1980 period). In 1985 versus 1980, the proportion of hydrocarbons in the energy balance was expected to decline from 64 percent to 59 percent, including a reduction from 36 percent to 32 percent for crude oil and petroleum products. While these reductions would "conserve" liquid hydrocarbons, they would not represent "pure" energy conservation when less efficient coal was used as a substitute fuel.[53]

In the 1981–1985 period, the government allocated approximately 12 percent of its total industrial investments to realize its targets for energy conservation. This occurred during a time of fiscal austerity when overall investments in industry were being sharply curtailed.[54] One-half of these monies were to finance large-scale projects to substitute various fuels and power for oil. These projects included the electrification of some 250 km of railways, the importation from the West of coal-fired power station equipment, and the hookup of an additional 100,000 to 120,000 residential dwellings to the natural gas network. The remaining monies, in the form of state subsidies, bank credits, and the development funds of enterprises, were to cover up to 30 percent (and, in some instances, 100 percent) of the investment funds needed for energy-saving and fuel-substitution projects at the enterprise level. Hungary has used a $109 million loan from the World Bank to this same end.[55]

Various initiatives sought to provide producers with an economic interest in energy conservation. Since 1979, ministries and major energy-consuming enterprises must include conservation programs in their annual and five-year plans, whose fulfillment determines financial rewards and perquisites.[56] In January 1980, the government initiated substantial increases in wholesale prices for energy resources designed to align them more closely with world market levels. A Soviet source criticized these increases for creating "artificial" profits in the energy production sector at the expense of other objectives, including projects to conserve energy.[57] Price increases also affected household and individual energy consumers. In 1982, the government raised the price of various home heating fuels by an average of 25 percent, although it mitigated the added economic burden through increases in pensions and income supplements to selected groups. The price increase reduced, but did not eliminate, the subsidy to the consumer for the affected fuels.[58] In January 1985, the government again enacted price increases that included a 30 percent rise in the price of home heating fuels and liquefied gas. These increases proved extremely unpopular with consumers.[59] Finally, prices for gasoline rose by 26 percent between 1981 and 1984.[60]

Hungarian data indicating that the annual rate of growth in energy consumption averaged 0.9 percent between 1981 and 1985—and in 1983 actually declined by 2 percent—seemingly demonstrate the effectiveness of these conservation measures.[61] Western data, although computed differently, also support this assessment at least through 1983.[62] A Hungarian source argued that increases in producer prices for energy were what "most forcefully" limited the growth in consumption of energy.[63]

Other analysts offer a contrasting assessment. First, they identify lower than anticipated economic growth and exceptionally mild weather as sources of much (upward of two-thirds) of the savings in energy realized during these years.[64] Several energy-intensive industrial sectors experienced especially sharp declines in output. In 1981, output in the metallurgy and mining sectors declined by 4.3 percent and 3.2 percent, respectively, compared with 1980. Similarly, production in the chemical industry was 3.9 percent lower in 1981 than in 1979.[65] Second, the relatively low indices of energy consumption attained in the 1981–1983 period were not repeated in 1984 and 1985.[66] Third, energy consumption in the communal sector increased by 4.6 percent annually between 1981 and 1985. The average increase would have been even higher but for a decline in consumption in 1983.[67] That the state continues to subsidize retail prices for energy accounts for this seeming disinterest in limiting consumption. In contrast, the price of gasoline did increase substantially between 1981 and 1984. During this period, while the national stock of automobiles expanded steadily, the consumption of gasoline declined by 7 percent.[68] Fourth, several economists argue that the "economic levers" introduced to date have not provided industrialists with meaningful economic incentives to conserve energy.[69]

Hungary appears to be reevaluating its market approach to energy conservation. In 1985, it established strict quotas of consumption for the nation's eighty four largest industrial energy consumers and stiff fines for noncompliance. One supporter of these measures conceded that "whatever way we look at it," they cannot be "easily explained as being in keeping" with prevailing theories of economic reform.[70] This conservation by decree approach also characterized measures to conserve fuels and power in the harsh winter of 1984–85. Labeled "draconian" by one observer, they included restrictions on television broadcast time, temperatures in public buildings, the supply of hot water, and the use of private automobiles.[71]

In the 1986–1990 period, Hungary expects to realize about 55 percent of its anticipated savings in energy by developing less energy intensive industries and production processes.[72] The targeted industries are to increase their share of industrial production from 28 percent in 1988 to 33 percent in 1990. These industries are to provide an increasing share of Hungary's exports to capitalist countries. Energy-intensive products hitherto predominated in these exports.

Romania

If the number of materials published on the subject, the stringency of targets pursued, and the sacrifices demanded of the population in its name measure a state's commitment to conserve energy, then Romania may be the most committed state in the world. Yet rhetoric and reality in the Romanian conservation program—similar to other aspects of its energy policy—often diverge. Only in the enormous sacrifices borne by a hapless and increasingly resentful population do stated and realized policy converge. In contrast, few discernible, and even fewer feasible, policies follow exhortations to conserve, while targets requiring a minimum reduction of 40 percent in the energy intensity of the economy during the 1980s cannot be taken seriously.[73]

A resident of Bucharest bitterly assessed the impact of successive reductions in power to the population by 20 percent in both 1979 and 1982, by 50 percent in 1983, by 12 percent in 1985, and by 30 percent in 1987: "We lived better during the war. Daily life has become a nightmare."[74] In February 1987, the government announced a further reduction of 20 percent in the power supplied to the population and promised the "most severe sanctions" against anyone who exceeded their permitted quota.[75]

Measures associated with these reductions include keeping temperatures in apartments and public buildings at no more than fifty degrees Fahrenheit (with theaters, movie houses, and libraries completely unheated), prohibiting the use of space and radiant heaters and "nonessential" household appliances (such as refrigerators), and placing stringent limitations on lighting in public and residential facilities. These initiatives are pursued under the campaign slogan "Every Watt Wasted Shows a Conscience That Has Experienced a Short Circuit." The government has established committees with the right of entry to dwellings to verify compliance with these regulations. Those found guilty of noncompliance are subject to criminal prosecution.[76]

Ironically, these draconian measures can have only a minimal impact on the overall consumption of electricity, since the industrial sector—which typically is exempted from the reductions in power[77]—accounts for approximately 85 percent of national consumption. And it is the industrial sector where the greatest waste in energy occurs. A Hungarian source reports that, depending on the branch of industry, "20, 30 and even 50 percent more energy is used in Romania" than in industrialized countries to produce the same (type, not quality) products and that "such great reserves" exist that "within a short time energy consumption could be decreased by even 10–15 percent" in industry.[78]

The Romanian leadership appears unwilling or unable to pursue decisive measures to limit the seemingly insatiable appetite of industry for energy. Indeed, at a time when it pursues such desperate measures to save fuel as substituting horses for tractors and resettling workers within walking distance of factories,[79] it continues to maintain and project the highest rates of growth in both national income and industrial production in Eastern Europe.[80] An understated commentary noted that such growth "obviously creates a supplementary demand for energy."[81]

Prospects

A respected Hungarian economist argues that there has been a "strikingly inadequate" response to energy conservation in Eastern Europe.[82] With the exception of East Germany, stagnant or declining rates of growth, not conservation measures, were the primary factor limiting demand for energy in most Eastern European economies in the 1980s.[83] In the assessment of another Hungarian analyst, only East Germany and Hungary can show "internationally competitive trends" in the conservation of energy (table 5–5).

A recent Western analysis expresses "guarded optimism" about the prospects for energy conservation in Eastern Europe. It argues that expected cutbacks in oil importation from the Soviet Union and the relatively high opportunity costs of importing crude oil from the Middle East "are bound" to foster this end.[84] If developments in Czechoslovakia and Poland during the current plan period (1986–1990) prove represent-

Table 5–5
Selected Countries: Average Annual Change
in Unit Energy Requirements per Unit
of National Income, 1981–1983
(percent)

United States	− 3.1
Japan	− 4.7
European Economic Community	− 2.7
Comecon	− 1.7
Bulgaria	− 1.6
Czechoslovakia	− 0.6
East Germany	− 2.9
Hungary	− 2.5
Poland	0.9
Romania	− 3.8*

Source: *Magyarorzag*, 7 July 1985, in JPRS-*EEI*, no. 75 (20 September 1985): 28–29; *Figyelo*, 27 June 1985, in JPRS-*EEI*, no. 64 (9 August 1985): 22, 24.

*One should treat this figure with extreme caution because of the notorious unreliability of official Romanian data overall and especially those relating to national income.

ative of other Eastern European states, this assessment seems overly optimistic.

In Czechoslovakia, the increase in consumption of fuels and power in 1986–87 exceeded the planned increase for these commodities in the entire plan period. Whereas Czechoslovakia sought to reduce the energy intensity of net material product by 2.9 percent annually between 1986 and 1990, the actual rates of reduction in 1986 and 1987 were 1.3 percent and 0.3 percent, respectively. In these years, Czechoslovakia assimilated only 6.3 percent of planned investments in energy conservation between 1986 and 1990.[85] In Poland, the State Council for the Energy Economy assessed the targets for conservation through 1990 as "unrealistic from the very beginning" because "no technical resources" were available for their realization. The director of the Institute of Mining and Metallurgy, a member of the State Council, asserts that the "situation is worse" than even the council anticipated. In his opinion, "it will be a lot" if Poland can achieve 25 percent of its current planned targets for energy conservation.[86] That Poland has now "given up" monitoring compliance with energy consumption norms by abolishing its Chief Inspectorate of the Energy Economy does not augur well for the realization of even this modest goal.[87]

The impediments to effective energy conservation are formidable. This end requires Eastern Europe to reduce substantially its reliance on supply-side initiatives to close the energy gap. The magnitude of investments devoted to produce energy ipso facto severely constrains its capacity to pursue other investment opportunities, including those for energy conservation. In lieu of significant capacities to substitute capital for energy in production, labor becomes the other potential source for substitution. Yet labor itself is a scarce resource in all economies of the region. Further, to the extent that supply-side initiatives include increased consumption of brown coal and lignite, they make the national economy more, not less, energy intensive (all things being equal). Finally, expanded supplies of energy make it easier for industrialists to ignore the dictates of sound conservation policies.

Altering this supply-side orientation will prove difficult. First, politically powerful bureaucratic actors—ministries and production units in the fuels and power complex and industrial managers in general—have a vested interest in its perpetuation. It is difficult to identify a bureaucratic constituency for energy conservation with commensurate political power. Second, the enormous sunken costs of operating existing power-producing facilities, and the long lead time required to construct new ones, effectively preclude rapid reallocation of investment resources, except in the unlikely event that states simply abandoned existing and under construction power projects. Third, the present era of fiscal stringency makes it difficult to justify expenditures for energy conservation that have no immediate economic payoff. Proponents claim that centrally planned economies provide a "macro" perspective that promotes the long-run interests of society. Empirical evidence pertaining to conservation of energy does not support this hypothesis.

Consumers also must have positive economic incentives to save energy. To date, regimes have used relatively few economic levers, particularly prices for energy that reflect marginal cost, to realize this end.

Identifing why this circumstance exists suggests why it likely will persist. An effective market approach to energy conservation is unthinkable without an overall marketization of the national economy—with all the deleterious consequences for the dominance of the Communist party that would entail. The fate of economic reform in Eastern Europe demonstrates that political considerations typically have subverted its implementation.[88]

The market approach necessarily raises the politically sensitive issue of increases in retail prices for energy. It is a truism that political elites (except in Romania) recognize that whatever popular legitimacy they possess rests primarily upon "goulash communism"—that is, satisfaction of consumer demand for higher standards of living. This recognition makes them reluctant to enact measures resulting in the short-run detriment of consumer welfare even if it is for the long-run welfare of the national economy—a category that includes increases in retail energy prices.

Finally, Eastern European economies will remain extraordinarily energy intensive as long as their traditional industrial backbone—steel, chemicals, mining, and so on—constitutes the primary consumer of energy. The enormous investment in existing plant and equipment effectively precludes any national economy from rapidly changing its production profile to emphasize less energy intensive goods and services. And Eastern Europe would not be promoting such changes under optimal circumstances. First, the requisite fiscal resources, especially of hard currency, for investment in new plants, and for retooling of existing ones are in short supply. Second, unemployment inevitably will accompany any major restructuring of the national economy as displaced workers are retrained and/or seek other jobs. Most of these individuals eventually will find employment, but this may provide little solace to regimes worried about the short-run threat of economic dislocations to their political power. Third, the widespread closure of obsolete energy-intensive production units would exacerbate already pervasive shortages of goods on the domestic market. A Polish source responded succinctly to the question "Can one close a plant for atrocious consumption of coal, electricity or gas when that plant is manufacturing goods that are in demand?": "It would be naive to assume that energy-devouring plants could be closed as of tomorrow."[89]

Of course, regimes may enact meaningful measures to conserve energy despite attendant economic and political costs. They may find the alternatives to conservation— such as limiting economic development to conform to existing supplies of energy—even less palatable. External developments also could enhance the prospects for conservation. The degree to which Mikhail Gorbachev's drive to reform the Soviet command economy impels similar reforms in Eastern Europe is an important example of this circumstance. Requisite reforms inevitably will alter those features of the command economy that foster excessive consumption of energy. Regimes also presumably would exhibit greater interest in conservation if prices for imported energy again began to escalate. Concomitantly, the persistence of today's relatively low prices for imported energy seemingly lessens the imperative for conservation. As with other methods of closing the energy gap, factors exogenous to Eastern Europe will influence the future course of energy conservation in the region.

6
Retrospection and Prospection

> It is impossible to further increase production and consumption of fuels and raw materials at the same rate as the overall economic growth rate and expand economic cooperation by increasing the exchange of fuel and raw materials for finished articles.
>
> —*Pravda*, 9 January 1989

Is Eastern Europe engaged in a Sisyphean pursuit to close the energy gap without considerable difficulties, painful dislocations, and manifest costs? That the energy gap itself will remain a vital issue of public policy seems clear. As a prominent Hungarian economist has contended, the "energy problem" in Eastern Europe is "lasting and irreversible," deriving from the seemingly insatiable appetite of the command economy for fuels and power.[1]

Retrospection

Substantial evidence in this study demonstrates that the past provides no sure guide to the future status of the energy gap. In the 1980s, the Soviet Union did not continue to increase its energy exports to Eastern Europe at the same rate as it had in the 1970s. Similarly, Eastern Europe was unable to maintain the rates of indigenous energy production it had achieved in the prior two decades. The now prevailing WMP for oil per barrel contrasts sharply with the comparable prices of the early 1980s that largely excluded Eastern Europe from the international energy market. Hungary and Poland plan to purchase substantial quantities of crude oil from Iran at the current WMP.

Yet it remains a tautology that the past gives birth to the future. What answers the past provides to the questions posed in chapter 1 constitute the sine qua non for a prospective assessment of the energy gap. The following propositions summarize the relevant findings of this study in respect to these questions:

1. *Eastern Europe must reduce its hitherto almost exclusive reliance on supply-side initiatives to close the energy gap.* A supply-side strategy remained viable as long as importation from the Soviet Union and indige-

nous production could meet incremental increases in demand for energy. These conditions existed in Eastern Europe approximately through the 1970s.

The situation changed dramatically in the 1980s. In 1987, the Soviet Union exported roughly the same volume of crude oil to Eastern Europe as it did in 1981. In contrast, Eastern Europe continues to receive more natural gas from the Soviet Union as repayment for its participation in joint projects such as the Progress pipeline. However, the Soviet Union has made incremental increases in exports of both oil and natural gas to Eastern Europe contingent upon payment in hard currency or goods. All states in Eastern Europe except East Germany and Romania also experienced a substantial deceleration in the rate of indigenous production of energy. This analysis indicates that, for the foreseeable future, Eastern Europe cannot anticipate appreciable increases in primary energy production from any resource except perhaps nuclear power.

These circumstances dictate a stress on demand-side policies to limit consumption of energy. Supply-side and demand-side policies are not always mutually exclusive, but substantial trade-offs do exist between them.

First, these policies compete with one another for investment resources. Demand-side policies will require enormous investments in energy-efficient equipment and production technologies. These investments must come largely from the monies now devoted to expanding the production of energy. The overall state of the economy and the concomitant amount of resources available for investment will decisively influence the acuteness of this competition.

Second, these policies seek different goals and ipso facto can require decision makers to choose between them. For example, demand-side policies must include prices for energy resources that reflect marginal cost, whereas such prices are antithetical to supply-side policies. Demand-side policies will close inefficient mining operations and power-generating facilities whereas supply-side policies will continue their operation. Demand-side policies will require extensive economic (and, inevitably, political) intercourse with Western states, whereas supply-side policies will require similar intercourse with the Soviet Union.

Third, these policies elicit support from different political constituencies because they distribute benefits and burdens differently. The political world is too fluid to stereotype the policy positions of political actors in any society. Yet it is likely that representatives of heavy industry, especially in the fuels and power complex, will oppose the pursuit of demand-side policies. Similarly, the average citizen may oppose these policies, fearing (correctly) that they will produce increases in consumer prices and dislocations in the work force. It is more difficult to identify the political constituency for demand-side policies. It probably includes representatives of the technical intelligentsia and academic disciplines such as economics. That many demand-side policies will bring only long-term and dispersed gains but immediate and concentrated losses constitutes a key political problem in mobilizing support for them.

2. A demand-side strategy requires fundamental change in the economic and political system. This strategy must eliminate those features of the command economy that promote the excessive consumption of energy. This end requires prices for energy resources that reflect marginal cost. Such prices are integral components of market, not command, economies. Command economies respond to the political preferences of elites, not the dictates of the marketplace.

Karl Marx correctly posited the nexus between economics and politics but incorrectly assumed the inevitable primacy of the former over the latter. The requisite conditions for market economies in Eastern Europe demonstrate that at times political change must precede economic change. Markets can exist only where Communist parties eschew their traditional role as "vanguards" imposing their political preferences on the polity. A demand-side strategy requires that the market, not the party, determine how energy resources will be consumed.

The successful implementation of Mikhail Gorbachev's program of economic perestroika in the Soviet Union would substantially enhance the prospects for demand-side policies in Eastern Europe. In many ways, perestroika is Gorbachev's version of a demand-side strategy. Proponents of a demand-side strategy seemingly are natural political allies of Gorbachev. The triumph of perestroika in the Soviet Union would strengthen the political position of Gorbachev and his allies in both the Soviet Union and Eastern Europe. Eastern European states that failed to enact similar reforms would incur both economic and political costs in their relations with the Soviet Union. They would encounter many of the same problems in trading with the Soviet Union as they now encounter in trading with capitalist states. They would become politically alienated from the Soviet Union, ever fearful that domestic political opponents would rally support in Moscow against the regime. Admittedly, the Soviet Union probably cannot impose its political desiderata unless it is willing to invade a recalcitrant Eastern European state. Yet it is naive to assume that in a struggle for power, support from Moscow cannot be exploited effectively by those who possess it.

3. The Soviet–Eastern European energy relationship exhibits the debates, conflicts, and pursuit of national interests normally associated with intercourse among democratic states. The Soviet Union remains primus inter pares in this relationship, but this analysis refutes any stereotypical view of the Soviet Union's imposing its will on a group of hapless and power-less states. Eastern Europe continues to pay for most Soviet energy with soft goods despite the insistence of the Soviet Union (first articulated in the 1950s) that payment be in hard goods. Romania does pay in hard goods for this energy, but it continues to pursue foreign policies often at variance with those of the Soviet Union. Czechoslovakia expresses consid-erable rhetorical support—but undertakes little substantive action—to im-plement perestroika and revitalize trade in Comecon. Various Eastern European states renege on their commitments to joint energy development projects, thereby undermining Soviet efforts to harden terms of trade.

These circumstances underscore the limited political utility of the en-ergy card to the Soviet Union. The energy card assumes that the Soviet Union can extract political advantage from Eastern Europe by threatening to withhold vital supplies of energy. Yet this threat must be credible before Eastern Europe will provide the requested political quid pro quo. Unfortunately for Moscow, both Eastern Europe and the Soviet Union understand that the national interest of the Soviets in the economic and political stability of the Eastern Europeans dictates that the energy card be played only in extremis. A relevant example of such an extreme situation may be the reported use of the energy card in 1981 to compel the Polish Regime to impose martial law. The Eastern Europeans adroitly exacerbate Soviet fears by reminding them of the potential economic and political chaos that would ensue from any sudden decision to cut off exports of energy. Ironically, then, it is Eastern Europe, not the Soviet Union, that often derives leverage from the energy relationship. The overwhelming dependence of its regimes on Soviet energy prevents the Soviet Union from pursuing policies that its national interest otherwise would dictate (for instance, significant reductions in, or substantial increases in prices for, energy).

Yet Eastern Europe does pay a price for dependence on the Soviet Union for energy. This dependence is one of the economic, political, and military links that constrain Eastern Europe's international autonomy and economic and political intercourse with Western states. Naturally, the nature of this price varies among regimes. Probably all regimes acknowl-edge a substantial economic price by being limited in their access to Western credits and technology. Some regimes (such as that in Czechoslo-vakia) may accept this price to prevent what they consider insidious West-ern influences from penetrating their societies.

Other regimes seemingly consider this price prohibitive. The coordi-nated efforts of the liberal Hungarian and conservative East German re-gimes to promote the autonomous international role of "small and medium size European countries" in East and West represent the most forceful explication of this position.[2] This so-called "Budapest–East Berlin axis" argues that through "dialogue and constructive relations," these states "can exert a favorable impact on the international atmosphere and improve relations between the Soviet Union and the United States."[3] Matyas Szuros, the ranking Hungarian Socialist Workers party official in charge of foreign affairs, explicitly endorsed the right of socialist states to pursue their own national interests. These interests, Szuros contended, can only be "subordinate" to the socialist community in an "extraordinary situation."[4] In 1984, the planned visit of Erich Honecker, secretary general of the Socialist Unity party to West Germany symbolized a substantive commitment to pursue these policies.

In the midst of the controversy over the North Atlantic Treaty Organization's planned deployment of Eurostrategic missiles in Western Europe, the Soviet Union forced Honecker to cancel his visit. This setback proved temporary. Under Mikhail Gorbachev, the Soviet Union has vigorously pursued a policy of Westpolitik designed to secure both economic and political advantage in Western Europe. Honecker himself made his long-planned visit to West Germany in 1987. Westpolitik facilitates Gorbachev's efforts to use Western credits and technology in the modernization of the Soviet economy. Similar benefits could accrue to Eastern European states pursuing their own Westpolitiks. This would, inter alia, enhance the capacity of these states to produce more of the hard goods the Soviet Union demands in payment for energy.

To be sure, this does not portend the imminent acquiescence of Mikhail Gorbachev in the "Finlandization" of Eastern Europe. It does suggest that the Soviet Union and Eastern Europe may discover mutual benefits from their respective pursuits of Westpolitik.

On balance, the Soviet Union has judiciously managed its energy relations with Eastern Europe. It has not treated Eastern Europe as a residual claimant on its energy resources after it satisfies domestic demand and requisite exports for hard currency. It has sought, with considerable success, to reduce energy exports to Eastern Europe to the lowest level possible while still maintaining minimally acceptable standards of economic welfare. This policy ensures that the Soviet Union will have the maximum amount of energy available for domestic consumption and export to the international market. Similarly, the Soviet Union exhibits flexibility in its efforts to harden terms of trade in energy. It simultaneously presses Eastern Europe to supply more hard goods while continuing to accept soft goods in payment for most of its energy. These are not altruistic policies. They represent a realistic assessment that economic and political stability in Eastern Europe serves the Soviet Union's national interest.

4. Eastern Europe derives short-run gains, but long-run losses, from abundant Soviet energy exports paid for with soft goods. Abundant Soviet energy exports immeasurably ease the immediate task of closing the energy gap. Not surprisingly, Eastern European officials charged with this task urge the Soviet Union to increase energy exports to the region and accept payment in soft goods. The Soviet Union is more likely to fulfill these appeals when WMPs for energy permit it to earn requisite hard currency without increasing exportation to the international market. This situation existed between 1976 and 1981. Then, the Soviet Union was able to increase oil exports to Eastern Europe while earning more hard currency from a diminishing volume of these exports to the world market. The converse occurred in the 1980s. The Soviet Union responded to declining WMPs for oil by increasing oil exports to the international market and decreasing them to Eastern Europe. The Soviet Union must make such trade-offs as long as its supply of energy does not exceed the demand from domestic, capitalist, and socialist markets.

Yet Eastern Europe incurred long-term losses from the ready availability of cheap Soviet energy. Eastern European economies became addicted to this energy, which they acquired for soft goods. Soviet energy provided essential underpinning to the economically inefficient command economy and its pursuit of extensive growth. Eastern Europe concomitantly became isolated from the competitive international market and integrated into the technologically backward socialist market. A Hungarian economist enumerates the deleterious consequences of dependence on the Soviet Union for energy and raw materials: "It has determined the development of the economic structure of the several countries, the development of their level of efficiency, the chief directions of technological development, the world market competitiveness of the industrial articles produced, etc."[5]

The continued addiction to Soviet energy acquired through soft terms of trade will only perpetuate the manifest inefficiencies in the Eastern European economies. These inefficiencies were tolerable as long as Eastern Europe was assured of steadily increasing volumes of Soviet energy with which to pursue extensive growth. This situation no longer exists. Eastern Europe now possesses an economic system designed for extensive growth but without sufficient inputs to implement this strategy.

5. The energy gap has become a subject of public discourse in Eastern Europe. This discourse often has involved popular protests against specific initiatives to close the energy gap. The nuclear debate that ensued in Communist Europe after Chernobyl included extensive participation by academicians, representatives of the technical intelligentsia, literary figures, and thousands of ordinary citizens. The Gabcikovo-Nagymaros barrage system on the Danube River has been embroiled in extended controversy involving masses of citizens in Hungary. Environmentalists have challenged the efficacy of crash programs to exploit coal that contributed to massive environmental degradation in Czechoslovakia, East Germany, and Poland. Demand-side policies that include increases in retail prices for fuels and power and threaten to close inefficient mining operations and obsolete energy-intensive production units predictably engender public protests. Only in Bulgaria and Romania are there few, if any, examples of this incipient political pluralism.

One cannot summarily reject the effectiveness of public involvement in these controversies. Overall, this involvement probably has circumscribed policymakers in undertaking initiatives to close the energy gap. The nuclear debate does appear to have heightened concern with issues of nuclear safety and the siting of NPS's in areas of dense population and high seismicity. The public controversy surrounding the Gabcikovo-Nagymaros project apparently helped initiate the unprecedented debate in the Hungarian National Assembly on its future status and the enactment of additional measures to mitigate its adverse impact on the environment. Popular concern with environmental degradation may have contributed to Czechoslovakia's decision to reduce its use of coal. Fear of popular opposition seemingly has inhibited regimes from undertaking certain initiatives. The failure of the East German regime to enact increases in retail prices for fuels and power provides a relevant example.

Admittedly, these are tentative judgments. Identifying the precise variables that determine public policy in any polity is a difficult task. The difficulty is compounded in Eastern Europe, where policy-making processes, even in the era of glasnost, remain largely removed from public scrutiny.

In general, public discourse has involved telling officials how *not* to close the energy gap. Opposition to nuclear power, to the use of coal, and to increases in retail prices for fuels and power (whatever their respective substantive merits) do not constitute a positive program to close the energy gap. Constructive public participation demands the development of such a program. Regimes might be willing to pursue hitherto unimplemented initiatives to close the energy gap if they perceived public support for them. Poland with its newly installed noncommunist government led by a prime minister from the ranks of Solidarity presents the first opportunity to test this hypothesis. It remains a truism that regimes will continue to respond in markedly different ways to public discourse on the energy gap.

6. *The United States and its allies gain more by mitigating than exacerbating the energy gap.* The United States and its allies should encourage the acquisition of Western equipment and technology to mitigate the en-

ergy gap. They can do so by eliminating trade barriers to facilitate commercial exchanges and by extending low-interest loans and credits to finance purchases in Western states. Assistance should be provided both bilaterally and multilaterally through organizations such as the World Bank. Policymakers should especially encourage the pursuit of demand-side policies by targeting assistance for these initiatives. They should avoid measures to exacerbate the energy gap. This prescription normally would preclude initiatives such as the failed U.S. attempt to prevent construction of the Siberian gas export line from the Soviet Union to Western Europe.

These are general prescriptions for policy. Political developments in Communist Europe and in East–West relations will determine how (or if) they are implemented at any particular moment. It is a tautology, for example, that a Soviet invasion of Poland hardly presents a propitious moment to pursue these prescriptions. These prescriptions are compatible with a policy of "differentiation" toward Eastern Europe.[6] That is, they can be applied selectively to reward those regimes that pursue policies of economic and political liberalization and maintain a modicum of autonomy from the Soviet Union.

The prescribed course of action serves the following desiderata of the United States and its allies:

1. It enhances the prospects for détente by promoting economic and political intercourse between East and West. Exacerbating the energy gap binds Eastern Europe more closely to the Soviet Union and frustrates Western efforts at bridge building and differentiation in the region.

2. It strengthens proponents of demand-side policies whose programs necessarily include substantial changes in the command economy and the vanguard role of the Communist party in society. Exacerbating the energy gap strengthens proponents of supply-side policies who resist efforts at economic and political liberalization.

3. It reduces any incentive the Soviet Union might have to use military force in the Third World to acquire energy for itself and its allies. Exacerbating the energy gap fosters this incentive and thereby increases the potential for confrontations between the Soviet Union and the United States.

4. It provides expanded markets for Western manufacturers. Exacerbating the energy gap closes this avenue for promoting mutually beneficial economic relations between East and West.

The capacity of Western states to realize these desiderata should not be overstated. Western assistance to mitigate the energy gap likely will never be of a magnitude to provide the United States and its allies with substantial influence over political and economic life within Communist Europe and between East and West. Nevertheless, the judicious implementation of these policy prescriptions can provide one link in an interpenetrating web of economic and political relations to promote international peace and stability.

7. *Political decisions created the energy gap, and only political decisions can resolve it.* In Harold Lasswell's felicitous phrase, politics is "who gets what, when and how." This truism explains the creation of the energy gap.

Political decisions determined that Eastern Europe would pursue extensive growth fueled by enormous increases in production and consumption of energy. Political decisions established arbitrary prices for energy resources that provided no incentive to conserve them. Political decisions dictated that energy-intensive heavy industries would compose the backbone of economic development. Political decisions created huge petrochemical industries that in all states, except Romania, necessarily relied on crude oil imported from the Soviet Union. Ironically, the Soviet Union, which now refuses to increase its exports of crude oil to Eastern Europe, was one of the principal proponents of this decision that contributed so decisively to the energy gap. Political decisions made Eastern Europe addicted to cheap Soviet energy provided in exchange for soft goods. Romania constitutes the exception to this circumstance because it made a political decision to pursue an autonomous foreign policy that alienated the Soviet Union.

If economic rather than political considerations prevailed, none of these decisions would have been made. Only if *Homo politicus* decides that henceforth *Homo economicus* determines the course of economic policy will the energy gap be resolved. The problem is that the latter would pursue initiatives deleterious to the political interests of the former. Is this problem surmountable? That is a question for prospection.

Prospection

This study claims no special prescience in forecasting the status of the energy gap. Such forecasting constitutes a tentative exercise whose utility diminishes as its perspective increases. At best, I can identify the most likely developments that will affect the energy gap through the 1990s.

The preceding analysis suggests the following relevant propositions:

• Primary energy production will not increase appreciably in any state.

- Primary energy consumption in the region will increase annually by an average of 2 to 3 percent.

- Sluggish economic growth will be the principal restraint on increases in primary energy consumption in the region.

- No state will receive appreciably more oil from the Soviet Union than it did in the 1986–1990 period.

- Exports of natural gas and electricity from the Soviet Union will continue to increase as repayment for Eastern European participation in joint Comecon energy development projects.

- Comecon will undertake no major joint projects to develop energy resources.

- Comecon will fail to enact the requisite reforms, especially in formation of prices, to revitalize trade among its members.

- Mikhail Gorbachev's program of economic perestroika will encounter only limited success in both the Soviet Union and Eastern Europe.

- No state, except perhaps Hungary, will pursue an effective demand-side strategy to limit consumption of energy.

- The international energy market will become more important as a supplementary source for supply of energy.

- Western states will make an increased, but still modest, contribution to close the energy gap.

- The imperatives of *Homo politicus*, not *Homo economicus*, will exercise decisive influence over the status of the energy gap.

These propositions will evoke déjà vu among observers of the energy gap. They suggest that Eastern Europe will experience no major changes in supply of and demand for energy throughout the early 1990s. They also ensure that policymakers will continue to grapple with the manifold dilemmas inherent in closing the energy gap. These dilemmas are similar to those encountered by the ancient mariners of Greek mythology who sailed the Strait of Messina past the twin dangers of Scylla and Charybdis: All alternatives contained danger, entailed costs, and offered no assurances that the sailors would be rescued from their peril.

How and with what consequences Eastern Europe closes the energy gap will remain questions of the keenest interest among analysts of political and economic life both inside and outside the region.

Appendix

Source: Directorate of Intelligence, *Handbook of Economic Statistics, 1987.*

Primary Energy Production, by Type
(thousands of barrels per day of oil equivalent)

	1970				1980				1986			
	Coal	Crude Oil	Natural Gas	Hydro/ Nuclear	Coal	Crude Oil	Natural Gas	Hydro/ Nuclear	Coal	Crude Oil	Natural Gas	Hydro/ Nuclear
Bulgaria	125	7	8	12	116	3	3	53	125	6	0	96
Czechoslovakia	861	4	17	23	905	2	9	51	885	2	10	90
East Germany	1,150	1	10	12	1,082	1	53	84	1,330	1	50	90
Hungary	182	39	56	1	140	41	99	1	120	40	113	38
Poland	1,790	8	84	11	2,364	7	104	18	2,390	4	100	20
Romania	125	281	460	13	178	241	639	57	210	227	690	60

Hard Coal Production
(millions of metric tons)

	1960	1970	1975	1980	1985	1986
Bulgaria	0.57	0.40	0.33	0.27	0.24	0.20
Czechoslovakia	26.40	28.20	28.12	28.20	26.22	25.70
East Germany	2.72	1.05	0.54	*	*	*
Hungary	2.85	4.15	3.02	3.07	2.64	2.32
Poland	104.44	140.10	171.62	193.12	191.64	192.08
Romania	3.40	6.40	7.32	8.06	8.66	8.80
Eastern Europe	140.38	180.30	210.95	232.72	229.40	229.10

*Amount less than 0.005.

Brown Coal and Lignite Production
(millions of metric tons)

	1960	1970	1975	1980	1985	1986
Bulgaria	15.42	28.85	27.52	29.95	30.66	35.00
Czechoslovakia	57.89	81.30	86.27	95.73	100.39	100.00
East Germany	225.47	261.48	246.71	258.10	312.00	311.00
Hungary	23.68	23.68	21.87	22.64	21.40	20.80
Poland	9.33	32.77	39.87	36.87	57.75	67.26
Romania	3.36	14.13	19.77	27.10	37.65	39.00
Eastern Europe	335.15	442.21	442.01	470.39	559.85	573.06

Natural Gas Production
(billions of cubic feet)

	1960	1970	1975	1980	1985	1986
Bulgaria	0	17	4	7	5	5
Czechoslovakia	51	43	33	23	25	21
East Germany	1	44	257	300	300	300
Hungary	12	123	183	217	247	231
Poland	19	183	211	224	225	195
Romania	352	847	1,115	1,179	960	940
Eastern Europe	435	1,257	1,803	1,950	1,762	1,692

Crude Oil Production
(thousands of barrels per day)

	1960	1970	1975	1980	1985	1986
Bulgaria	4	7	2	6	6	6
Czechoslovakia	3	4	3	2	2	2
East Germany	1	1	1	1	1	1
Hungary	24	39	40	41	40	40
Poland	4	8	11	7	4	4
Romania	241	281	306	242	225	227
Eastern Europe	277	340	363	299	278	280

Abbreviations

ADN	Allgemeiner Deutscher Nachrichtendienst
AFP	Agence France-Presse
BTA	Bulgarsko Telegrafna Agentsiia
CTK	Ceskoslovenska Tiskova Kancelar
DIW	Deutsches Institut fur Wirtschaftsforschung
DPA	Deutsche Presse Agentur
FBIS	Foreign Broadcast Information Service
FBIS-EEDR	*East Europe Daily Report*
FBIS-EEU	*East Europe Daily Report*
FBIS-SOV	*Soviet Union Daily Report*
GPO	Government Printing Office
IRNA	Iranian News Agency
JPRS	Joint Publications Research Service
JPRS-EEI	*East Europe Report—Industrial Affairs*
JPRS-EER	*East Europe Report*
JPRS-EPS	*East Europe Report—Political, Sociological, and Military Affairs*
MTI	Magyar Tavirati Irada
PAP	Polska Agencja Prasowa
RFE	Radio Free Europe
RL	Radio Liberty
TASS	Telegrafnoe Agentstvo Sovetskogo Soiuza

Notes

Chapter 1

1. Radio Moscow, 10 August 1979.
2. Eastern European states do not publish comprehensive statistics on their reserves of primary energy. Data in this discussion are drawn from N.V. Alisov and E.B. Valev, eds., *Economic Geography of the Socialist Countries of Europe* (Moscow: Progress Publishers, 1984). Data on reserves of natural gas are from *Petroleum Economist*, August 1988, 257.
3. L. Csaba, "CMEA and the Challenge of the 1980s," *Soviet Studies*, April 1988, 269.
4. For example, a Soviet source reported in 1987 that the European members of Comecon "consume approximately 40 percent more power per unit of output on average than do European Economic Community countries" (*New Times*, 12 January 1987, 32). *Planovane hospodarstvi*, no. 3 (1984), reports that Czechoslovakia consumes between 50 and 80 percent more energy than does Austria, France, or Japan to produce similar units of national income. Cited in RFE *Situation Report*, no. 17 (Czechoslovakia), 21 September 1984.
5. *Kulgazdasag*, no. 1 (January 1984), in JPRS-*EEI*, no. 30 (13 March 1984): 13; *Kulpolitika*, no. 3 (1985), in JPRS-*EEI*, no. 69 (30 August 1985): 15.
6. *Heti Vilaggazdasag*, 11 October 1986, in JPRS-*EER*, no. 33 (6 March 1987): 3.
7. *New York Times*, 12 October 1986.
8. Istvan Dobozi, "Intra-CMEA Mineral Cooperation: Implications for Trade with OECD and Third World Countries," *Resources Policy*, September 1986, 187.
9. *Trybuna ludu*, 3–4 January 1981, cited in RFE *Situation Report*, no. 18 (Poland), 18 October 1981.

Chapter 2

1. Data derived from Directorate of Intelligence, *International Energy Statistics Review* (Washington, D.C.: GPO, DI IESR 88–005, 31 May 1988), 16–18. See also *Izvestiia*, 26 April 1988.
2. *Budapest Domestic Service*, 18 June 1984, in FBIS-*EEDR*, 18 June 1984, AA8.
3. J.G. Polach, "The Development of Energy in East Europe," in U.S. Congress, Joint Economic Committee, *Economic Developments in Countries in*

Eastern Europe (Washington, D.C.: GPO, 1970), 348–433, provides a comprehensive analysis of energy policies in Eastern Europe in the 1950s and 1960s.

4. For details on the origins and construction of the Druzhba pipeline, see RFE, *Situation Report*, no. 5 (Czechoslovakia), 9 February 1977. Mikoyan's comments are reported in *New York Times*, 21 December, 1958.

5. See *New York Times*, 30 October 1964, for an analysis of the charges against Khrushchev, including those pertaining to Eastern Europe.

6. For an assessment that these agreements represented a conscious decision by the Soviet Union to subsidize these countries, see Marie Lavigne, "The Soviet Union Inside Comecon," *Soviet Studies*, April 1983, 138. For details of the agreements, see Jozef van Brabant, "The USSR and Socialist Economic Integration—A Comment," *Soviet Studies*, January 1984, 129–30. Also see *Izvestiia*, 26 September 1966. Radio Prague, 7 November 1967, as reported in RFE *Situation Report*, no. 43 (Czechoslovakia), 28 November 1973, carries an account accusing the Soviet Union of economically exploiting Czechoslovakia.

7. Central Intelligence Agency, *USSR: Development of the Gas Industry* (Washington, D.C.: ER78–10393, Library of Congress, July 1978), 21–22.

8. Polach, "The Development of Energy in East Europe," 405–406. See also *New York Times*, 29 October 1963.

9. See, for example, *Voprosy ekonomiki*, no. 12 (1971). *New York Times*, 29 November 1969, reported that an official in Czechoslovakia said that that country would get less oil from the Soviet Union in the 1970s because "Soviet output would be shifting to Siberia."

10. *Pravda*, 27 June 1979. For an overall analysis of these exports during the 1970s, see Office of Technology Assessment, *Technology and Soviet Energy Availability* (Washington, D.C.: GPO, 1981), 286–90.

11. *Pravda*, 27 June 1979 carries Kosygin's remarks. Kosygin was referring to trade with all Comecon states, although the overwhelming share of this trade is with Eastern Europe. Data on exports from 1981 to 1985 are calculated from Office of Technology Assessment; *Technology and Soviet Energy Availability*, table 73, 305.

12. Honecker's remarks appear in *Neues Deutschland*, 12 April 1981. See also *Ekonomicheskaia gazeta*, no. 45 (1981).

13. *Wall Street Journal*, 11 February 1982.

14. *Kozgazdasagi Szemle*, December 1987, in JPRS-EER, no. 24 (25 March 1988): 40. This source provides an extensive empirical analysis to support this contention. For a similar assessment, see *Figyelo*, 13 October 1983, in JPRS-EPS, no. 84892 (6 December 1983): 8. For an overall analysis of the relationship between energy and economic growth, see Robin Watson, "The Linkage between Energy and Growth Prospects in Eastern Europe," in U.S. Congress, Joint Economic Committee, *East European Economic Assessment, Part 2* (Washington, D.C.: GPO, 1981), 476–508.

15. *Rude pravo*, 19 October 1983.

16. See the article by Marshall Goldman in *Wall Street Journal*, 23 November 1981, for examples of the Soviet Union playing the oil card. Jaruzelski's remarks are reported in *Washington Post*, 23 July, 1989.

17. In 1973, a Romanian source reported that Romania wanted part of its need for imported oil "guaranteed by means of cooperation with the Soviet Union" [*Viata Economica*, 23 February 1973, quoted in RFE *Situation Report*, no. 9 (Romania), 27 February 1973].

18. For background materials on this trade, see RFE *Background Report*, no. 132 (14 June 1982); RFE *Situation Report*, no. 4 (Romania), 2 March 1984.

19. RFE *Situation Report*, no. 16 (Romania), 14 September 1979, carries the comment about the Soviet Union's "friends" receiving oil on preferential terms. *Stuttgarter Zeitung*, 1 February 1984, reports the Soviet Union supplying Romania with oil on "preferential conditions." For an assessment of the validity and significance of this report, see RFE *Situation Report*, no. 5 (Romania), 13 March 1985.

20. *Scinteia*, 28 December 1987.

21. RFE *Situation Report*, no. 3 (Romania), 22 April 1987. The Soviet Union exported 6.4 MT and 4.6 MT of crude oil to Romania in 1986 and 1987, respectively [*Vneshniaia torgovlia SSSR 1987* (Moskva: Financy i Statistika, 1988)]. I am unaware of any public explanation for the decrease in deliveries in 1987. Plausible hypotheses include Romania's having insufficient hard commodities to pay for more oil or the Soviet Union's desire to average out its oil exports to Romania at around 5 to 5.5 MT annually.

22. The Radio Moscow report is cited in RL *Research Bulletin*, no. 13 (8 January 1988). On this subject, see also TASS, 27 February 1987, in FBIS-*SOV*, 3 March 1987, F1. RFE *Situation Report*, no. 3 (Romania), 22 April 1987, provides an excellent summary of Romanian trade in hard goods for Soviet energy.

23. Sandor Sipos, "Energy Cooperation between East and West," paper presented at Forum European, Paris, 23 April 1987, 3.

24. Central Intelligence Agency, *Prospects for Soviet Oil Production* (Washington, D.C.: ER 77-10277, April 1977). An account of the CIA's amended prediction is in *New York Times*, 19 May 1981. *New York Times*, 3 September 1981, provides a summary of the prediction by the DIA. See the article by Marshall Goldman in *Washington Post*, 19 August 1979, for a critique by a private scholar of the CIA's predictions.

25. See, for example, Office of Technology Assessment, *Technology and Soviet Energy Availability*; Marshall Goldman, *The Enigma of Soviet Petroleum: Half Full or Half Empty?* (London: Allen and Unwin, 1981); Leslie Dienes and Theodore Shabad, *The Soviet Energy System: Resource Use and Policies* (New York: Halsted Press, 1979); Edward A. Hewett, *Energy, Economics, and Foreign Policy in the Soviet Union* (Washington D.C.: Brookings Institution, 1984). For a Soviet analysis of the subject, see A.I. Zybkov, ed., *Toplivno-cyrevaya problema v usloviyakh sotsialisticheskoi ekonomicheskoi integratsy* (Moskva: Nauka, 1979), 266–92.

26. *Wall Street Journal*, 9 June 1983. The analyst is Edward A. Hewett of the Brookings Institution.

27. Unless otherwise noted, all data on production of energy resources in the Soviet Union are drawn from *Narodnoe khoziaistvo SSSR za 70 Let* (Moskva: Financy i Statistika, 1987), 163.

28. All data on output targets in the current economic plan are from *Pravda*, 19 June 1986.

29. Jeremy Russell, *Energy as a Factor in Soviet Foreign Policy* (Lexington, Mass.: Lexington Books, 1976), 48. For an analysis by General Secretary Gorbachev of problems besetting the petroleum industry, see *Pravda*, 5 September 1985.

30. For an overview of the development of nuclear power in the Soviet Union, see Fedor Ovchinnikov et al., *Mezhdunarodnoe sotrudnichestvo stran chlenov SEV v oblasti atomnoi energetiki* (Moskva: Energoatomizat, 1986), 76–99 (hereafter cited as *atomnoi energetiki*). See also David Marples, *Chernobyl and Nuclear Power in the USSR* (New York: St. Martin's Press, 1986). Data on output of nuclear power in 1988 are from *Argumenty i fakty*, 6–12 January 1989, 8.

31. On this subject, see, inter alia, Judith Thornton, "Chernobyl and Soviet Energy," *Problems of Communism*, November/December 1986, 1–16. The announcement that the Soviet Union will halt construction at six NPS's was reported by TASS, 23 December 1988, in FBIS-SOV, 27 December 1988, 66.

32. The following discussion, unless otherwise noted, is drawn from John M. Kramer, "Chernobyl and the Nuclear 'Debate' in Communist Europe: The Role of Public Opinion," testimony presented before the U.S. Congress, Commission on Cooperation and Security in Europe, Washington, 26 April 1988; RL *Supplement*, no. 1 (16 February 1988); *RL Research Bulletin*, no. 135 (21 March 1988); *RL Research Bulletin*, no. 392 (2 September 1988).

33. *Literaturna Ukraina*, 21 January 1988.

34. *Izvestiia*, 10 February 1988.

35. *Izvestiia*, 9 March 1988.

36. For example, see the comments by V. Masol, chairman of the Council of Ministers, Ukrainian SSR, as carried by Radio Kiev, 17 August 1988, in FBIS-SOV, 22 August 1988, 55. This official reported that public opinion influenced the decision to halt construction at NPS's in Odessa and Kharkov and to reduce the number of reactors planned for a station in the Crimea. On the work of the Interdepartmental Council for Information and Ties with the Public, see *Argumenty i fakty*, 6–12 January 1989, 8.

37. For a detailed analysis of the prospects for natural gas production in the 1980s, see Edward A. Hewett, "Near-Term Prospects for Soviet Natural Gas Industry and the Implications for East–West Trade," in U.S. Congress, Joint Economic Committee, *Soviet Economy in the 1980's: Problems and Prospects*, Part 1 (Washington, D.C.: GPO, 1982), 391–413.

38. TASS, 11 September 1987, in FBIS-SOV, 15 September 1987, 39. The meaning of Yamburg in the Nenets language is cited in L. Csaba, "CMEA and the Challenge of the 1980s," *Soviet Studies*, April 1988, 27. The comments of the environmentalists were reported by TASS, 2 September 1988.

39. Data on exports of crude oil and petroleum products in 1980 and 1985 are calculated from *International Energy Statistics Review*, 31 May 1988, 16. See the data on exports of crude oil to Eastern Europe in 1986 and 1987 in *Vneshniaia torgovlia SSSR 1987*. As noted, crude oil deliveries to Romania declined from 6.4 MT in 1986 to 4.6 MT in 1987.

40. Prime Minister Grosz of Hungary reported that the Soviet Union was "ready to maintain existing ratios" in exports of energy to Hungary through 1995 (*Nepszabadsag*, 9 July 1988). The Soviet trade advisor to Poland stated that in the 1991–1995 period, Soviet exports of crude oil to Poland will be "on an unchanged basis" (*Zycie partii*, 1 June 1988, in FBIS-*EER*, 30 August 1988, 65). A Polish source reports that the projection of the volume of Soviet oil deliveries to Poland in the 1991–1995 period was so contentious that it could be resolved only by the respective prime ministers of the two countries [*Tygodnik kulturalny*, 4 September 1988, in JPRS-*EER*, no. 100 (23 November 1988): 2].

41. Treatments of Soviet trade in hard currency during these years include William Cooper, "Soviet–Western Trade," in U.S. Congress, Joint Economic Committee, *Soviet Economy in the 1980's: Problems and Prospects*, Part 1, 454–78; Joan Parpart Zoeter, "USSR: Hard Currency Trade and Payments," in U.S. Congress, Joint Economic Committee, *Soviet Economy in the 1980's: Problems and Prospects*, Part 1, 479–506.

42. Unless otherwise noted, all data on Soviet energy exports are drawn from *Narodnoe khoziaistvo SSSR za 70 Let*, 640–48; *International Energy Statistics Review*, 31 May 1988, 16–17.

43. For a detailed analysis of the pipeline project, see Jonathan Stein, *The Soviet Bloc, Energy, and Western Security* (Lexington, Mass.: Lexington Books, 1983), 59–84.

44. For an overall exposition and analysis of these issues, see George Hoffman, *The European Energy Challenge: East and West* (Durham, N.C.: Duke University Press, 1985), 117–32.

45. *Wall Street Journal*, 16 March 1983. A Hungarian economist explicitly links the reduction in exports to Eastern Europe with the increase in exports to the capitalist market (*Kulgazdasag*, January 1984, in JPRS-*EEI*, no. 30, 13 March 1984), 17. On this point, see also Edward A. Hewett, "Soviet Primary Products Export to Comecon and the West," in R.G. Jensen, ed., *Soviet Natural Resources in the World Economy* (Chicago: University of Chicago Press, 1983), 639–657.

46. *Wall Street Journal*, 9 June 1983.

47. Plan Econ, Inc., *Plan Econ Report: Developments in the Economies of the Soviet Union and Eastern Europe* (4, nos. 1–2, 15 January 1988).

48. *Izvestiia*, 10 October 1987; *Literaturnaia gazeta*, 21 October 1987.

49. See the data on exports of selected commodities by Eastern European states in *Statisticheskii ezhegodnik stran chlenov Soveta Ekonomicheskoi Vzaimopomoshchi 1987* (Moskva: Financy i Statistika, 1987), table 139, 313–68.

50. A Hungarian source agrees that when formulating its energy export policy, the Soviet leadership has been keenly aware of its "significant interest in protecting the economic and political stability of the small East European socialist countries" [*Kozgazdasagi Szemle*, November 1987, in JPRS-*EER*, no. 10 (8 February 1988): 45].

51. See, for example, Sipos, "Energy Cooperation between East and West," 13; the analysis by Jonathan Stern as reported in *Petroleum Economist*, May 1988, 148–49. For an earlier analysis by Stern on this subject, see Jonathan Stern,

Soviet Natural Gas Development to 1990: Implications for the CMEA and the West (Lexington, Mass.: Lexington Books, 1980).

52. For an explication of the procedures entailed in the Bucharest formula, see RFE *Background Report*, no. 67 (25 March 1977).

53. Polach, "The Development of Energy in East Europe," 400–402, asserts that Soviet prices for fuels to Eastern Europe were above comparable world prices. For a view that argues overall that the Soviet Union "lost" in its trade with Eastern Europe during these years, see Lavigne, "The Soviet Union Inside Comecon," 135. Calculations by Hungarian economists lend support to Lavigne's position. They indicate that in 1964, prices for machinery and equipment in Comecon trade were 25.9 percent above WMPs, while respective prices for raw materials were only 15.4 percent above WMPs [*Kozgazdasagi Szemle*, March 1967, cited in RFE *Background Report*, no. 21 (16 February 1988)].

54. For a discussion of these issues, see Raimund Dietz, "Advantages and Disadvantages in Soviet Trade with Eastern Europe," U.S. Congress, Joint Economic Committee, *East European Economies: Slow Growth in the 1980's*, vol. 2 (Washington, D.C.: GPO, 1986), 292–93.

55. For a detailed discussion of problems encountered in ascertaining the real prices charged for goods in Comecon trade, see RFE *Background Report*, no. 155 (24 August 1984).

56. For example, at the 1983 session of the Comecon Council, Soviet premier Nikolai Tikhonov asserted that "mutual advantage" must prevail in Comecon trade. This requires Eastern Europe to supply the Soviet Union with "goods intended for export" (that is, hard goods). "Understandably," Tikhonov continued, the willingness of the Soviet Union to meet Eastern Europe's demand for energy "depends considerably on the extent that the Comecon countries provide goods that are needed by the national economy of the USSR" (*Pravda*, 19 October 1983). A Hungarian source reported that as early as the 1960s, the Soviet Union asserted that it would accept only hard goods for much of the energy it sold to Eastern Europe [*Kozgazdasagi Szemle*, November 1979, cited in RFE *Situation Report*, no. 22 (Hungary), 5 December 1979].

57. Thus, a Polish source asserts that Poland attaches artificially high prices to many of the goods it exports to the Soviet Union. (PAP, 23 September 1981, in FBIS-*EEDR*, 24 September 1981, G3). In contrast, a recent Western study, drawing on calculations by Hungarian economists, finds that "there is little basis for assuming" that exports of machinery and equipment now are overpriced in Comecon trade, although they may have been overpriced in the 1960s (Kazimierz Poznanski, "Opportunity Cost in Soviet Trade with Eastern Europe: Discussion of Methodology and New Evidence," *Soviet Studies*, April 1988, 292).

58. According to calculations of the Vienna Institute for Comparative Economic Studies, the Soviet Union has accumulated a surplus of almost 18 billion TR since 1960 in trade with Eastern Europe [cited in RFE *Background Report*, no. 251 (30 December 1988)]. In 1987, the Soviet Union ran an overall trade surplus with Eastern Europe of 493 million rubles. Bulgaria, Czechoslovakia, and Hungary actually achieved trade surpluses with the Soviet Union (calculated from data in *Vneshniaia torgovlia SSSR v 1987*, table 4).

59. *Kozgazdasagi Szemle*, November 1979, in RFE. *Situation Report*, no. 22 (Hungary) 5 December 1979.

60. Romania has been especially outspoken on this subject. For example, at the 1986 meeting of the Comecon Council in Bucharest, Prime Minister Constantin Dascalescu asserted that "we must immediately proceed to convening steps on concrete economic incentives, including appropriate prices, for the production and export of agricultural and food produce" (*Scinteia*, 5 November 1986). Similarly, a Hungarian source asserted that prices paid for agricultural commodities in Comecon trade "do not, or barely, bring us satisfactory income" (*Nepszabadsag*, 7 July 1988).

61. The evidence for this comes from Hungary. Matyas Szuros, a secretary of the Central Committee, reports that in the present plan period, "the Soviet Union is examining what kinds of goods it can buy from Hungary for dollars which it purchases from capitalist markets" (*Budapest Domestic Service*, 20 January 1987, in FBIS-*EEU*, 21 January 1987, F2). A Czechoslovak source also reported that the Soviet Union, Czechoslovakia, East Germany, and Poland pay in dollars for 45 percent of the 2 MT of wheat that they annually import from Hungary (*Rude pravo*, 8 August 1988).

62. Comprehensive data on this hard currency trade are lacking. Reportedly, in 1978, Hungary paid in hard currency for 2 MT of the 8 MT of crude it imported from the Soviet Union. [*Heti Vilaggazdasag*, 21 July 1979, cited in RFE *Situation Report*, no. 1 (Hungary), 22 January 1980].

63. The argument that the "joint projects" represent a "hardening" of trade is made forcefully in L. Csaba, "Joint Investments and Mutual Advantages in the CMEA: Retrospection and Prognosis," *Soviet Studies*, April 1985, 239. Hungarian economists report that investment credits in joint projects are repaid in TR over twelve years at an annual interest rate of 2 percent [Balint Balkay and Sandor Sipos, "Gas in Eastern Europe and the USSR," in Melvin Conant, ed., *The World Gas Trade: Resource for the Future* (Boulder, Colo.: Westview Press, 1986), 17].

64. RL *Research Bulletin*, no. 330, (20 July 1988).

65. *Vneshniaia torgovlia SSSR v 1987*, table 17, provides the following data on prices charged to individual Eastern European states for Soviet crude oil and natural gas in 1986 and 1987:

Country	1986		1987		Percent Decrease 1987–1986	
	Oil[a]	*Natural gas*[b]	*Oil*	*Natural gas*	*Oil*	*Natural gas*
Bulgaria	170.08	120.10	147.62	108.85	13.2	9.4
Czechoslovakia	172.32	120.34	153.06	110.55	11.2	8.1
East Germany	160.34	119.88	143.08	109.92	10.8	8.3
Hungary	161.87	116.80	144.12	106.09	11.0	9.2
Poland	165.97	119.99	148.45	110.54	10.6	7.9
Romania	150.78	120.40	149.72	109.38	0.7	9.1

[a]All oil values given in rubles per ton.
[b]All natural gas values given in rubles per thousand cubic meters.

66. Wharton Econometric Forecasting Associates, Centrally Planned Economies, *Analysis of Current Issues*, 21 January 1987.

67. *Vneshniaia torgovlia SSSR v 1987*, table 17.

68. *Ibid.*, table 4.

69. *Pravda*, 7 July 1988.

70. Michael Marrese and Jan Vanous, *Soviet Subsidization of Trade with Eastern Europe—A Soviet Perspective* Berkeley: Institute of International Studies (University of California, 1983).

71. See, for example, van Brabant, "The USSR and Socialist Economic Integration—A Comment," 127–38; Poznanski, "Opportunity Cost in Soviet Trade with Eastern Europe," 290–307. Other contributions to this discussion include Josef Brada, "Soviet Subsidization of Eastern Europe: The Primacy of Economics over Politics?" *Journal of Comparative Economics*, no. 9 (1985); Dietz, "Advantages and Disadvantages in Soviet Trade with Eastern Europe"; Franklyn D. Holzman, "The Significance of Soviet Subsidies to Eastern Europe," *Comparative Economic Studies*, no. 1 (Spring 1986); Lavigne, "The Soviet Union Inside Comecon," 135–53.

72. The importance of soft goods in exchange for energy is made forcefully in RFE *Background Report*, no. 21 (16 February 1988). Eastern Europe derives other advantages, including lower transportation charges and greater stability in prices, by importing principally from the Soviet Union rather than the world market.

73. *Trybuna ludu*, 19 October 1987.

74. *Rzeczywistosc*, 17 July 1988, in FBIS-*EEU*, 2 August 1988, 2.

75. Nemeth was quoted in the Soviet newspaper *Ekonomicheskaia gazeta*, no. 6 (February 1988).

76. For an overall analysis of these projects, see L. Csaba, "Joint Investments and Mutual Advantages in the CMEA," 227–47; John Hannigan and Carl McMillan, "Joint Investment in Resource Development: Sectoral Approaches to Socialist Integration," in U.S. Congress Joint Economic Committee, *East European Economic Assessment, Part 2*, 259–95.

77. Csaba, "Joint Investments and Mutual Advantages in the CMEA," 242.

78. Reportedly, the first such arrangement involved only Eastern European states. This entailed an agreement in 1957 whereby Czechoslovakia and East Germany extended credits to Poland for the development of coal mining with repayment from output of completed facilities [Michael Kaser, *Comecon: Integration Problems of the Planned Economies* (Oxford: Oxford University Press, 1967), 78–79].

79. For a discussion of joint projects under the 1971 Comprehensive Program, see Hannigan and McMillan, "Joint Investment in Resource Development," 262–65.

80. Csaba, "CMEA and the Challenge of the 1980s," 276.

81. The assessment of the Hungarian economist is from *Kulgazdasag*, January 1984, in JPRS-*EEI*, no. 30 (13 March, 1985): 5. The Western assessment is from Hannigan and McMillan, "Joint Investment in Resource Development," 282. These authors hypothesize that the higher estimate of the Hungarian scholar derives from including contributions to bilateral as well as joint projects.

82. Hannigan and McMillan, "Joint Investment in Resource Development," 274–82, provides a detailed analysis of this project. Unless otherwise noted, materials on this subject are drawn from this source.

83. For example, Hungary compensated the Soviet Union with Ikarus buses (which are considered hard goods in Comecon trade) for its subcontract work (*Nepszabadsag*, 20, 23, 24 August 1976, cited in Hannigan and McMillan, "Joint Investment in Resource Development," 278).

84. *Nepszabadsag*, 21 February 1987. This source reports that the figures for Bulgaria and Czechoslovakia are 9 percent and 4 percent respectively.

85. *Magyar Hirlap*, 13 December 1986, in JPRS-*EER*, 11 June 1987, 78–79; Radio Hvezda, 23 July 1986, cited in RFE *Background Report*, no. 124 (9 September 1986). Hungary also has complained publicly about "certain partners" who "rather frequently" consume more than their authorized share of electricity from the Mir network. Gyorgy Lazar, head of the Hungarian delegation at the 1986 session of the Comecon Council in Bucharest, asserted that these "irregularities" have necessitated "immediate, at times drastic governmental measures, causing extremely serious harm to the Hungarian economy" (MTI, 4 November 1986, in FBIS-*EEU*, 4 November 1986, AA12). Although not publicly identified as such, Romania appears to be a principal culprit in these irregularities.

86. For details of the project, see Ovchinnikov et al., *atomnoi energetiki*, 89. Cost estimates for the project are from RFE *Background Report*, no. 77 (2 April 1979). To understand why nominal and actual costs for this project may diverge, see the discussion later in the text regarding factors that drive up actual costs in joint projects.

87. *Radyanska Ukraina*, 30 December 1987.

88. Ovchinnikov et al., *atomnoi energetiki*, 89.

89. Csaba, "CMEA and the Challenge of the 1980s," 276.

90. For details of the project, see TASS, 11 September 1987, in FBIS-*SOV*, 15 September 1987, 39.

91. TASS, 14 August 1986, in FBIS-*SOV*, 15 August 1986, S2.

92. For an optimistic assessment of the pace of construction on Progress, see *Moscow Domestic Service*, 28 December 1987, in FBIS-*SOV*, 30 December 1987, 35. Assessments that contrast sharply with this view include *Otechestven front*, 19 August 1987, in FBIS-*EEU*, 2 September 1987, B1–2; *Zemedelske noviny*, 23 July 1987, in FBIS-*EEU*, 28 July 1987, C7.

93. *Petroleum Economist*, May 1988, 148.

94. *Dziennik Baltycki*, 12 July 1988, in FBIS-*EEU*, 22 July 1988, 42.

95. *Planovoe khoziaistvo*, August 1976, 72.

96. *Nepszabadsag*, 7 July 1988.

97. *Smena*, 29 October 1986, cited in RFE *Background Report*, no. 160 (7 November 1986). A Hungarian economist reported that two to three years may elapse before the technical documentation is completed for an already agreed upon project (Csaba, "Joint Investments and Mutual Advantages in the CMEA," 238).

98. Eastern European sources advancing this argument include *Polityka-Eksport-Import*, no. 8 (April 1988), in JPRS-*EER*, no. 46 (13 June 1988): 12; *Rude pravo*, 14 October 1987; *Scinteia*, 5 November 1986. For a Soviet account that agrees with this argument, see *Pravda*, 7 September 1987. The Hungarian

official, now retired deputy prime minister Joszef Marjai, was quoted by MTI, 21 October 1988, in FBIS-*EEU*, 24 October 1988, 32.

99. Reportedly, at the 1984 and 1985 sessions of the Comecon Council, an almost "unanimous chorus" of creditor states in joint projects demanded that precise terms of repayment be stipulated before the initiation of a project (Csaba, "CMEA and the Challenge of the 1980s," 277).

100. *Kulgazdasag*, January 1984, in JPRS-*EEI*, no. 30 (13 March 1985): 7.

101. *Pravda*, 12 October 1988. The assessment that "no progress" was made on this issue is by Wladyslaw Gwiazda, Poland's minister for foreign economic relations, as reported by PAP, 12 October 1988, in FBIS-*SOV*, 12 October 1988, 6.

102. *Scinteia*, 5 November 1986.

103. *Kulgazdasag*, January 1984, in JPRS-*EEI*, no. 30 (13 March, 1985): 7, provides a comprehensive summary of Soviet objections to the joint projects. For a Western analysis that argues that the Eastern Europeans have received a "fantastic rate of return" from joint energy projects and that the Soviet Union has suffered a "sizable opportunity cost" from these projects, see van Brabant, "The USSR and Socialist Economic Integration—A Comment," 130.

104. *Planovoe khoziaistvo*, August 1981, 19. However, this circumstance is becoming less important in the late 1980s as terms of trade shift in favor of the Eastern Europeans.

105. Wharton Econometric Forecasting Associates, Centrally Planned Economies, Analysis of Current Issues, 29 June 1984, 3.

106. *Kulgazdasag*, January 1984, in JPRS-*EEI*, no. 30 (March 1985): 6.

107. Unless otherwise noted, the following discussion is drawn from John M. Kramer, "Council for Mutual Economic Assistance," in Richard Staar, ed., *1988 Yearbook on International Communist Affairs* (Stanford: Hoover Institution Press, 1988), 371–74.

108. As quoted in *Figyelo*, 16 October 1986, in JPRS-*EER*, no. 18 (4 December 1986): 21.

109. As Premier Strougal contended at the 1988 session of the Comecon Council in Prague, "Like certain other countries, we are convinced that no significant progress can be attained without a consistent development of goods-money relations between the member countries. We most urgently need realistic domestic and contractual prices, rates of exchange, interest rates, and so forth" (*Rude pravo*, 8 July 1988).

110. Ibid.

111. *Rude pravo*, 11 July 1988. A Polish source argues that Comecon "is not an organization whose individual members have common or at least complementary goals . . . The existing goals . . . are divergent, and often even contradictory." *Polityka-Eksport-Import*, no. 16 (August 1988), in *JPRS-EER*, no. 87 (18 October 1988): 27.

112. *Kozgazdasagi Szemle*, November 1987, in FBIS-*EEU*, 17 February 1988, 26.

113. The text of Grosz's speech was carried in *Pravda*, 6 July 1988. Grosz made a similar demand in an interview carried by *Budapest Domestic Service*, 14 October 1987, in FBIS-*EEU*, 15 October 1987, 53.

114. *Pravda*, 7 July 1988.

115. *Pravda*, 22 February 1988.

116. *Budapest Domestic Service*, 2 July 1988, in FBIS-*EEU*, 5 July 1988, 16. Data on the 1989 trade pact from MTI, 2 March, 1989 in FBIS-*EEU*, 6 March, 1989, 31-32.

117. *Budapest Domestic Service*, 2 July, 1988 in FBIS-*EEU*, 5 July, 1988, 16.

118. *Heti Vilaggazdasag*, 8 October 1988, quoted in RFE *Situation Report*, no. 16 (Hungary), 28 October 1988.

119. *Budapest Television Service*, 17 September 1987, in FBIS-*EEU*, 2 October 1987, 29.

120. MTI, 11 October 1988, in FBIS-*EEU*, 13 October 1988, 34.

121. *Hospodarske noviny*, 22 June 1988, in JPRS-*EER*, 12 February 1988, 20.

122. Officially, Strougal "requested" that he be removed from the premiership, but it seems clear that he actually was ousted by more conservative forces in the leadership. Strougal's letter of resignation was carried by *Prague Domestic Service*, 11 October 1988, in FBIS-*EEU*, 12 October 1988, 11.

123. *Kulgazdasag*, January 1984, in JPRS-*EEI*, no. 30 (11 January 1984): 11.

124. *Moscow Domestic Service*, 6 July 1988, in FBIS-*SOV*, 12 July 1988, 3.

Chapter 3

1. Previous treatments of nuclear power in Eastern Europe include J.G. Polach, "Nuclear Power in East Europe," *East Europe*, no. 5 (1968): 3–12; J. Wilczynski, "Atomic Energy for Peaceful Purposes in the Warsaw Pact Countries," *Soviet Studies*, October 1974, 568–91; Lesley J. Fox, "Soviet Policy in the Development of Nuclear Power in Eastern Europe," in U.S. Congress, Joint Economic Committee, *Soviet Economy in the 1980's: Problems and Prospects*, Part 1 (Washington, D.C.: GPO, 1982), 457–507. A comprehensive treatment of this subject by Eastern European analysts is Fedor Ovchinnikov et. al,. *Mezhdunarodnoe sotrudnichestvo stran chlenov SEV v oblasti atomnoi energetiki* (Moskva: Energoatomizat, 1986) (hereafter cited as *atomnoi energetiki*).

2. TASS, 3 November 1986, in FBIS-*SOV*, 4 November 1986, BB8. These targets are scaled back from those that Comecon announced in 1979. Then, Comecon projected that by the year 2000, nuclear power would account for 50 percent of the electricity generated in the member states [TASS, 29 June 1979, as discussed in RFE *Background Report*, no. 150 (3 July 1979)].

3. All reactors in Eastern Europe are pressurized-water reactors (of either 440 MW or 1,000 MW capacity) using water as both moderator and coolant and lightly enriched uranium as fuel. In contrast, the type of reactor at the Chernobyl NPS and many other NPS's in the Soviet Union is graphite moderated, water cooled, and fueled with either natural or lightly enriched uranium. For a discussion of the different types of reactors manufactured in the Soviet Union and Eastern Europe, see Office of Technology Assessment, *Technology and Soviet Energy Availability* (Washington, D.C.: GPO, 1981), 114–16. For a detailed sur-

vey of official reactions in Eastern Europe to the disaster at Chernobyl, see RFE *Background Report*, no. 72 (30 May 1986).

4. *Pravda* (Bratislava), 10 July 1984, in FBIS-*EEU*, 12 July 1984, D1; *Rzeczpospolita*, 1 May 1985, in JPRS-*EEI*, no. 60 (22 July 1985): 5–6; *New York Times*, 15 April 1979, 27.

5. *Planovane hospodarstvi*, no. 2 (1985): 24–37, in JPRS-*EER*, no. 55 (10 June 1985). This source provides a detailed analysis of the relative costs of nuclear and nonnuclear sources of power.

6. For example, one source estimated that in Poland it costs almost three times more to build an NPS than a hard coal–fired power plant of equal capacity. PAP, 5 October 1988, in FBIS-*EEU*, 6 October 1988, 36.

7. *Rzeczpospolita*, 28 December 1984, in JPRS-*EPS*, no. 26 (26 February 1985): 191. John M. Kramer, "The Environmental Crisis in Eastern Europe: The Price for Progress," *Slavic Review*, Summer 1983, 204–21, provides a comprehensive analysis of environmental pollution in the region. See RFE *Background Report*, no. 74 (27 May 1986), for an analysis of the dilemma that environmentalists in Eastern Europe face in opposing nuclear power.

8. *Pravda* (Bratislava), 6 November 1985, in JPRS-*EPS*, no. 123 (17 December 1985): 25.

9. As quoted in *New York Times*, 2 January 1980.

10. The traditionally insouciant attitude toward nuclear power is reflected in the remark made by a director of a Soviet NPS to Valerii Legasov, the individual who headed the official investigation into the causes of the accident at the Chernobyl NPS. "What are you worried about?" the director asked Legasov. "A nuclear reactor is only a samovar . . . nothing will ever happen" (*Pravda*, 20 May 1988).

11. TASS, 24 June 1986, in FBIS-*SOV*, 25 June 1986, S6.

12. *Pravda*, 18 January 1955, carried the offer of nuclear cooperation between the Soviet Union and its allies. Unless otherwise noted, the following discussion is drawn primarily from the works cited in note 1.

13. Polach, "Nuclear Power in Eastern Europe," 3–4, sets forth the economic rationale for nuclear power in the region.

14. J.G. Polach, "Nuclear Energy in Czechoslovakia: A Study in Frustration," *Orbis*, July 1968, 849.

15. Ibid., 851.

16. The dissident group Charter 77 alleges that the A-1 plant suffered two serious accidents that included loss of life and radioactive steam escaping into the atmosphere in 1976 and 1977 and that the second mishap so damaged both the primary and secondary cooling circuits and the reactor itself that the plant had to be closed. Czechoslovakia has never officially acknowledged that the accidents occurred, but in 1980 a member of the Czechoslovak Nuclear Energy Commission did disclose that there had been a "defect" at the A-1 plant that damaged the reactor and led to the closure of the plant. Radio Prague, 8 August 1980, in RFE *Background Report*, no. 207 (14 August 1980), provides an extensive analysis of all these issues. The assertion that the A-1 plant was built with the "active assistance" of the Soviet Union is in RFE *Situation Report*, no. 8 (Czechoslovakia), 26 May 1986.

17. For a discussion of the technical and operating characteristics of this reactor, see Ovchinnikov et al., *atomnoi energetiki*, 33–42.

18. *New York Times*, 26 July 1984; *New York Times*, 23 November 1968.

19. *New York Times*, 5 March 1972.

20. BTA, 21 June 1974, in RFE *Background Report*, no. 5 (28 June 1974).

21. For details of these agreements, see Ovchinnikov et al., *atomnoi energetiki*, 114.

22. RFE *Background Report*, no. 150 (3 July 1979).

23. Unless otherwise noted, all material on these organizations is drawn from Ovchinnikov et al., *atomnoi energetiki*, 133–39.

24. Paul Josephson, "Atomic Energy in Eastern Europe: Trends and Prospects for the Year 2000," paper presented at the Annual Convention of the American Association for the Advancement of Slavic Studies, Monterey, Calif., November 1981, 6.

25. CTK, 24 May 1987, in FBIS-*EEU*, 3 June 1987, AA1.

26. *Krasnaia zvezda*, 27 August 1985.

27. Detailed analyses of Czechoslovakia as an exporter of nuclear equipment include *Hospodarske noviny*, no. 48 (1985), in JPRS-*EEI*, no. 34 (11 March 1986); *Planovane hospodarstvi*, no. 2 (1985) in JPRS-*EEI*, no. 55 (10 June 1985). For information on Czechoslovakia's role in the breeder reactor program, see CTK, 28 September 1988, in FBIS-*EEU*, 30 September 1988, 32.

28. On this subject, see *Hospodarske noviny*, no. 40 (1985), in JPRS-*EEI*, no. 92 (9 December 1985): 7.

29. For Premier Strougal's criticism, see *Prague Domestic Television*, 4 July 1981, in FBIS-*SOV*, 8 July 1981, AA13; *Rude pravo*, 19 October 1983. *Zivot strany*, no. 14 (1982), in RFE *Situation Report*, no. 15 (Czechoslovakia), 25 August 1982, admits that Czechoslovakia also has been criticized for lagging in the fulfillment of Comecon projects.

30. See *Rude Pravo* (18 May 1989) for a detailed analysis of the status of orders for Czechoslovak nuclear equipment by Comecon states. Premier Ryzhkov's remarks were reported by TASS, 3 November 1986. Ironically, the Soviet Union may also be guilty of reneging on commitments to purchase reactors from Czechoslovakia. A Western source reports that the Soviet Union seeks to conclude an agreement with Canada for the purchase of reactors that were to be supplied by Czechoslovakia (*Washington Post*, 21 August 1988).

31. Premier Strougal's comments were reported in *Prague Domestic Service*, 10 June 1982, in FBIS-*SOV*, 11 June 1982, AA4. On alleged Eastern European dissatisfaction with Soviet technology, see *Washington Post*, 17 December 1985.

32. TASS, 14 October 1987. The "new generation" of pressurized water reactors is supposed to be ready by 1992 (*Moscow Domestic Service*, 20 April 1988, in FBIS-*SOV*, 28 April 1988, 74.

33. *Pravda* (Bratislava), 10 July 1984, in FBIS-*EEU* (2 July 1984), D1. Chairman Havel's comments were carried by *Czechoslovak Television*, 18 April 1986, in RFE *Situation Report*, no. 8 (Czechoslovakia), 26 May 1986. *Hospodarske noviny*, no. 48 (1985), in JPRS-*EEI*, no. 34 (11 March 1986), noted the alterations—reportedly "on the recommendation of Soviet specialists"—in Soviet designed reactors.

34. *Washington Post*, 7 May 1986. On the informal procedures that Comecon purportedly has developed to exchange information on mishaps at NPS's, see *Jaderna energie*, no. 3 (1984), in RFE *Situation Report*, no. 8 (Czechoslovakia), 26 May 1986.

35. TASS, 25 September 1987. The consequences of any radiation accident are to be eliminated by the state on whose territory the accident has taken place or its consequences have manifested themselves. All expenses incurred in eliminating these consequences are to be paid by the state responsible for the accident.

36. *Izvestiia*, 13 October 1987.

37. *Moscow International Service*, 20 January 1988, in FBIS-*SOV*, 21 January 1988, 6–7. This source reported that the new commission will deal with "construction of NPS, nuclear heating plants, securing their safety, construction of large thermal and hydropower stations, and the preparations of cadres." This broad functional mandate would appear to overlap considerably with the activities of Interatominstrument and Interatomenergo.

38. Unless otherwise noted, all the material on national nuclear programs is drawn from Ovchinnikov et al., *atomnoi energetiki*, 56–105.

39. *Energetika*, no. 2 (1985), in JPRS-*EEI*, no. 61 (23 July 1985), provides a detailed discussion of these plans.

40. On the difficulties encountered in construction at Kozloduy and Belene, see, respectively, *Energetika*, no. 10 (1983), in JPRS-*EEI*, no. 15 (3 February 1984), and *Sofia Domestic Service*, 26 November 1985, in FBIS-*EEU*, 29 November 1985, C3, C4. *Sofia Domestic Service*, 23 December 1987, in FBIS-*EEU*, 28 December 1987, reported that the fifth block at Kozloduy had been connected to the national power grid. *Zemedelsko zname*, 13 February 1986, cited in RFE *Background Report*, no. 72 (23 May 1986), reported on the use of foreign workers at Bulgarian nuclear projects. For details of the dispute over the price of reactors for Belene, see *Rude pravo* (18 May, 1989). *Mlada Fronta*, 23 May, 1989, in FBIS-*EEU*, 1 June 1989, 31.

41. An Austrian source charged that many residents of Jaslovske Bohunice were dying as a result of an accident at the A-1 plant in 1976 that led to extensive radioactive contamination of the surrounding environment. (*Kurier*, 4 March 1987, in FBIS-*EEU*, 5 March 1987, D1). For a Czechoslovak account that characterizes these charges as "obvious nonsense," see *Rude pravo*, 7 March 1987.

42. *Kurier*, 1 February 1988, in FBIS-*EEU*, 2 February 1988, 10.

43. For details of these plans, see *Ibid.*; *Rude pravo*, 26 June 1986; *Rude pravo*, 4 March 1988. The account in *Rude pravo*, 26 June 1986, indicates that two reactors at Kecerovice may be operational by the year 2000.

44. *Mlada Fronta*, (31 May, 1989), in FBIS-*EEU*, 7 June 1989, 21.

45. *Hospodarske noviny*, no. 26 (1987), in JPRS-*EER*, no. 156 (18 November 1987): 10.

46. *Smena*, 11 January 1984, quoted in RFE *Situation Report*, no. 2 (Czechoslovakia), 6 February 1984, provides the comments about the Mochovce NPS. The deadline for putting the first reactor into trial operation at Mochovce will not be met as a result of "unprepared building schemes, problems with recurring

deliveries, and, in particular, a shortage of professionals at the building site" [*Pravda* (Bratislava), 22 September 1988, in FBIS-*EEU*, 29 September 1988, 26].

47. *Rude pravo*, 19 July 1983. For a discussion of the decrees issued by the Communist party and the government on these issues, see *Hospodarske noviny*, no. 48 (1985), in JPRS—*EEI*, no. 34 (11 March 1986).

48. Analyses of these problems include *Hospodarske Noviny*, no. 48 (1985), in JPRS-EEI, no. 34 (11 March 1986); *Pravda* (Bratislava), 22 September 1988, in FBIS-*EEU*, 29 September, 1988, 26.

49. See Premier Strougal's comments in *Rude pravo*, 21 September 1985, in FBIS-*EEU*, 1 October 1985, directed toward problems of administrative fragmentation in NPS projects. Material on the "conflict ridden" Soviet–Czechoslovak relationship is from *Hospodarske noviny*, no. 26 (1987), in JPRS-*EER*, no. 156 (18 November 1987), 10–16.

50. *Rude pravo*, 27 April 1984, quoted in RFE *Situation Report*, no. 9 (Czechoslovakia), 11 May 1984.

51. The western assessment of the Czechoslovak nuclear program appeared in RFE *Situation Report*, no. 14 (Czechoslovakia), 9 August 1983; Deputy Premier Gerle's comments were reported in *Rude pravo*, 19 July 1983. Premier Strougal expressed similar sentiments in *Rude pravo*, 21 September 1985, in FBIS-*EEU*, 1 October 1985.

52. The comment about East Germany being committed to nuclear power is made in RFE *Background Report*, no. 102 (25 June 1985); Secretary General Honecker's remarks were made to *Dagens Nyheter*, reprinted in *Neues Deutschland*, 25 June 1986.

53. *Das Parlament*, 9 August 1986, in JPRS-*EER*, no. 11 (26 January 1987): 22.

54. On projections for nuclear power in the 1986–1990 state plan, see *Neues Deutschland*, 23 April 1986, in FBIS-*EEU*, 10 June 1986, E26. For contrasting assessments on the future status of the Stendal NPS, see *IWE Tagesdienst*, 16 December 1986, in JPRS-*EER*, no. 11 (26 January 1987): 38; *Svet hospodarstvi*, 15 October 1987, in JPRS-*EER*, no. 3 (15 January 1988): 12.

55. MTI, 12 January 1974, in FBIS-*EEDR*, 15 January 1974, F2; RFE *Situation Report*, no. 10 (Hungary), 9 September 1974. *Magyar Hirlap*, in RFE *Situation Report*, no. 10 (Hungary), 9 September 1974, is the source of the estimate for nuclear capacities in the year 2000.

56. RFE *Situation Report*, no. 1 (Hungary), 11 January 1983, provides a detailed analysis of the many problems encountered in making the power blocks at Paks operational. Data on cost overruns at Paks are from *Heti Vilaggazdasag*, 11 January 1986, in RFE *Situation Report*, no. 5 (Hungary), 25 March 1986. Data on expenditures for safety measures are from MTI, 3 October 1986, in FBIS-*EEU*, 10 October 1985, F5.

57. *Budapest Domestic Service*, 16 August 1987, in FBIS-*EEU*, 21 August 1987, H9.

58. The agreement on Paks was signed by Soviet and Hungarian representatives on 4 February 1986, as reported in RFE *Situation Report*, no. 5 (Hungary), 25 March 1986. See *Nepszabadsag*, 18 October 1985, in JPRS-*EEI*, no. 94 (12

December 1985); 76, for information regarding debates on the future expansion of Paks.

59. *Izvestiia*, 16 August 1986, reports the agreement for 1,000 MW reactors. *Heti Vilaggazdasag*, 11 March 1989, in JPRS-*EER*, no. 50 (3 May 1989), 14, reports that neither of these reactors will become operational before 1998. Data on projections for nuclear power by 2015 are from *Magyar Hirlap*, 31 October 1986, in FBIS-*EEU*, 14 November 1986, F5.

60. For details of the negotiations with Canada, see RFE *Background Report*, no. 19 (15 February 1988). The talks with France were reported by MTI, 26 August 1988, in FBIS-*EEU*, 1 September 1988, 21–22.

61. *Rzeczpospolita*, 26 June 1982, cited in RFE *Situation Report*, no. 13 (Poland), 27 July 1982.

62. *Zycie Warszawy*, 2 February 1978, as discussed in RFE *Situation Report*, no. 3 (Poland), 3 March 1978, intimates at Poland's exclusion from Comecon nuclear projects and Soviet apprehensions regarding Poland's national nuclear program. *Washington Post*, 17 December 1985, asserts categorically that the Soviet Union effectively blocked Poland's nuclear program.

63. RFE *Situation Report*, no. 13 (Poland), 27 July 1982. This source argues that the decision to move ahead with the project was motivated primarily by political considerations: "It is not possible to escape the feeling . . . that this project is . . . merely intended to show the general public that the authorities are launching useful projects in the best public interest, even if their feasibility seems rather doubtful."

64. *Trybuna ludu*, 6 April 1984; *Trybuna ludu*, 14 November 1985; *Gwiazda morza*, no. 16 (August 1987) in JPRS-*EER*, no. 151 (30 October 1987): 13–15.

65. *Zycie Warszawy*, 5 September 1986, in FBIS-*EEU*, 15 September 1986, G14.

66. The lack of suitable concrete that, among other materials, led to the halt in construction in 1986 could prove devastating to the future of the project. One source reports:

> The result of all of this is that nothing is being done to proceed with the concrete foundations for the project. It has even been proposed that in view of the lack of the right kinds of concrete, the thousands and thousands of square meters of iron structures should be dismantled so that they do not become rusty in the rain . . . . This would be a technological and primarily an economic howler.

> What to do to find out . . . if this nuclear power station is to go ahead at all!
> *Zycie Warszawy*, 5 September 1986, in FBIS-*EEU* (15 September 1986), G14.

Data on underfulfillment of the plan for capital investment at Zarnowiecz and the reasons why this has occurred are from *Zycie Warszawy*, 23 October 1986, in JPRS-*EER*, no. 193 (19 October 1986): 13. That the construction site had only one heavy crane—and even it was not "fully suited" to its task—reflects the shortage of requisite equipment at Zarnowiecz [*Glos wybrzeza*, 19 December 1986, in JPRS-*EER*, no. 43 (20 March 1987): 20].

67. *Rzeczpospolita*, 8 July 1987, in FBIS-*EEU*, 17 July 1987, P17.

68. *Zycie Warszawy*, 23 October 1986, in JPRS-*EER*, No. 193 (19 October 1986), 12.

69. *Zycie Warszawy*, 22 June 1988, in JPRS-*EER*, no. 71 (31 August 1988): 69.

70. *Zycie Warszawy*, 23 October 1986, in JPRS-*EER*, no. 193 (19 October 1986), 12.

71. PAP, 24 February 1989, in FBIS-*EEU* (27 February 1989), 38.

72. RFE *Background Report*, no. 129 (8 November 1985).

73. Ibid. collates a variety of official estimates for nuclear power capacities. See Agerpres, 9 July 1985, in FBIS-*EEU*, 11 July 1985, H5, for an official estimate of these capacities through the year 2000.

74. For background on this project, see Radio Bucharest, 24 March 1974, in RFE *Situation Report*, no. 28 (Romania), 7 December 1978; RFE *Background Report*, no. 165 (18 August 1982); RFE *Background Report*, no. 129 (18 November 1985).

75. The Hungarian press report on the project appeared in *Magyar Hirlap*, 14 January 1986, in FBIS-*EEU*, 4 February 1986, H1. RFE *Situation Report*, no. 5 (Romania), 13 March 1985, provides background material on the subject.

76. Compare the Romanian announcement of the Moldova project in Agerpres (in English from Moscow), 9 September 1982, with the Soviet announcement over Radio Moscow (in Romanian), 9 September 1982. RFE *Background Report*, no. 129 (18 November 1985), discusses the rationale behind Romania's policy of silence on these matters. This is the source reporting that Romania must pay with hard goods for much of the nuclear assistance from the Soviet Union.

77. Radio Bucharest, 25 October 1977, carried the announcement of the agreement. RFE *Situation Report*, no. 33 (Romania), 9 November 1977, provides an extensive analysis of the project.

78. Agerpres, 9 September 1981, in FBIS-*EEU*, 10 September 1981, H1; RFE *Background Report*, no. 165 (18 August 1982). On the role of Italy and the United States in the Cernavoda project, see *Financial Times*, 3 March 1981; *Wall Street Journal*, 27 August 1982.

79. Agerpres, 9 July 1985, in FBIS-*EEU*, 11 July 1985, H1, informs about Canadian interest in speeding up work on the project.

80. RFE *Situation Report*, no. 15 (Romania), 29 October 1985. This source quotes Radoslav Selucky, a prominent émigré economist from Czechoslovakia, that Romania must have made these financial arrangements "out of despair," for they are "hardly the best way to accomplish an international transfer of technology."

81. *Wall Street Journal*, 27 August 1982, provides background material on the American decision to suspend its credit to Romania. For additional material on this matter, see also RFE *Situation Report*, no. 16 (Romania), 16 September 1983; RFE *Situation Report*, no. 15 (Romania), 29 October 1985.

82. *Scinteia*, 24 April 1985, and 3 April 1986, both quoted in RFE *Situation Report*, no. 7 (Romania), 2 July 1986, reported General Secretary Ceausescu's

remarks. RFE *Situation Report*, no. 15 (Romania), 29 October, 1985, discusses the apprehensions of Canadian officials regarding these initiatives.

83. Agerpres, 31 July 1982, in FBIS-*EEU*, 3 August 1982, reported the proposed NPS in Transylvania. Agerpres, 9 July 1985, in FBIS-*EEU*, 11 July 1985, H1 noted that Romania and Canada want "to identify new mutually profitable forms of cooperation in the field, the realization of projects in third markets included."

84. For a comprehensive analysis of these protests, see John M. Kramer, "Chernobyl' and the Nuclear 'Debate' in Communist Europe: The Role of Public Opinion," testimony presented before the U.S. Congress, Commission on Cooperation and Security in Europe, Washington, 26 April 1988.

85. *Tygodnik powszechny*, 27 July 1986, in FBIS-*EEU*, 12 August 1986, G5.

86. DPA, 1 June 1986, in FBIS-*EEU*, 2 June 1986, G2. The text of the letter sent by the nuclear experts was carried by DPA, 16 May 1986, in FBIS-*EEU*, 19 May 1986, G3.

87. *Gwiazda morza*, no. 19 (September 1987), in JPRS-*EER*, no. 155 (17 November 1987): 7.

88. The petition further asserted that official assurances about the safety of nuclear power were "not credible" DPA, 1 June 1986 (in FBIS-*EEU*, 2 June 1986), G2. The Sejm, in a detailed response to the petition, strongly reiterated the need for nuclear power. It did acknowledge that the petitioners were "motivated by a true concern for the future of the country and its inhabitants" but asserted that nuclear power is "indispensable" in Poland's energy future because of the "limited possibilities" to increase indigenous production of other fuels and the "lack of possibilities" to increase importation of liquid fuels (PAP, 10 June 1986, in FBIS-*EEU*, 13 June 1986, G5–7).

89. *Gwiazda morza*, no. 19 (September 1987) in JPRS-*EER*, no. 155 (17 November 1987): 7.

90. *Zycie Warszawy*, 18 October 1985, in JPRS-*EER*, no. 25 (25 February 1986): 38. For the opposition of environmentalists to the site, see *Wprost*, 11 October 1987, discussed in RFE *Situation Report*, no. 2 (Poland), 8 February 1988.

91. *Tygodnik powszechny*, 27 July 1986, in FBIS-*EEU* (2 August 1986): 65.

92. The comments of the mayor of Miedzyrzec were reported in *Prawo zycie*, 21 November 1987, in JPRS-*EER*, no. 13 (22 February 1988): 13. For background material on this controversy, see Marek Kossakowski, "Leave the Bunkers to the Bats!" *Across Frontiers*, Spring/Summer 1988, 10–11, 48–49.

93. The official is head of the Department of Energy, Institute of Basic Technical Problems, Polish Academy of Sciences. He was interviewed in *Nowosci*, 12 January 1988, in RFE *Situation Report*, no. 2 (Poland), 8 February 1988.

94. The text of the petition was published in *Across Frontiers*, Fall 1986, 10.

95. For the text of the letter of protest sent to the Council of Ministers, see *Die Tageszeitung*, 17 May 1986, discussed in RFE *Background Report*, no. 102 (21 July 1986). This also provides information on the antinuclear deliberations at the synod of the Evangelical Church.

96. On the anxiety of citizens regarding nuclear power, see *Luxemburger Wort*, 12 May 1986, in JPRS-*EER*, no. 96 (7 July 1986): 44; *Rude pravo*, 28 July 1986, in FBIS-*EEU*, 1 August 1986, D2.

97. On the activities of Antiatom, see *Kurier*, 9 May 1986, in FBIS-*SOV*, 12 May 1986, M1.

98. *Die Presse*, 6–8 June 1987, in JPRS-*EER*, no. 118 (19 June 1987): 15–16. Charter 77 also has criticized official reticence regarding the scope and consequences of the explosion at the Chernobyl NPS. See *Dokumenty charty*, 6 May 1986, in JPRS-*EER*, no. 91 (20 June 1986): 102–3.

99. For materials on Nahlas, see *Kurier*, 1 February 1988, in FBIS-*EEU*, 2 February 1988, 10. *Kurier*, 14 November 1987, in FBIS-*EEU*, 19 November 1987, 12, reports the protests of the concerned scientists.

100. Reservations about nuclear power per se have, however, been expressed: for example, "After Chernobyl, after taking stock of the country's economic situation, and in view of the 100 billion forint construction cost of a nuclear plant, I think it is not completely unfounded to ask: How much do we need nuclear power?" (*Magyar Hirlap*, 31 October 1986, in FBIS-*EEU*, 14 November 1986, F5).

102. *Profil*, 20 June 1988, in JPRS-*EER*, no. 60 (28 July 1988): 8. All material on this controversy is drawn from this source. For a Soviet account of the controversy, see *Izvestiia*, 14 May 1988.

103. *Glos wybrzeza*, 1 September 1986, in FBIS-*EEU*, 15 September 1986.

104. For material on the training center using Japanese computers, see *Kurier*, 1 February 1988, in FBIS-*EEU* (2 February 1988): 10. *Rude pravo*, 31 August 1988, reported on the plan to purchase safety equipment with hard currency earned from the exportation of electricity.

105. BTA, 28 May 1986, in FBIS-*EEU*, 4 June 1986, C4.

106. *Scinteia*, 5 November 1986.

107. TASS, 23 May 1988, in FBIS-*SOV*, 24 May 1988, 12.

108. *Moscow Domestic Service*, 24 May 1988, in FBIS-*SOV*, 25 May 1988, 11.

109. As one Soviet proponent of the project asserted; "Chernobyl was the result of the unprecedented coincidence of circumstances generated by the personnel's mistakes. The same reasons were behind the accident at the atomic power station near Harrisburg, USA. We can and should organize joint personnel training with account of the experience gained" (TASS, 17 June 1988, in FBIS-*SOV*, 20 June 1988, 70).

110. See, respectively, ADN, 3 May 1988, in FBIS-*EEU* (5 May 1988): 16; *Neues Deutschland*, 6 March 1987, in FBIS-*EEU* (18 March 1987): 87; ADN, 4 August 1987, in FBIS-*EEU*, 5 August 1987, G1.

111. See, respectively, ADN, 29 March 1988, in FBIS-*EEU*, 30 March 1988, 7; ADN, 16 March 1987, in FBIS-*SOV*, 17 March 1987, F3; *Neues Deutschland*, 29–30 October 1988.

112. PAP, 5 November 1986, in FBIS-*EEU*, (5 November 1986): AA12.

113. *Jaderna energie*, no. 6 (1986), as summarized in RFE *Situation Report*, no. 13 (Czechoslovakia), 11 September 1987. A similar argument is made in

Planovane hospodarstvi, no. 4 (1985), in JPRS-*EEI*, no. 71 (9 September 1985): 21.

114. *Planovane hospodarstvi*, 4 (1985) in JPRS-*EEI*, no. 71 (9 September 1985): 21.

115. This was the assessment of Deputy Premier Ladislav Gerle, the official in charge of Czechoslovakia's nuclear program. Gerle's words were reported in *Pravda* (Bratislava), 15 November 1984, in FBIS-*EEU*, (23 November 1984): D3.

116. *Kommunist*, no. 14 (1979).

117. *Tribuna*, 29 October 1986, in FBIS-*EEU*, 13 November 1986, D4.

118. *Pravda*, 20 May 1988.

119. *Rude pravo*, 16 February 1983, as quoted in RFE *Situation Report*, no. 11 (Czechoslovakia), 24 June 1983.

120. All data on production in gross tonnage and oil equivalent are derived from appendix unless otherwise noted.

121. For example, in the Soviet Union, this factor may cause output figures for coal to be overstated by as much as 20 to 40 percent. (Office of Technology Assessment, *Technology and Soviet Energy Availability*, 83).

122. In 1984, the fuel and energy sector in Eastern Europe accounted for upward of 60 percent of primary energy consumption, much of it used to convert coal into energy. United Nations Economic Commission for Europe, *Economic Survey of Europe in 1986–1987* (New York: UN, 1987), 201.

123. *Trybuna ludu*, 3–4 January 1981, cited in RFE *Situation Report*, no. 18 (Poland), 18 October 1981. For a discussion of similar practices in Romania, see RFE *Situation Report*, no. 13 (Romania), 26 November 1986.

124. *FS-Analysen*, no. 1 (1987), in JPRS-*EER*, no. 121 (6 August 1987): 79.

125. *Voprosy ekonomiki*, no. 12 (1980): 98.

126. Material on plans for coal in the 1976–1980 period is from John Haberstroh, "Eastern Europe: Growing Energy Problems," in U.S. Congress, Joint Economic Committee, *East European Economies Post-Helsinki* (Washington, D.C.: GPO, 1977), 390.

127. *Figyelo*, 19 September 1985, in JPRS-*EEI*, no. 90 (21 November 1985): 110.

128. *Figyelo*, 13 October 1983, in JPRS-*EEI*, No. 84892 (6 December 1983): 6–8, includes an extended discussion of these issues. This source provides the following data illustrating the decline in the growth rate of labor productivity (in percent) in the mining sector in the 1970s:

Country	1971–1975	1976–1980
Bulgaria	10.9	4.1
Czechoslovakia	3.4	1.8
Hungary	7.2	3.9
East Germany	3.9	3.1
Poland	5.1	0.5
Romania	4.2	1.4*

*Also includes crude oil and natural gas mining.

129. *Magyarorzag*, 11 December 1983, in JPRS-*EPS*, no. 21 (8 February 1984): 11.

130. *Hetofi Hirek*, 3 August 1985, in JPRS-*EEI*, no. 76 (27 September 1985): 25.

131. Data on plan targets are from Ibid., 22.

132. *Energetika*, no. 1 (1986), in JPRS-*EER*, no. 69 (5 May 1986): 28.

133. Naturally, such a large increase in production arouses suspicions that to meet strenuous plan targets, collieries are inflating output data and/or neglecting sound mining practices while increasingly extracting coal of declining caloric content. Published data are unavailable to substantiate these suspicions.

134. Bulgaria originally projected an output target for coal of between 42 and 45 MT in 1990. See, for example, *Energetika*, no. 2 (1985), in JPRS-*EEI*, no. 61, (23 July 1985): 3; *Rabotnichesko delo*, 21 February 1986. *Rabotnichesko delo*, 26 December 1986, publishes the national economic plan for 1986–1990 that includes targets for production of coal.

135. Data on planned reductions in extraction of coal in 1990 and 2000 are from *Hospodarske noviny*, no. 34 (1986), in JPRS-*EER*, no. 189 (10 December 1986): 35; *Planovane hospodarstvi*, no. 4 (1985), in JPRS-*EEI*, no. 71 (9 September 1985): 22–23; CTK, 2 January 1989, in FBIS-*EEU*, 9 January 1989, 18. For a discussion of the requisite conditions to realize this reduction, see *Hospodarske noviny*, no. 43 (1985), in JPRS-*EER*, no. 8 (21 January 1986): 3.

136. The consumption of primary energy in 1986 and 1987 exceeded plan targets by 1.1 MT and 1.8 MT of black coal units, respectively, even though the targets for creation of national income were underfulfilled. CTK, 2 June 1988, in FBIS-*EEU* (7 June 1988): 11.

137. *Planovane hospodarstvi*, no. 5 (1987), cited in RFE *Situation Report*, no. 13 (Czechoslovakia), 11 September 1987; CTK, 2 January 1989, in FBIS-*EEU* (9 January 1989): 18.

138. These trends were apparent in the late 1970s. The caloric content of the coal then being mined was between 3,000 and 3,500 kilocalories per kilogram versus a comparable figure of 4,500 kilocalories in the coal previously mined. Further, the average content of cinders in mined coal had risen from approximately 6 percent to 15 percent, and the volume of sulfur and dust particles had increased "markedly" [*Pravda* (Plzen), 20 June 1979, cited in RFE *Situation Report*, no. 23 (Czechoslovakia), 22 September 1980]. Western sources report that the sulfur content of coal now being mined in Czechoslovakia ranges between 10 and 20 percent. See, for example, Leslie Dienes and Victor Merkin, "Energy Policy and Conservation in Eastern Europe," in U.S. Congress, Joint Economic Committee, *East European Economies: Slow Growth in the 1980's*, vol. 1 (Washington, D.C.: GPO, 1985), 335; *Die Welt*, 7 February 1986, in JPRS-*EER*, no. 59 (16 April 1986): 102.

139. *Tribuna*, 2 July 1986, in JPRS-*EER*, no. 148 (1 October 1986): 1.

140. CTK, 24 February 1982, in FBIS-*EEDR*, 25 February 1982, D5.

141. Ibid.; *Rude pravo*, 12 September 1988.

142. *Hospodarske noviny*, no. 45 (1983), in JPRS-*EEI*, no. 22 (21 February 1984): 11.

143. For example, twenty-nine towns and hamlets in the North Bohemian region alone are scheduled for destruction to make new coal seams accessible for exploitation (Dienes and Merkin, "Energy Policy and Conservation in Eastern Europe," 335).

144. *Rude pravo*, 12 September 1988. On the deleterious consequences of the "coal at any cost" philosophy, including those involving the safety of miners, see *Pravda* (Bratislava), 9 September 1985, in JPRS-*EEI*, no. 77 (1 October 1985): 34. These consequences include "frequent unforeseen cave-ins" and other "negative phenomena" that have "enhanced . . . the risks of the miners' work."

145. A detailed discussion of these issues is found in *Hospodarske noviny*, no. 43 (1985), in JPRS-*EER*, no. 8 (21 January 1986): 3. For an overview of ecological deterioration in Czechoslovakia, see Kramer, "The Environmental Crisis in Eastern Europe: The Price for Progress."

146. The comment was made in an interview with *IWE Tagesdienst*, 24 March 1987, in JPRS-*EER*, no. 66 (28 April 1985): 75.

147. Ibid.; *Presse Informationen*, 27 December 1985, in JPRS-*EER*, no. 54 (9 April 1986): 36.

148. *Das Parlament*, 9 August 1986, in JPRS-*EER*, no. 11 (26 January 1987): 16.

149. *East Berlin Domestic Service*, 6 January 1982, in FBIS-*EEDR*, 13 January 1982, E4; *IWE Tagesdienst*, 24 March 1987, in JPRS-*EER*, no. 66 (28 April 1987): 75.

150. *IWE Tagesdienst*, 24 March 1987, in JPRS-*EER*, no. 66 (28 April 1987): 75.

151. For a general discussion of the various steps that must be taken in populated areas to make coal reserves accessible for exploitation, see *Wasserwirtschaft-Wassertechnik*, May 1988, in JPRS-*EER*, no. 58 (22 July 1988): 47.

152. *Nepszava*, 21, 22, 23 October 1985, in JPRS-*EEI*, no. 92 (9 December 1985): 78–87.

153. *Figyelo*, 19 September 1985, in JPRS-*EEI*, no. 90 (21 November 1985): 110.

154. *Hetofi Hirek*, 3 August 1985, in JPRS-*EEI*, no. 76 (27 September 1985): 22.

155. Computed from data reported by MTI, 17 July 1986, in FBIS-*EEU*, 18 July 1986, F2.

156. Data on investment monies computed from materials in *Nepszava*, 23 October 1985, in JPRS-*EEI*, no. 92 (9 December 1985): 86; *Figyelo*, 19 September 1985, in JPRS-*EEI*, no. 90 (21 November 1985): 110. The latter, on page 111, reports on escalating costs in coal mining.

157. Data on monies allocated for coal mining in the 1986–1990 period are from *Nepszava*, 23 October 1985, in JPRS-*EEI*, no. 92 (9 December 1985): 86. This source adds that, as a result of inadequate investment, coal production "will obviously decline by 1990." Similar sentiments were expressed in *Figyelo*, 19 September 1985, in JPRS-*EEI*, no. 90 (21 November 1985): 112.

158. *Budapest Domestic Service*, 29 August 1986, in FBIS-*EEU*, 4 September 1986, F5.

159. *Budapest Domestic Service*, 29 October 1988, in FBIS-*EEU*, 30 October 1988, 35; *Figyelo*, 19 September 1985, in JPRS-*EEI*, no. 90 (21 November 1985): 111.

160. *Nepszava*, 22 October 1985, in JPRS-*EEI*, no. 92 (9 December 1985): 83.

161. Ibid.

162. Radio Budapest, 30 November 1985, quoted in RFE *Situation Report*, no. 1 (Hungary), 3 January 1986. This RFE *Situation Report* provides detailed data on economic benefits and other perquisites designed to attract and retain workers in coal mining. Ironically, miners themselves often feel that they are underpaid and unappreciated by the public. For the expression of such sentiments, see *Nepszava*, 21 October 1985, in JPRS-*EEI*, no. 92 (9 December 1985): 79.

163. *Figyelo*, 19 September 1985, in JPRS-*EEI*, no. 90 (21 November 1985): 111; *Nepszabadsag*, 18 May 1985.

164. On these practices, see *Nepszava*, 29 November 1985, and *Partelet*, October 1985, both of which are cited in RFE *Situation Report*, no. 1 (Hungary), 3 January 1986. Reportedly, a new source of guest workers has been found among immigrants of Hungarian nationality who are fleeing oppression in neighboring Romania *Budapest Domestic Service*, 29 October 1988, in FBIS-*EEU*, (30 October 1988): 36.

165. *Nepszava*, 23 October 1985, in JPRS-*EEI*, no. 92 (9 December 1985): 85.

166. *Ibid.*, 86. This source is skeptical that even substantial technological modernization can compensate for the precipitous decline in the mining force: "Such a large decrease could not be made up for even with the most modern techniques—if there was money for it."

167. Radio Budapest, 30 November 1985, in RFE *Situation Report*, (Hungary), 3 January 1986.

168. *Nepszava*, 22 October 1985, in JPRS-*EEI*, no. 92 (9 December 1985): 82.

169. A representative exposition of this argument is found in *Hetofi Hirek*, 3 August 1985, in JPRS-*EEI*, no. 76 (27 September 1985): 24.

170. As one such skeptic asked, "What is the guarantee that industry will be capable—with the money taken from coal mining—of increasing its export to such a degree that it can provide the additional hundreds of millions of dollars for increased importation of fuels?" *Nepszava*, 23 October 1985, in JPRS-*EEI*, no. 92 (9 December 1985): 87.

171. Ibid., 84–85.

172. *Nepszava*, 22 October 1985, in JPRS-*EEI*, no. 92 (9 December 1985): 83.

173. Unless otherwise noted, material on the strike is from RFE *Situation Report*, no. 15 (Hungary), 5 October 1988.

174. *Budapest Domestic Service*, 29 October 1988, in FBIS-*EEU* (30 October 1988): 35.

175. *Rzeczpospolita*, 17 June 1985, in JPRS-*EEI*, no. 72 (10 September 1985): 63; *Trybuna ludu*, 4–5 April 1987.

176. Stanley Kabala, "Poland: Facing the Hidden Costs of Development," *Environment*, no. 9 (1985): 11.

177. *Nowe drogi*, November 1986, in JPRS-*EER*, no. 49 (30 March 1987): 111.

178. See, for example, the analysis in *Zycie Warszawy*, 30 December 1986, in JPRS-*EER*, no. 40 (17 March 1987): 41.

179. Dienes and Merkin, "Energy Policy and Conservation in Eastern Europe," 335.

180. Commentaries advancing this argument include PAP, 22 March 1985, in FBIS-*EEU*, 25 March 1985, G7; PAP, 7 August 1986, in FBIS-*EEU*, 8 August 1986, G21.

181. *Gosc niedzielny*, 29 May 1988, in JPRS-*EER*, no. 64 (5 August 1988): 46–47. This source notes that these arguments are "commonly pointed out by economic journalists."

182. *Zycie Warszawy*, 22 June 1988, in JPRS-*EER*, no. 71 (30 August 1988): 69.

183. Cited in Dienes and Merkin, "Energy Policy and Conservation in Eastern Europe," 335.

184. *Trybuna ludu*, 3 November 1986.

185. The comments of the critics are reported in *Rzeczpospolita*, 3 December 1985, in JPRS-*EER*, no. 13 (29 January 1986): 17–18. The proposal that other Comecon states participate in the Lublin project can be found in K. Barcikowski, "Fraternal Cooperation Is the Way to Overcome Difficulties," *World Marxist Review*, no. 7 (1985): 9. A similar proposal was carried in *Warsaw Domestic Service*, 24 September 1985, in FBIS-*EEU*, 26 September 1986, AA1.

186. *Gosc niedzielny*, 29 March 1987, in JPRS-*EER*, no. 116 (24 July 1987): 78. Other commentaries making this argument include *Trybuna ludu*, 25 October 1985; *Rzeczpospolita*, 1–2 March 1986, in JPRS-*EER*, no. 62 (21 April 1986): 12.

187. *Gosc niedzielny*, 29 March 1987, in JPRS-*EER*, no. 116 (24 July 1987): 78, 79. On this subject, see also *Rzeczpospolita*, 1–2 March 1986, in JPRS-*EER*, no. 62 (21 April 1986): 12. The former source reports that the safety of work is routinely subordinated to the task of plan fulfillment:

> In the mining industry, it is common knowledge that, if all occupational safety and hygiene regulations were to be observed, most Polish mines would have to take up mushroom farming rather than coal production. Miners work with the understanding that regulations are or have to be violated in order not to disrupt the pace of production.

188. *Gosc niedzielny*, 29 March 1987, in JPRS-*EER*, no. 116 (24 July 1987): 80.

189. In 1989, Poland planned to export 12 MT of hard coal to the interna-

tional market, a decline of almost 70 percent from the 1988 level of exportation. *Rzeczpospolita*, 5 January 1989, in FBIS-*EEU*, 1 February 1989, 54.

190. Agerpres, 23 October 1985, in FBIS-*EEU*, 24 October 1985, H4.

191. Agerpres, 5 June 1984, in FBIS-*EEU*, 6 June 1984, H6.

192. United Nations Economic Commission for Europe, *Economic Survey of Europe in 1986–1987*, 204.

193. Plan target for 1986 is from *Scinteia*, 7 February 1986.

194. The CIA reported a production figure of 8.80 MT for 1986, an increase of 1.6 percent over the 1985 level of production. Directorate of Intelligence, *Handbook of Economic Statistics 1987* (Washington, D.C.: GPO, 1987), 139.

195. *Revista Economica*, 18 April 1986, in JPRS-*EER*, no. 106 (21 July 1986): 46.

196. *Romania Libera*, 28 February 1986, in JPRS-*EER*, no. 76 (19 May 1986): 36. Another account stressing the critical need to enhance the productivity of labor is *Revista Economica*, 28 February 1986, in JPRS-*EER*, no. 80 (30 May 1986): 72.

197. On measures to transfer workers from other sectors to mining, see *Scinteia*, 30 March 1983. On measures to combat absenteeism and turnover among workers, see *Revista Economica*, 28 February 1986, in JPRS-*EER*, no. 80 (30 May 1986): 74.

198. *Scinteia*, 21 August 1982, cited in RFE *Situation Report*, no. 4 (Romania), 7 March 1983. Reportedly, power plants in Romania are burning lignite with an energy value as low as 1,000 kilocalories per kilogram. The lignite is of such low quality that in "many cases" oil must be used to help it burn [RFE *Situation Report*, no. 13 (Romania), 26 November 1986].

199. For an analysis of the impact of coal on the environment in Eastern Europe, see John M. Kramer, "Energy and the Environment in Eastern Europe," in Joan Debardeleben, ed., *Environmental Problems and Policies in Eastern Europe* (Montreal: McGill University Press, 1989).

200. TASS, 15 July 1988, in FBIS-*SOV*, 20 July 1988, 7–8.

201. Agerpres, 20 May 1986, in JPRS-*EER*, 30 June 1986, 58; Agerpres, 26 July 1986, in FBIS-*EEU*, 29 July 1986, H2.

202. Agerpres, 6 October 1981, in FBIS-*EEDR*, 7 October 1981, H6.

203. Material on the program is from *Rude pravo*, 30 August 1986.

204. The government already has a program to encourage both socialist organizations and private individuals to construct hydroelectric generators with capacities of less than 100 kw. Under its provisions, the state extends credits for the construction or renovation of such generators. It then purchases excess electricity from their output and imposes no taxes on the income derived therefrom. For details of the program, see *Budapest Domestic Service*, 15 February 1984, in FBIS-*EEU*, 17 February 1984, D3–4.

205. *Rude pravo*, 19 September 1986. For another account defending the cost-effectiveness of hydroelectric power, see *Rude pravo*, 30 August 1986.

206. Minister Ehrenberger reported that the repair of aging hydroelectric facilities is an "increasingly difficult issue" involving expensive "general repairs of basic installations." *Rude pravo*, 19 September 1986.

207. Background material on the project is from RFE *Situation Report*, no. 12 (Hungary), 21 November 1986; RFE *Situation Report*, no. 16 (Hungary), 28 October 1988. Planning for the project actually began in the 1950s before Stalin's death.

208. For a Czechoslovak account of Hungarian objections to the project, see *Tribuna*, 1 October 1986, in JPRS-*EER*, no. 172 (12 November 1986): 13. The former president of the Hungarian Academy of Sciences reports that in 1983, the academy's board unanimously and "emphatically" recommended that Hungary abandon, or at least suspend, work on the project (MTI, 7 October 1988, in FBIS-*EEU*, 11 October 1988, 7). The government stamped the academy's report "highly confidential" and suppressed its publication [*Heti Vilaggazdasag*, 1 October 1988, cited in RFE *Situation Report*, no. 16 (Hungary), 28 October 1988].

209. Detailed discussions of these issues in the Czechoslovak press include *Praca*, 16 June 1986, in JPRS-*EER*, no. 144 (26 September 1986): 15; *Pravda* (Bratislava), 18 August 1986, in FBIS-*EEU*, 22 August 1986, D5.

210. *Budapest Television Service*, 6 October 1988, in FBIS-*EEU*, 19 October 1988, 21.

211. Among the voluminous material on these protests is an especially informative account in RFE *Situation Report*, no. 4 (Czechoslovakia), 12 March 1988. Public criticism of the project in Czechoslovakia has been muted. For evidence that some opposition to the project does exist, see RFE *Situation Report*, no. 13 (Czechoslovakia), 1 September 1988.

212. For publicly unexplained reasons, the House of Culture canceled the film on the day of its planned showing. Subsequently, however, Radio Budapest (12 October 1988) reported that the president of the Soviet Society for the Protection of Nature called construction of huge flatland barrage systems an "ecological sin." All material cited in RFE *Situation Report*, no. 4 (Czechoslovakia), 12 March 1988.

213. Material on the debate is from RFE *Situation Report*, no. 16 (Hungary), 28 October 1988. For summaries and texts of several of the speeches at the National Assembly, see MTI, 7 October 1988, in FBIS-*EEU* (11 October 1988): 7–9; *Budapest Television Service*, 6 October 1988, in FBIS-*EEU* (19 October 1988): 21–29.

214. *Budapest Television Service*, 9 October 1988, in FBIS-*EEU* (25 October 1988): 30.

215. The Hungarian decision to suspend construction at Nagymaros is carried in *Nepszabadsag*, 20 May 1989. For the Czechoslovak position on compensation see *Rude pravo*, 19 August 1989. The Austrian position on compensation is reported in *Budapest Domestic Service*, 25 May 1989, in FBIS-*EEU* (1 June 1989): 49.

216. For a detailed discussion of these issues, see *Magyar Hirlap*, 25 April 1981, in FBIS-*EEDR*, 7 May 1981, F8. An exception to these conditions may have occurred in the region around Fuzesgyarmat, where Hungary reported discovering "large stocks of natural gas with a high caloric value and considerable oil layers." Hungary hoped to begin exploiting these reserves by the end of 1989 (*Nepszabadsag*, 10 February 1988).

217. For a prediction that production will decline as early as 1990, see *Heti Vilaggazdasag*, 28 September 1985, in JPRS-*EEI*, no. 96 (23 December 1985): 125. Assessments that see this circumstance occurring by the end of the century include *Nepszava*, 26 March 1988, in FBIS-*EEU*, 29 March 1988, 34; *Nepszabadsag*, 28 October 1987. The latter source maintains that even to extract 1 MT of oil and 6 billion m³ of natural gas in the year 2000 "will require considerable efforts."

218. Material on exploitation of the continental shelf is from RFE *Situation Report*, no. 4 (Romania), 29 May 1987. For a Romanian account of these efforts, see Agerpres, 25 March 1989, in FBIS-*EEU* (29 March, 1989): 44.

219. RFE *Situation Report*, no. 11 (Romania), 15 June 1982.

220. *Era Socialista*, 15 October 1986, in JPRS-*EER*, no. 65 (24 April 1987): 48.

221. *Petroleum Economist*, August 1988, 257.

222. On anticipated increases in the extraction of oil and natural gas, respectively, see *Lidova demokracie*, 16 April 1987, in JPRS-*EER*, no. 82 (26 May 1987): 42. *Prague Domestic Service*, 7 June 1986, in JPRS-*EER*, no. 99 (9 July 1986): 43. For reports of discoveries of new deposits of oil and natural gas, see *Zemedelske noviny*, 3 November 1988, in FBIS-*EEU*, 14 November 1988, 15.

223. PAP, 7 July 1987, in FBIS-*EEU*, 14 July 1987, P14.

224. *Rzeczpospolita*, 17 June 1985, in JPRS-*EEI*, no. 72 (10 September 1985): 63. One of the problems in energy exploration is that almost all the equipment used for this purpose is "nearly obsolete" [*Zycie Warszawy*, 30 December 1986, in JPRS-*EER*, no. 40 (17 March 1987): 42].

225. As one source explained, "Coal mining has been and is a deadly foe of oil exploration" *Zycie Warszawy*, 22 January 1981, quoted in George Hoffman, *The European Energy Challenge: East and West* (Durham, N.C.: Duke University Press, 1985), 33.

226. The consortium has announced that it will bring its first oil field, located in the territorial waters of the Soviet Union, on line in 1989. The Soviet Union will receive one-half of the output from the field, with East Germany and Poland equally dividing the remaining output (*Petroleum Economist*, September 1986, 351–352).

227. For an overview of initiatives to develop these energies in Comecon states, see *Ekonomicheskoe sotrudnichestvo stran-chlenov SEV*, no. 8 (1987): 72–75. This source, pages 67–71, provides material on the utilization of geothermal water. All material on this subject, unless otherwise noted, is from these sources.

228. Agerpres, 27 March 1989, in FBIS-*EEU* (29 March 1989): 44.

229. For details of these efforts, see Agerpres, 27 August 1987, in FBIS-*EEU* (28 August 1987): 26. I have found no evidence that these efforts have born fruition.

230. *Hospodarske noviny*, no. 40 (1985), in JPRS-*EEI*, no. 92 (9 December 1985): 6.

231. Ibid.

Chapter 4

1. For comprehensive data on exports and imports of all types of energy to the international market by Eastern European states between 1960 and 1985, see *Plan Econ Report: Developments in the Economies of the Soviet Union and Eastern Europe*, 2, nos. 12–13 (31 March 1986): 17.

2. *Svet hospodarstvi*, 1 October 1985, in JPRS-*EEI*, no. 97 (28 December 1985): 44.

3. *Warsaw Domestic Service*, 2 February 1988, in FBIS-*EEU* (4 February 1988): 42.

4. See the comments by a Czechoslovak official as reported in *New York Times*, 24 November 1969.

5. For example, in 1974 the Soviet Union and Libya concluded an arms for oil deal in which the former supplied the latter with surface-to-air missiles in exchange for crude [Jonathan Stern, "CMEA Oil Acquisition Policy in the Middle East and the Gulf: The Search for Economic and Political Strategies," in U.S. Congress, Joint Economic Committee, *Soviet Economy in the 1980's: Problems and Prospects, Part 1* (Washington, D.C.: GPO, 1982), 418].

6. As calculated from data in National Foreign Assessment Center, *Energy Supplies in Eastern Europe: A Statistical Compilation* (ER79-10624, December 1979), table 19, appendixes A–F.

7. *Nepszabadsag*, 23 January 1974, in RFE *Hungarian Press Survey*, no. 2338 (1974).

8. *Heti Vilaggazdasag*, 2 November 1973, cited in RFE *Situation Report*, no. 44 (Hungary), 11 December 1973.

9. For background material on Adria, see RFE *Background Report*, no. 12 (19 October 1973); *Washington Post*, 10 January 1974.

10. Radio Prague, 19 March 1969, reported in RFE *Situation Report*, no. 35 (Czechoslovakia), 11 October 1972.

11. RFE *Background Report*, no. 12 (19 October 1973).

12. Data on financial contributions from Kuwait and Libya are from *Financial Times*, 18 February 1975. RFE *Situation Report*, no. 1 (Hungary), 22 January 1980, reported on the cost of Adria to Czechoslovakia and Hungary.

13. MTI, 24 August 1987, in FBIS-*EEU*, 25 August 1987, H2.

14. As calculated by John Haberstroh, "Eastern Europe: Growing Energy Problems," in U.S. Congress, Joint Economic Committee, *East European Economies Post-Helsinki* (Washington, D.C.: GPO, 1977), 387.

15. *Heti Vilaggazdasag*, 26 January 1974, cited in RFE *Situation Report*, no. 8 (Hungary), 19 February 1974.

16. One Western analyst reported that after 1974, the amount of crude oil that Eastern Europe received in barter trade with the Middle East "declined dramatically" but by precisely how much is not publicly known" (Haberstroh, "Eastern Europe: Growing Energy Problems," 388).

17. The most important example of this was the financing that Kuwait and Libya extended for construction of the Adria pipeline. See *New York Times*, 13 October 1975, for other examples of recycled petrodollars in Eastern Europe.

18. Quoted in RFE *Situation Report*, no. 8 (Romania), 15 March 1976.

19. RFE *Situation Report*, no. 33 (Romania), 23 September 1976.

20. Quotations are from *The London Times*, 12 March 1976.

21. *The London Times*, 3 March 1976.

22. Ronald G. Oechsler and John A. Martens, "Eastern European Trade With OPEC: A Solution to Emerging Energy Problems?" in U.S. Congress, Joint Economic Committee, *East European Economic Assessment, Part 2* (Washington, D.C.: GPO, 1981), 521.

23. Ibid., 514.

24. Ibid., 515.

25. RFE *Situation Report*, no. 19 (Czechoslovakia), 19 June 1979. For a detailed analysis of the Soviet–Iranian natural gas agreements, see J.B. Hannigan and C.H. McMillan, "The Soviet–Iranian Gas Agreements: Nexus of Energy Policies, East–West Relations, and Middle East Politics," *Soviet Union*[, Vol. 9, Part 2,] (1982): 131–153.

26. Quoted in *Washington Post*, 25 February 1980.

27. Quoted in RFE *Situation Report*, no. 19 (Czechoslovakia), 19 June 1979.

28. Quoted in *Washington Post*, 15 July 1979.

29. Quoted in RFE *Situation Report*, no. 20 (Romania), 1 October 1981.

30. Material on the loan from the Arab Bank consortium is from RFE *Situation Report*, no. 19 (Romania), 12 May 1981. RFE *Situation Report*, no. 19 (Romania), 23 September 1981, discusses the loan from the International Monetary Fund. *Scinteia*, 14 July 1981, reports that, solely as a result of price increases, Romania paid $1.5 billion more for imported oil in 1980 than in 1979.

31. *Petroleum Economist*, May 1983, 190.

32. RFE *Situation Report*, no. 14 (Romania), 8 August 1979.

33. RFE *Situation Report*, no. 6 (Romania), 30 May 1980, provides a detailed discussion of these contacts.

34. Ibid.

35. For background material on the proposed role of Kuwait in constructing the petrochemical complex, see RFE *Situation Report*, no. 9 (Romania), 12 May 1981.

36. For details of the 1979 agreement with Libya, see RFE *Situation Report*, no. 6 (Romania), 25 March 1985. See *Scinteia*, 25 January 1983; *Scinteia*, 28 July 1984; *Scinteia*, 7 March 1985, for complaints that existing contracts between Romania and Libya were being underfulfilled. Part of the problem may arise from Libya's reported attempt to play the oil card against Romania. When Romania's Ceausescu visited Libya in 1985, Libyan leader Muammar Qaddafi warned him that Romania would suffer unspecified "consequences" because of its political ties with Israel and Arab "moderates" such as the Palestine Liberation Organization. I have been unable to determine if any of Qaddafi's threatened consequences materialized. For details of this incident, see *Associated Press* reporting from Tripoli on 5 March 1985.

37. Calculated from data in *Petroleum Economist*, June 1986, 216; and *Plan Econ Report: Developments in the Economies of the Soviet Union and Eastern Europe*, 2, nos. 17–18 (30 December 1985): 15.

38. For a detailed analysis of Soviet bloc trade in arms for oil, see Atef Gawad, "Moscow's Arms for Oil Diplomacy," *Foreign Policy*, Summer 1986, 147–68. See also *Washington Post*, 4 August 1984.

39. CTK, 10 February 1982, in FBIS-*EEU*, 11 February 1982, D2.

40. AFP, 15 February 1982, in FBIS-*SOV*, 16 February 1982, H5. The Soviet Union did agree to resume work (which had been discontinued when the Khomeini regime came to power) on construction of power stations at Isfahan and Ahwaz.

41. *Financial Times*, 10 March 1982.

42. *Financial Times*, 6 October 1981. This source speculated that the price for at least part of the oil would be below the official OPEC price.

43. *Pravda* (Bratislava), 31 May 1984, in FBIS-*EEU*, 6 June 1984, D1. For additional details of both the 1984 and 1985 agreements, see RFE *Situation Report*, no. 17 (Czechoslovakia), 29 October 1985.

44. *Zemedelske noviny*, 9 February 1984, in FBIS-*EEU*, 17 February 1984, D2.

45. According to this agreement, Iran will ship 5 MT of crude oil annually to the Soviet Union in exchange for refined petroleum products [TASS, 17 October 1987, cited in RL *Research Bulletin*, no. 424 (1987)].

46. CTK, 15 January 1987, in FBIS-*EEU*, 16 January 1987, D6.

47. MTI, 28 October 1988, in FBIS-*EEU*, 31 October 1988, 33. According to this source, Hungary offered Iran a hard currency credit worth $200 million to finance the importation of Hungarian capital goods. Although Hungary reportedly faces "tough competition" on the Iranian market, Iranian sources indicated that if its trade proposals were competitive, "Hungary would come into consideration because it was a reliable supplier during Iran's eight-year war with Iraq."

48. For details of this agreement, see *Trybuna ludu*, 21–22 January 1989. Another Polish source reports that "a further increase in purchases is possible in the following years, provided Poland can present a sufficiently broad export offer" (PAP, 17 February 1989, in FBIS-*EEU*, 22 February 1989, 57).

49. *Moscow World Service*, 25 July 1989, in FBIS-*SOV* (26 July 1989): 15. The agreement to resume exports was announced. Kashirov's remarks are reported by *TASS*, 10 March 1989, cited in RL *Report on the USSR* (17 March 1989): 43.

50. These remarks were reported by IRNA (Tehran), 20 January 1989, in FBIS-*EEU*, 24 January 1989, 51.

51. Premier Ladislav Adamec explained that a concern to improve the quality of the environment through increased use of low-polluting natural gas in the Prague and central Bohemian regions provided the principal rationale for the proposal. *Pravda* (Bratislava), 20 February 1989, in FBIS-*EEU*, 27 February 1989. *Rude pravo*, 7 April 1989, reported the comments of the minister of fuels and power.

52. *Trud*, 19 June 1989, in FBIS-*EEU*, 21 June 1989, 8.

53. President Carter himself asserted that the Soviet invasion of Afghanistan represented a "stepping stone to possible control over much of the world's oil supplies" (*New York Times*, 9 January 1980). Caspar Weinberger, President Reagan's secretary of defense, predicted that the Soviet Union would "almost

certainly" become a net importer of energy (*New York Times*, 19 May 1981). "The worry," Weinberger added, "is that they would move down through Iran, Iraq, and Afghanistan and try to seize the oil fields" (*New York Times*, 8 February 1982). Of course, the Soviet Union has not become a net importer of energy in general or oil in particular.

54. *Plan Econ Report: Developments in the Economies of the Soviet Union and Eastern Europe*, 2, nos. 12–13 (31 March 1986): 17.

55. *Rzeczpospolita*, 5 January 1989, in FBIS-*EEU*, 1 February 1989, 54. The assertion that these exports have become "entirely unprofitable" was reported in *Zycie Warszawy*, 22 September 1988, in FBIS-*EEU*, 14 December 1988, 57.

56. *Plan Econ Report: Developments in the Economies of the Soviet Union and Eastern Europe*, 1, nos. 17–18 (30 December 1985): 16.

57. For materials on East Germany's "cost plus" contract with West Germany for oil, see Jan Vanous, "Soviet and East European Trade and Financial Relations with the Middle East," *Soviet–East European Foreign Trade*, Spring/Summer/Fall 1985, 90. For various estimates of the dimensions of East Germany's export trade in oil, see *Frankfurter Allgemeine*, 12 September 1986, in JPRS-*EER*, no. 158 (22 October 1986): 8; *Frankfurter Allgemeine*, 24 December 1987, in JPRS-*EER*, no. 13 (22 February 1988): 39; *FS-Analysen*, no. 4 (1986), in JPRS-*EER*, no. 61 (16 April 1987): 34.

58. It is the "guess" of one Western analyst that most of the crude oil imported from the Middle East is directly reexported (Jochen Bethkenhagen, "The GDR's Energy Policy and Its Implications for the Intensification Drive," *Studies in Comparative Communism*, Spring 1987, 65). In contrast, Vanous, "Soviet and East European Trade and Financial Relations with the Middle East," 90, asserts that it is "believed" that East Germany has "never" reexported Middle Eastern crude directly but always in refined form.

59. *DIW-Wochenbericht* 53, no. 47 (1986), in JPRS-*EER*, no. 23 (18 February 1987): 18.

60. For a discussion of such transactions, see Vanous, "Soviet and East European Trade and Financial Relations with the Middle East," 90.

61. C.H. McMillan, "Eastern Europe's Relations with OPEC Suppliers," in U.S. Congress, Joint Economic Committee, *East European Economies: Slow Growth in the 1980's, vol. 1* (Washington, D.C.: GPO, 1985), 375.

62. Hungary did publish data on the volume of these exports in the 1970s. See, for example, *Statisticheskii ezhegodnik stran-chlenov Soveta Ekonomicheskoi Vzaimopomoshchi 1981* (Moskva: Financy i Statistica, 1981), 352.

63. As estimated by *Petroleum Economist*, April 1986, 215.

64. *Plan Econ Report: Developments in the Economies of the Soviet Union and Eastern Europe*, 1, nos. 17–18 (30 December 1985): 15, 16. *Washington Post*, 8 November 1985, speculates that the reduction in exports may be due to cutbacks in Soviet oil deliveries.

65. *Plan Econ Report: Developments in the Economies of the Soviet Union and Eastern Europe*, 1, nos. 17–18 (30 December 1985): 18.

66. Data from *Rude pravo*, 20 October 1988.

67. Ibid.

68. *Rude pravo*, 20 December 1988.

69. Stern, "CMEA Oil Acquisition Policy in the Middle East and the Gulf," 415.

70. See the survey of these impediments in *Rynki zagraniczne*, August 9–12 1986, in JPRS-*EER*, no. 157 (21 October 1986): 42. A similar analysis of this subject concludes that "the socialist countries have very little or no experience in how to organize economic cooperation with these countries" [*Kulpolitika*, no. 3 (1985), in JPRS-*EEI*, no. 67 (22 August 1985): 5]. For an overall assessment of Eastern Europe's trade with the Third World, see Marie Lavigne, "Eastern Europe–LDC Economic Relations in the Eighties," in U.S. Congress, Joint Economic Committee, *East European Economies: Slow Growth in the 1980's*, vol. 2 (Washington, D.C.: GPO, 1986), 31–61.

71. For a detailed exposition of the difficulties Poland encounters in trade with Libya, see *Rynki zagraniczne*, 29–30 December 1986, in JPRS-*EER*, no. 64 (22 April 1987): 15.

72. According to Strougal, Czechoslovakia advanced such proposals to its partners in Comecon on three occasions. (*Rude pravo*, 19 October 1983).

Chapter 5

1. *Figyelo*, 27 June 1979, quoted in RFE *Situation Report*, no. 14 (Hungary), 18 July 1979.

2. *Rzeczpospolita*, 21 May 1986, in JPRS-*EER*, no. 122 (13 August 1986): 36.

3. As reported by TASS, 3 November 1986, in FBIS-*SOV*, 4 November 1986, BB7.

4. An exposition of this position appeared in *Wirtschaftswissenschaft* 34 (January 1986), in JPRS-*EER*, no. 42 (21 March 1986): 14. Similar arguments were made in *Rude pravo*, 21 September 1985; *Hospodarske noviny*, 9 September 1983, in JPRS-*EEI*, no. 84615 (26 October 1983): 40.

5. Reported in RFE *Situation Report*, no. 13 (Czechoslovakia), 17 September 1987.

6. See, for example, *Wirtschaftswissenschaft* 34 (January 1986), in JPRS-*EER*, no. 42 (21 March 1986): 14, 15.

7. See the citations in note 4, chapter 1.

8. *Hospodarske noviny*, no. 40 (1985), in JPRS-*EEI*, no. 92 (9 December 1985): 6.

9. Western analysts usually measure and compare the relative energy efficiency of the Comecon states in unit energy requirements needed to generate x amount of aggregate output as expressed in dollars of gross national product (GNP). The following data represent a typical example of such calculations. They reflect comparative levels of relative energy consumption in Communist European and selected Western states (in thousands of barrels per day oil equivalent per $1 billion of GNP in constant 1984 prices).

Energy Efficiency, Selected Countries, 1983

Country	Energy per Dollar of GNP (megajoules)
France	8.6
Sweden	8.6
Japan	9.7
West Germany	11.8
United Kingdom	17.2
United States	19.3
Yugoslavia	21.5
Poland	26.9
East Germany	29.0
Czechoslovakia	30.1
Soviet Union	32.3
Romania	37.6
China	40.9
Hungary	49.5

Source: William U. Chandler, "The Changing Role of Market in National Economies," Worldwatch Paper 72, reprinted in Hilary French, "Industrial Wasteland," *Worldwatch*, November/December 1988, 28.

However, respected Western analysts have expressed concern that such calculations overstate the relative energy inefficiency of the Comecon states vis-á-vis the developed West, primarily because of the tentative nature of Western estimates of Eastern European dollar GNP levels. In their opinion, these estimates typically understate the actual aggregate output of the Eastern European economies and thereby overstate the amount of energy they consume per unit of GNP.

The debate here is not over whether the Comecon states are less energy efficient than their Western counterparts—all analysts agree that they are—but over the relative degree of inefficiency of the former versus the latter. For more details of the arguments presented here, see *Plan Econ Report: Developments in the Economies of the Soviet Union and Eastern Europe*, 2, nos. 12–13 (31 March 1986): especially 6–7.

10. These issues are discussed in United Nations Economic Commission for Europe, *Economic Survey of Europe in 1986–1987* (New York: UN, 1986–87), 200.

11. *Rude pravo*, 2 August 1988.

12. *Zycie Warszawy*, 22 June 1988, in JPRS-EER, no. 71 (31 August 1988): 68. Of course, the Stalinist model is not sui generis in this regard. Clearly, capitalist entrepreneurs will waste energy when economic self-interest dictates. The converse also is true, however; the capitalist will save energy when it is economically rational to do so. The following analysis makes clear that integral components of the Stalinist model inherently vitiate the conservation of energy.

13. *Figyelo*, 27 June 1979, in RFE *Situation Report* no. 14 (Hungary) 18 July 1979; *Rude pravo*, 18 November 1981; *Rabotnichesko delo*, 7 October 1985, in JPRS-*EER*, no. 116 (21 November 1985): 40.

14. *Pogled*, 8 July 1985, in JPRS-*EEI*, no. 77 (1 October 1985): 27. This source identifies another disincentive for industrialists to conserve energy: "If you were to ask an economic manager if he is interested in economy, his honest answer would be no. The reason is simple: he finds it much more convenient to absorb the one-time economy incentive than to wonder how to make ends meet subsequently when the plan for subsequent periods absorbs any discovered reserves."

15. A Czechoslovak source argued:

The fact is that, notwithstanding all efforts to use fuels and energy efficiently, we have failed to make use of instruments such as tax breaks for energy saving investments, state subsidies, price supports for energy-efficient products, . . . instruments that led to rapid consumption cuts abroad. It is likely that under the administrative method of managing the national economy they would not even have shown the desired effect. (*Rude pravo*, 2 August 1988).

16. *Voprosy ekonomiki*, no. 12 (1980): 101.

17. *Rude pravo*, 21 September 1985. On this subject, see also *Hospodarske noviny*, 3 August 1984, in JPRS-*EEI*, no. 111 (3 October 1984): 23.

18. *Zycie Warszawy*, 22 June 1988, in JPRS-*EER*, no. 71 (31 August 1988): 68.

19. Istvan Dobozi, "The 'Invisible' Source of 'Alternative' Energy: Comparing Energy Conservation Performance of the East and the West," *Natural Resources Forum*, no. 3 (1983): 213, notes the introduction of many oil-intensive technologies and equipment in the mid-1970s. Analysis of the national economic plans for the 1981–1985 period is from *Voprosy ekonomiki*, no. 8 (1983): 105–13. On this subject, see also *Voprosy ekonomiki*, no. 12 (1980): 99.

20. *Zycie Warszawy*, 22 June 1988, in JPRS-*EER*, no. 71 (31 August 1988): 68.

21. Leslie Dienes and Victor Merkin, "Energy Policy and Conservation in Eastern Europe," in U.S. Congress, Joint Economic Committee, *East European Economies: Slow Growth in the 1980's*, vol. 1 (Washington, D.C.: GPO, 1985), 351.

22. *Trybuna ludu*, 10 August 1981, cited in Dienes and Merkin, "Energy Policy and Conservation in Eastern Europe," 343.

23. *Rude pravo*, 2 August 1988.

24. Dobozi, "The 'Invisible' Source of 'Alternative' Energy," 206, elaborates on this point.

25. For an overall summary of these measures, see RFE *Background Report*, no. 274 (15 December 1978). For material on initiatives in individual countries, see the following: for Bulgaria—RFE *Situation Report*, no. 41 (Bulgaria), 23 November 1973; *Rabotnichesko delo*, 4 August 1974, in FBIS-*EEDR*, 8 August 1974, C1–C3; for Czechoslovakia—*Svet hospodarstvi*, 18 November 1980, in JPRS-*EEI*, no. 77157 (12 January 1981); *Svet hospodarstvi*, 30 July 1974, dis-

cussed in RFE *Situation Report*, no. 47 (Czechoslovakia), 18 December 1974; for Hungary—*Penzugyi Szemle*, June 1974, discussed in RFE *Situation Report*, no. 28 (Hungary), 23 July 1974; for Poland—Radio Warsaw, 24 November 1973, summarized in RFE *Situation Report* (Poland), 30 November 1973; for Romania—*Scinteia*, 18 November 1973, in FBIS-*EEDR*, 21 November 1973, H1–H12.

26. For an analysis of the economic plans and the energy requirements of those plans, see John Haberstroh, "Eastern Europe: Growing Energy Problems," in U.S. Congress, Joint Economic Committee, *East European Economies Post-Helsinki* (Washington, D.C.: GPO, 1977), 394–95.

27. *Nepszabadsag*, 22 March 1975, quoted in RFE *Situation Report*, no. 17 (Hungary), 9 April 1975.

28. This circumstance paralleled developments in Western Europe and the United States where meaningful increases in real energy prices typically occurred from 1979 on. For details, see Dobozi, "The 'Invisible' Source of 'Alternative' Energy," 204–5.

29. *Voprosy ekonomiki*, no. 12 (1980): 102. For a summary of these initiatives, see Martin J. Kohn, "Consumer Price Developments in Eastern Europe," in U.S. Congress, Joint Economic Committee, *East European Economic Assessment, Part 2* (Washington, D.C.: GPO, 1981), 334–36. For further details, see the following RFE *Situation Reports*: no. 7 (Poland), 20 March 1980; no. 22 (Czechoslovakia), 24 July 1979; no. 15 (Hungary), 1 August 1979; no. 14 (Romania), 8 August 1979.

30. *Washington Post*, 5 August 1979.

31. *New York Times*, 22 July 1979, carried the report of "heavy police patrols" attendant upon announcement of the price increases. Kohn, "Consumer Price Developments in Eastern Europe," 336, also stresses the political sensitivity of the price increases.

32. *New York Times*, 22 July 1979.

33. For details of these initiatives, see Kohn, "Consumer Price Developments in Eastern Europe," 336. The Czechoslovak and Hungarian measures, respectively, are discussed in RFE *Situation Report*, no. 22 (Czechoslovakia), 24 July 1979; RFE *Situation Report*, no. 15 (Hungary), 15 August 1979.

34. This conclusion was reached by, among others, *Figyelo*, 19 November 1980, in JPRS-*EEI*, no. 77178 (14 January 1981): 65; *Planovane hospodarstvi*, no. 4 (1984), in JPRS-*EEI*, no. 100 (5 September 1984): 41. For Western analyses making the same point, see Central Intelligence Agency, "East European Energy Outlook through 1990," in U.S. Congress, Joint Economic Committee, *East European Economies: Slow Growth in the 1980's*, vol. 1 (Washington, D.C.: GPO, 1985), 307; Office of Technology Assessment, *Technology and Soviet Energy Availability* (Washington, D.C.: GPO, 1981), 302.

35. Dobozi, "The 'Invisible' Source of 'Alternative' Energy," 212; *Kulpolitika*, no. 3 (1985), in JPRS-*EEI*, no. 69 (30 August 1985): 14; *Kulgazdasag*, no. 10 (October 1983), in JPRS-*EEI*, no. 5 (11 January 1984): 16.

36. Hungarian sources especially stress how cheap Soviet energy impeded efforts to conserve in Eastern Europe [*Kozgazdasagi Szemle*, no. 11 (1987), in

FBIS-*EEU*, 17 February 1988, 26; *Kozgazdasagi Szemle*, no. 12 (1987), in JPRS-*EER*, no. 24 (25 March 1988): 40].

37. *Pogled*, 8 July 1985, in JPRS-*EEI*, no. 77 (1 October 1985): 25. Polish sources have expressed similar sentiments. For example, one source remarked that "the unit consumption of energy in Poland is still about the highest in the world . . . and frankly speaking, not much has changed in this picture" [*Zycie gospodarcze*, 26 August 1984, in JPRS-*EEI*, no. 112 (5 October 1984): 108]. Another said that in energy conservation, "Poland has neither acquired any good experience nor can it boast any notable achievements in this respect during the past 40 years" [*Zycie Warszawy*, 9 July 1985, in JPRS-*EEI*, no. 68 (26 August 1985): 63.

38. *Energietechnik*, December 1983, in JPRS-*EEI*, no. 18 (9 February 1984): 37.

39. A detailed discussion of these measures is found in *Energieanwendung*, no. 6 (December 1986), in JPRS-*EER*, no. 53 (3 April 1987): 43–44.

40. *Deutschland Archiv*, December 1985, in JPRS-*EER*, no. 52 (8 April 1986): 31.

41. For details on the system of consumption norms, see *Energietechnik*, December 1983, in JPRS-*EEI*, no. 84965, 16 December 1983): 44. An extended analysis of the problems encountered in implementing this system is Jochen Bethkenhagen, "GDR's Energy Management Facing Difficult Tasks," *DIW-Wochenbericht* 48, no. 5 (29 January 1981): 57–62.

42. For detailed material on these initiatives, see *Presse Informationen*, 27 December 1985, in JPRS-*EER*, no. 54 (9 April 1986): 40.

43. *Presse Informationen*, 14 April 1988, in JPRS-*EER*, no. 45 (9 June 1988): 32. On page 33, this source reports that in the 1986–1990 period, East Germany will electrify an additional 1,500 km of rail lines. On these measures, see also Jochen Bethkenhagen, "The GDR's Energy Policy and Its Implications for the Intensification Drive," *Studies in Comparative Communism*, Spring 1987, 60–61.

44. *Presse Informationen*, 27 December 1985, in JPRS-*EER*, no. 54 (9 April 1986): 48.

45. These and other measures to conserve energy in the military are discussed in *Militaertechnik*, no. 6 (1983), in JPRS-*EPS*, no. 28 (24 February 1984): 6; *Militaertechnik*, no. 2 (1984), in JPRS-*EPS*, no. 93 (27 July 1984): 1–5. A Western source for similar materials is DPA, 25 June 1982, in FBIS-*EEU*, 28 June 1982, E21.

46. *Energieanwendung*, no. 6 (December 1986), in JPRS-*EER*, no. 53 (3 April 1987): 57.

47. *Energietechnik*, December 1983, in JPRS-*EEI*, no. 86965 (16 December 1983): 43–46; *Presse Informationen*, 11 October 1983, in JPRS-*EPS*, no. 84858 (1 December 1983): 85.

48. Bethkenhagen, "The GDR's Energy Policy and Its Implications for the Intensification Drive," 61.

49. Ibid., 64, reports that per capita primary energy consumption is about 20 percent higher in East Germany than in West Germany, although per capita

national product is approximately 25 percent lower in the former than in the latter.

50. Ibid.

51. One analyst has argued:

> In the final analysis, the economy's energy demand can only really decrease if we increase the production of high value, modern goods that can be efficiently marketed in world markets. All of this is far from being primarily a question of energetics. It shows, however, that the tasks of energy management harmonize in many respects with the tasks of increasing our competitiveness and improving our efficiency. (*Nepszabadsag*, 18 May 1985).

52. Dobozi, "The 'Invisible' Source of 'Alternative' Energy," 215.

53. For discussions of these plans, see *Nepszabadsag*, 20 January 1981; *Figyelo*, 24 December 1980, in JPRS-*EEI*, no. 77502 (4 March 1981).

54. *Nepszabadsag*, 19 October 1983; *Heti Vilaggazdasag*, no. 5 (1983), in JPRS-*EEI*, no. 13 (25 January 1984): 59.

55. *Magyar Kozlony*, no. 96 (24 December 1980), in JPRS-*EEI*, no. 77550 (10 March 1981): 29; *Nepszabadsag*, 20 January 1981. *Heti Vilaggazdasag*, no. 5 (1983), in JPRS-*EEI*, no. 13 (25 January 1984): 58, provides information on the World Bank loan and the projects for which it will be used.

56. Dobozi, "The 'Invisible' Source of 'Alternative' Energy," 211.

57. The Soviet criticisms are expressed in *Voprosy ekonomiki*, no. 12 (1980): 101–2. For a typical defense of the price increases, see Dobozi, "The 'Invisible' Source of 'Alternative' Energy," 213.

58. The 1982 price increases were reported in *Budapest Domestic Service*, 14 April 1982, in FBIS-*EEU*, 15 April 1982, F1–F2. This source also provides data on the magnitude of subsidies for consumer prices.

59. For details, see RFE *Situation Report*, no. 1 (Hungary), 3 January 1986.

60. *Nepszabadsag*, 16 October 1985.

61. *Magyar Hirlap*, 2 October 1985, in FBIS-*EEU*, 29 October 1985, F7.

62. *Plan Econ Report: Developments in the Economies of the Soviet Union and Eastern Europe*, 2, nos. 12–13 (13 March 1986), reports that in 1984 and 1985 primary energy consumption increased by 9.21 percent and 9.8 percent, respectively.

63. *Heti Vilaggazdasag*, no. 24 (1984), in JPRS-*EEI*, no. 93 (16 August 1984): 72.

64. Accounts expressing this conclusion include *Magyar Hirlap*, 2 October 1985, in FBIS-*EEU* (29 October 1985), F7; *Nepszabadsag*, 23 October 1985. Indeed, one source contended that the energy intensity of the Hungarian economy actually increased in the 1981–1984 period [*Heti Vilaggazdasag*, no. 38 (1985), in JPRS-*EEI*, no. 96 (23 December 1985): 126].

65. Dobozi, "The 'Invisible' Source of 'Alternative' Energy," 214. As a result of this circumstance, Dobozi notes, the "real" saving in energy "becomes significantly smaller than the recorded saving. Some of the 'recorded' saving will probably disappear with any upswing in these sectors."

66. *Magyar Hirlap*, 2 October 1985, in FBIS-*EEU* (29 October 1985): F8. Also see the data cited in note 62.

67. Energy consumption in this sector increased by 5.6 percent annually between 1980 and 1982 and by 6.1 percent in 1984 (*Nepszabadsag*, 16 October 1985). *Nepszabadsag*, 28 October 1987, reports that in both 1986 and 1987, this sector again substantially exceeded its planned targets for energy consumption.

68. *Nepszabadsag*, 16 October 1985.

69. For example, a recent study found in industry a "continual lack of strong managerial incentives to minimize cost" in the expenditure of energy. (Istvan Dobozi, "An Empirical Estimation of Price Responsiveness of the Hungarian Economy: The Case of Energy Demand," paper prepared for the Tenth U.S.–Hungarian Economic Roundtable, Budapest, 1–5 December 1986).

70. *Magyar Hirlap*, 2 October 1985, in FBIS-*EEU* (29 October 1985): F8. This source also expresses concern that these new measures will force industrialists to ask: "Will it be worthwhile to increase production to a certain level so that bearing the burdens of the tariff for extra energy consumption will be worth it?"

71. *Budapest Domestic Service*, 12 January 1985, in FBIS-*EEU*, 14 January 1985, F4. *Magyar Hirlap*, 2 October 1985, in FBIS-*EEU* (29 October 1985): F8 labeled the measures "draconian."

72. *Nepszabadsag*, 21 February 1987, provides extensive commentary on these initiatives. Less energy intensive sectors targeted for development include the electronics, pharmaceutical, rubber, and synthetic materials processing industries. *Nepszabadsag*, 27 August 1987, reports that Hungary has signed contracts with the Bechtel Corporation whereby the latter will supply sundry energy-saving technologies to facilitate this restructuring of industry.

73. Energy conservation targets in the 1980s are from *Revista Economica*, 26 December 1980, in JPRS-*EEI*, no. 77403 (17 February 1981): 51; Agerpres, 18 January 1982, in FBIS-*EEU*, 21 January 1982, H5.

74. Quoted by AFP, 25 November 1985, in FBIS-*EEU*, 27 November 1985, H8. For materials on the several reductions in supply of electricity to the population, see *Buletinul Oficial*, no. 67 (31 July 1979), discussed in RFE *Situation Report*, no. 13 (Romania), 9 July 1982; *Bucharest Domestic Service*, 25 November 1983, in FBIS-*EEU*, 28 November 1983, H4; *Scinteia*, 4 December 1985.

75. *Scinteia*, 7 February 1987.

76. A good summary of these measures is found in the Hungarian publication *Magyarorzag*, 11 December 1983, in JPRS-*EPS*, no. 21 (8 February 1984): 10–11. See also Radio Bucharest, 28 April 1982, as summarized in RFE *Situation Report*, no. 18 (Romania), 13 January 1983; *Scinteia*, 4 December 1985.

77. The February 1987 decree is typical in this respect. After announcing the latest steep cut in electricity for the population, it informed that "the consumption regime for enterprises will remain in accordance with the norms, but in this field, too, decisive measures are required to keep the consumption of every unit below the quotas" (*Scinteia*, 7 February 1987).

78. *Magyarorzag*, 11 December 1983, in JPRS-*EPS*, no. 21 (8 February 1984): 12. The assessment that consumption could be cut sharply "within a short time," this source informs, is "how the Romanian political leadership judges the situation."

79. RFE *Situation Report*, no. 4 (Romania), 20 March 1986.

80. See *New Times*, 12 January 1987, 32, for data on rates of growth (actual and projected) for national income and industrial production.

81. *Magyarorzag*, 11 December 1983 in JPRS-*EPS*, no. 21 (8 February 1984): 12.

82. Dobozi, "The 'Invisible' Source of 'Alternative' Energy," 213.

83. Poland is the most obvious example of this circumstance. As the director of the Institute of Mining and Metallurgy in Poland has bluntly asserted, "If industry operated now as it did in 1978 and 1979, we would already have a permanent energy shortage" [*Zycie Warszawy*, 22 June 1988, in JPRS-*EER*, no. 71 (31 August 1988): 69].

84. *Plan Econ Report: Developments in the Economies of the Soviet Union and Eastern Europe*, 2, nos. 12–13 (31 March 1986). For a contrasting assessment, see Central Intelligence Agency, "East European Energy Outlook through 1990," 317. Inter alia, the CIA argues, "The bleak supply picture is forcing Eastern Europe to tackle problems on the demand side, and nearly all the regimes are now focusing more closely on energy conservation. But energy savings are more likely to continue to reflect stagnant economies rather than improved efficiency."

85. *Rude pravo*, 2 August 1988.

86. *Zycie Warszawy*, 22 June 1988 in JPRS-*EER*, no. 71 (31 August 1988): 69.

87. Ibid., 70.

88. For a detailed analysis of the fate of economic reform in Eastern Europe, see Morris Bornstein, "Economic Reform in Eastern Europe," in U.S. Congress, Joint Economic Committee, *East European Economies Post-Helsinki*, 102–34. As a Polish source has argued, the fate of economic reform in Eastern Europe "will hinge on political factors . . . [I]n our countries politics still dominate over economics regardless of whether we approve or deplore this phenomenon" [*Polityka-Eksport-Import*, no. 8 (April 1988), in JPRS-*EER*, no. 46 (13 June 1988): 13].

89. *Zycie Warszawy*, 24 June 1988, in JPRS-*EER*, no. 83 (5 October 1988): 48.

Chapter 6

1. L. Csaba, "CMEA and the Challenge of the 1980s," *Soviet Studies*, April 1988, 269.

2. The quoted words are those of Matyas Szuros, secretary of the Hungarian Socialist Workers party Central Committee [*Magyar Hirlap*, 4 April 1984, in RFE *Background Report*, no. 158 (25 August 1984)]. This RFE publication provides extensive documentation on the positions of East Germany and Hungary and the reactions of the Soviet Union and other socialist states to them.

3. Ibid.

4. *Tarsadalmi Szemle*, January 1984, in RFE *Background Report*, no. 158 (25 August 1984).

5. *Kozgazdasagi Szemle*, October 1984, in JPRS-*EEI*, no. 133 (10 December 1984): 39–40.

6. The substance of, and rationale for, a policy of differentiation toward Eastern Europe is forcefully made in Charles Gati, *Hungary and the Soviet Bloc* (Durham, N.C.: Duke University Press, 1986).

Bibliography

Alisov, N.V., and E.B. Valev, eds., *Economic Geography of the Socialist Countries of Europe* (Moscow: Progress Publishers, 1984).

Balkay, Balint, "Some Macroeconomic Aspects of the CMEA Countries Mineral Economy," *Research Report*, no. 105 (Vienna: Vienna Institute for Comparative Economic Studies, 1985).

Balkay, Balint, and Sandor Sipos, "Gas in Eastern Europe and the USSR," in Melvin Conant, ed., *The World Gas Trade: Resource for the Future* (Boulder, Colo.: Westview Press, 1986).

Barcikowski, K., "Fraternal Cooperation Is the Way to Overcome Difficulties," *World Marxist Review*, no. 7 (1985).

Barry, Donald D., "Political and Legal Aspects of the Development and Use of Nuclear Power in the USSR and Eastern Europe," in Peter Maggs, Gordon Smith, and George Ginsburgs, eds., *Law and Economic Development in the Soviet Union* (Boulder, Colo.: Westview Press, 1982).

Becker, Abram S., "Oil and the Persian Gulf in Soviet Policy in the 1970's," in Michael Confino and Shimon Shamier, eds., *The USSR and the Middle East* (Jerusalem: Israel University Press, 1973).

Bethkenhagen, Jochen, "GDR's Energy Management Facing Difficult Tasks," *DIW-Wocenbericht*, 48, no. 5, 29 January 1981.

———. "The GDR's Energy Policy and Its Implications for the Intensification Drive," *Studies in Comparative Communism*, Spring 1987.

———. "Joint Energy Projects and their Influence on Future COMECON Energy Autarchy Ambitions," in NATO Directorate of Economic Affairs, *COMECON: Progress and Prospects* (Brussels: NATO, 1977).

Bornstein, Morris, "Economic Reform in Eastern Europe," in U.S. Congress, Joint Economic Committee, *East European Economies Post Helsinki* (Washington, D.C.: GPO, 1977).

Bozyk, Pawel, and M. Guzek, "Joint Planning and Forecasting in the CMEA," *Studies in International Relations*, no. 9 (Warsaw: Polish Institute of International Affairs, 1977).

Brada, Josef, "Soviet Subsidization of Eastern Europe: The Primacy of Economics over Politics?" *Journal of Comparative Economics*, no. 9 (1985).

Burger, Ethan S., *Eastern Europe and Oil: The Soviet Dilemma*, no. P-6368 (Santa Monica: Rand Corporation, 1979).

Central Intelligence Agency, *Prospects for Soviet Oil Production* (Washington, D.C.: ER77-10270, April 1977).

——, *USSR: Development of the Gas Industry* (Washington, D.C.: Library of Congress, ER78-10393, July 1978).

——, "East European Energy Outlook through 1990," in U.S. Congress, Joint Economic Committee, *East European Economies: Slow Growth in the 1980's*, vol. 1 (Washington, D.C.: GPO, 1985).

Chadwick, Margaret, David Long, and Machiko Nissanke, *Soviet Oil Exports: Trade Adjustments, Refinery Constraints, and Market Behavior* (Oxford: Oxford University Press, 1987).

Chandler, William U., "The Changing Role of Market in National Economies," Worldwatch Paper no. 42; reprinted in Hilary French, "Industrial Wasteland," *Worldwatch*, November-December, 1988.

Cooper, William, "Soviet–Western Trade," in U.S. Congress, Joint Economic Committee, *Soviet Economy in the 1980's: Problems and Prospects*, Part 2 (Washington, D.C.: GPO, 1982).

Crovitz, Gordon, *Europe's Siberian Gas Pipeline: Economic Lessons and Strategic Implications*, Occasional Paper no. 6 (London: Alliance Publishers, Ltd., for the Institute for European Defence & Strategic Studies, 1983).

Csaba, L., "Joint Investments and Mutual Advantages in the CMEA: Retrospection and Prognosis," *Soviet Studies*, April 1985.

——, "CMEA and the Challenge of the 1980s," *Soviet Studies*, April 1988.

Debardeleben, Joan, "Esoteric Policy Debate: Nuclear Safety in the Soviet Union and the German Democratic Republic," *British Journal of Political Science*, April 1985.

Dienes, Leslie, and Victor Merkin, "Energy Policy and Conservation in Eastern Europe," in U.S. Congress, Joint Economic Committee, *East European Economies: Slow Growth in the 1980's*, vol. 1 (Washington, D.C.: GPO, 1985).

Dienes, Leslie, and Theodore Shabad, *The Soviet Energy System: Resource Use and Policies* (New York: Halsted Press, 1979).

Dietz, Raimund, "Advantages and Disadvantages in Soviet Trade with Eastern Europe," in U.S. Congress, Joint Economic Committee, *East European Economies: Slow Growth in the 1980's*, vol. 2 (Washington, D.C.: GPO, 1986).

Directorate of Intelligence (Central Intelligence Agency), *Handbook of Economic Statistics* (Washington, D.C.: GPO). Annual edition.

——, *International Energy Statistics Review* (Washington, D.C.: GPO, 88-005, 31 May 1988).

Dobozi, Istvan, ed., "Economic Cooperation between Socialist and Developing Countries," *Trends in World Economy*, no. 25 (Budapest: Hungarian Scientific Council for World Economy, 1978).

——, "World Raw Material Markets Until the Year 2000—Implications for Eastern Europe," *Raw Materials Report*, no. 2 (1983).

——, "The 'Invisible' Source of 'Alternative' Energy: Comparing Energy Conservation of the East and the West," *Natural Resources Forum*, no. 3 (1983).

————, "Prospects for East–South Economic Interaction in the Changing International Environment," *Soviet and East European Foreign Trade*, Spring/Summer/Fall 1985.

————, "Are the Centrally Planned Economies Over-Consuming Metals?" paper presented at the Conference on Metal Demand, Pennsylvania State University, 19–22 May 1986.

————, "Intra-CMEA Mineral Cooperation: Implications for Trade with OECD and Third World Countries," *Resources Policy*, September 1986.

————, "An Empirical Estimation of Price Responsiveness of the Hungarian Economy: The Case of Energy Demand," paper prepared for the Tenth U.S.–Hungarian Economic Roundtable, Budapest 1–5 December 1986.

Ellis, James L., "Eastern Europe: Changing Trade Patterns and Perspectives," in U.S. Congress, Joint Economic Committee, *East European Economies: Slow Growth in the 1980's*, vol. 2 (Washington, D.C.: GPO, 1986).

Fallenbuchl, Zbigniew, "East European Integration: COMECON," in U.S. Congress, Joint Economic Committee, *Reorientation and Commercial Relations of the Economies of Eastern Europe* (Washington, D.C.: GPO, 1974).

————, "The Commodity Composition of Intra-COMECON Trade and the Industrial Structure of the Member Countries," in NATO Directorate of Economic Affairs, *COMECON: Progress and Prospects* (Brussels: NATO, 1977).

————, "Industrial and Economic Integration in CMEA and EEC," in Paul Marer and John Michael Montias, eds., *East European Integration and East–West Trade* (Bloomington: Indiana University Press, 1980).

Fallenbuchl, Zbigniew, and C.H. McMillan, eds., *Partners in East–West Economic Relations: The Determinants of Choice* (Elmsford, New York: Pergamon Press, 1980).

Fox, Lesley J., "Soviet Policy in the Development of Nuclear Power in Eastern Europe," in U.S. Congress, Joint Economic Committee, *Soviet Economy in the 1980's: Problems and Prospects*, Part 1 (Washington, D.C.: GPO, 1982).

Gati, Charles, *Hungary and the Soviet Bloc* (Durham: Duke University Press, 1986).

Gawad, Atef, "Moscow's Arms for Oil Diplomacy," *Foreign Policy*, Summer 1986.

Goldman, Marshall, *The Enigma of Soviet Petroleum: Half Full or Half Empty?* (London: Allen and Urwin, 1981).

Gorst, Isabel, "Soviet Union—Oil Exports Rise to Record Level," *Petroleum Economist*, February 1988.

Gustafson, Thane, "Energy and the Soviet Bloc," *International Security*, Winter 1981–82.

————, "Soviet Energy Policy," in U.S. Congress, Joint Economic Committee, *Soviet Economy in the 1980's: Problems and Prospects*, Part 1 (Washington, D.C.: GPO, 1982).

Haberstroh, John, "Eastern Europe: Growing Energy Problems," in U.S. Congress, Joint Economic Committee, *East European Economies Post-Helsinki* (Washington, D.C.: GPO, 1977).

Hannigan, J.B., and C.H. McMillan, *The Energy Factor in Soviet–East European*

Relations (Ottawa: Institute of Soviet and East European Studies, Carleton University, 1981).

———, "Joint Investment in Resource Development: Sectoral Approaches to Socialist Integration," in U.S. Congress, Joint Economic Committee, *East European Economic Assessment*, Part 2 (Washington, D.C.: GPO, 1981).

———, *The Soviet Energy Stake in Afghanistan and Iran: Rationale and Risk for Natural Gas Imports*, Research Report no. 16, East–West Commercial Relations Series (Ottawa: Institute of Soviet and East European Studies, Carleton University, 1981).

———, "The Soviet–Iranian Gas Agreements: Nexus of Energy Policies, East–West Relations, and Middle East Politics," *Soviet Union*, Vol. 9, Part 2, (1982).

Hardt, John, "West Siberia: The Quest for Energy," *Problems of Communism*, May/June 1973.

———, "Soviet Energy Policy in Eastern Europe," in Sarah Terry, ed., *Soviet Policy in Eastern Europe* (New Haven: Yale University Press, 1984).

Hewett, Edward A., *Foreign Trade Prices in the Council for Mutual Economic Assistance* (Cambridge, England: Cambridge University Press, 1974).

———, "Recent Developments in East–West European Economic Relations and Their Implications for U.S.–East European Economic Relations," in U.S. Congress, Joint Economic Committee, *East European Economies Post-Helsinki* (Washington, D.C.: GPO, 1977).

———, "Near-Term Prospects for Soviet Natural Gas Industry and the Implications for East–West Trade," in U.S. Congress, Joint Economic Committee, *Soviet Economy in the 1980's: Problems and Prospects*, Part 1 (Washington, D.C.: GPO, 1982).

———, "Soviet Primary Products Export to Comecon and the West," in R.G. Jensen, ed., *Soviet Natural Resources in the World Economy* (Chicago: University of Chicago Press, 1983).

———, *Energy, Economics, and Foreign Policy in the Soviet Union* (Washington, D.C.: Brookings Institution, 1984).

Hoffman, George, "Energy Projections—Oil, Natural Gas and Coal in the USSR and Eastern Europe," *Energy Policy*, September 1979.

———, "Energy Dependence and Policy Options in Eastern Europe," in R.G. Jensen, ed., *Soviet Natural Resources in the World Economy* (Chicago: University of Chicago Press, 1983).

———, *The European Energy Challenge: East and West* (Durham, N.C.: Duke University Press, 1985).

Holzman, Franklyn, D., *Foreign Trade under Central Planning* (Cambridge, Mass.: Harvard University Press, 1974).

———, *International Trade Under Communism—Politics and Economics* (New York: Basic Books, 1976).

———, "The Significance of Soviet Subsidies to Eastern Europe," *Comparative Economic Studies*, no. 1 (Spring 1986).

Jack, Emily, J. Richard Lee, and Howard Lent, "Outlook for Soviet Energy," in U.S. Congress, Joint Economic Committee, *Soviet Economy in a New Perspective* (Washington, D.C.: GPO, 1976).

Josephson, Paul, "Atomic Energy in Eastern Europe: Trends and Prospects for the Year 2000," paper presented at the annual convention of the American Association for the Advancement of Slavic Studies, Monterey, Calif.: 1981.

Kabala, Stanley, "Poland: Facing the Hidden Costs of Development," *Environment*, no. 9 (1985).

Kaser, Michael, *Comecon: Integration Problems of the Planned Economies* (Oxford: Oxford University Press, 1967).

Knirsch, Peter, "COMECON and the Developing Nations," in NATO Directorate of Economic Affairs, *COMECON: Progress and Prospects* (Brussels: NATO 1977).

Kohn, Martin J., "Developments in Soviet–Eastern European Terms of Trade, 1971–75," in U.S. Congress, Joint Economic Committee, *Soviet Economy in a New Perspective* (Washington, D.C.: GPO, 1976).

———, "Consumer Price Developments in Eastern Europe," in U.S. Congress, Joint Economic Committee, *East European Economic Assessment*, Part 2 (Washington, D.C.: GPO, 1981).

Kohn, Martin J., and Nicholas R. Lang, "The Intra-CMEA Foreign Trade System: Major Price Changes, Little Reform," in U.S. Congress, Joint Economic Committee, *East European Economies Post-Helsinki* (Washington, D.C.: GPO, 1977).

Kossakowski, Marek, "Leave the Bunkers to the Bats!" *Across Frontiers*, Spring/Summer 1988.

Kramer, John M., "The Energy Gap in Eastern Europe," *Survey*, Spring/Summer 1975.

———, "Between Scylla and Charybdis: The Politics of Eastern Europe's Energy Problem," *Orbis*, Winter 1979.

———, "The Policy Dilemmas of East Europe's Energy Gap," in U.S. Congress, Joint Economic Committee, *East European Economic Assessment*, Part 2 (Washington, D.C.: GPO, 1981).

———, "The Environmental Crisis in Eastern Europe: The Price for Progress," *Slavic Review*, Summer 1983.

———, "Soviet–CMEA Energy Ties," *Problems of Communism*, July/August 1985.

———, "Nuclear Power in Eastern Europe," *Problems of Communism*, November/December 1986.

———, "Chernobyl' and the Nuclear 'Debate' in Communist Europe: The Role of Public Opinion," testimony presented before the U.S. Congress, Commission on Cooperation and Security in Europe, Washington, 26 April 1988.

———, "Council for Mutual Economic Assistance," in Richard Staar, ed., *1988 Yearbook on International Communist Affairs* (Stanford: Hoover Institution Press, 1988).

———, "Energy and the Environment in Eastern Europe," in Joan Debardeleben, ed., Environmental Problems and Policies in Eastern Europe (Montreal: McGill University Press, forthcoming).

Lavigne, Marie, "The Soviet Union Inside COMECON," *Soviet Studies*, April 1983.

———, "Eastern Europe–LDC Economic Relations in the Eighties," in U.S. Congress, Joint Economic Committee, *East European Economies: Slow Growth in the 1980's*, vol. 2 (Washington, D.C.: GPO, 1986).

Lemoine, Francoise, "Trading Prices within the CMEA," *Soviet and East European Foreign Trade*, Spring 1979.

Levine, Herbert S., "Energy and Grain in Soviet Hard Currency Trade," in U.S. Congress Joint Economic Committee, *Soviet Economy in a Time of Change* (Washington, D.C.: GPO, 1979).

Lewin, Joseph, "The Russian Approach to Nuclear Reactor Safety," *Nuclear Safety*, July/August 1977.

Marakova, A.A., ed., *Tendentsii razvitiia i metody prognozirovaniia energetiki stran-chlenov SEV* (Moskva: Energoatomizdat, 1987).

Marer, Paul, "Has Eastern Europe Become a Liability to the Soviet Union—The Economic Aspects," in Charles Gati, ed., *The International Politics of Eastern Europe* (New York: Praeger, 1976).

———, "The Political Economy of Soviet Relations with Eastern Europe," in Sarah M. Terry, ed., *Soviet Policy in Eastern Europe* (New Haven: Yale University Press, 1984).

Marer, Paul, and John Michael Montias, eds., *East European Integration and East–West Trade* (Bloomington: Indiana University Press, 1980).

———, "CMEA Integration: Theory and Practice," in U.S. Congress, Joint Economic Committee, *East European Economic Assessment*, Part 2 (Washington, D.C.: GPO, 1981).

Marples, David, *Chernobyl and Nuclear Power in the USSR* (New York: St. Martin's Press, 1986).

Marrese, Michael, "CMEA: Effective but Cumbersome Political Economy," *International Organization*, Spring 1986.

Marrese, Michael, and Jan Vanous, *Soviet Subsidization of Trade with Eastern Europe—A Soviet Perspective* (Berkeley: Institute of International Studies, University of California, 1983).

Martens, John A., "Quantification of Western Exports of High-Technology Products to Communist Countries," in U.S. Congress, Joint Economic Committee, *East European Economies: Slow Growth in the 1980's*, vol. 2 (Washington, D.C.: GPO, 1986).

McMillan, C.H. "Eastern Europe's Relations with OPEC Suppliers in the 1980s," in U.S. Congress, Joint Economic Committee, *East European Economies: Slow Growth in the 1980's*, vol. 1 (Washington, D.C.: GPO, 1985).

Meyerhoff, Arthur A., "Energy Base of Communist–Socialist Countries," *American Scientist*, December 1981.

Montias, John Michael, "The Structure of COMECON Trade and the Prospects for East–West Exchanges," in U.S. Congress, Joint Economic Committee, *Reorientation and Commercial Relations of the Economies of Eastern Europe* (Washington, D.C.: GPO, 1974).

Narodnoe khoziaistvo (Moskva: Financy i Statistika). Annual edition.

Narodnoe khoziaistvo SSSR za 70 Let (Moskva: Financy i Statistika, 1987).

National Foreign Assessment Center (Central Intelligence Agency), *Energy Supplies in Eastern Europe: A Statistical Compilation* (ER79-10624, December 1979).

Neuberger, Egon, and Laura D'Andrea Tyson, eds., *The Impact of International Economic Disturbances on the Soviet Union and Eastern Europe: Transmission and Response* (Elmsford, N.Y.: Pergamon Press, 1980).

Oechsler, Ronald G., and John A. Martens, "Eastern European Trade with OPEC: A Solution to Emerging Energy Problems?" in U.S. Congress, Joint Economic Committee, *East European Economic Assessment*, Part 2 (Washington, D.C.: GPO, 1981).

Office of Technology Assessment, *Technology and Soviet Energy Availability* (Washington, D.C.: GPO, 1981).

O'Reiley, A. Edward, "Hungarian Agricultural Performance and Policy during the NEM," in U.S. Congress, Joint Economic Committee, *East European Economies Post-Helsinki* (Washington, D.C.: GPO, 1977).

Ovchinnikov, Fedor, K. Toot, V. Solov'ev, V. Fateev, and S. Sharoiko, *Mezhdunarodnoe sotrudnichestvo stran chlenov SEV v oblasti atomnoi energetiki* (Moskva: Energoatomizat, 1986).

Park, J.D., *Oil and Gas in COMECON Countries* (New York: Nichols Publishing Company, 1979).

Pecsi, Kalman, *The Future of Socialist Integration* (Armonk, N.Y.: M.E. Sharpe, 1981).

Plan Econ Inc., *Plan Econ Report: Developments in the Economies of the Soviet Union and Eastern Europe*, 1, nos. 17–18 (30 December 1985).

———, 2, nos. 12–13 (31 March 1986).

———, 3, no. 52 (30 December 1987).

Polach, J.G., "Nuclear Power in East Europe," *East Europe*, no. 5 (May 1968).

———, "Nuclear Energy in Czechoslovakia: A Study in Frustration," *Orbis*, July 1968.

———, "The Energy Gap in the Communist World," *East Europe*, April 1969.

———, "The Development of Energy in East Europe," in U.S. Congress, Joint Economic Committee, *Economic Developments in Countries in Eastern Europe* (Washington, D.C.: GPO, 1970).

Poznanski, Kazimierz, *Technology, Competition, and the Soviet Bloc in the World Market* (Berkeley: Institute of International Studies, University of California, 1987).

———, "Opportunity Cost in Soviet Trade with Eastern Europe: Discussion of Methodology and New Evidence," *Soviet Studies*, April 1988.

Pryde, P., "Nuclear Energy Development in the Soviet Union," *Soviet Geography*, February 1978.

Radio Free Europe, *Background Reports; Situation Reports; Press Surveys* (Munich: Radio Free Europe Research, RFE/RL, Inc.)

Radio Liberty, *Research Bulletin Report on the USSR* (Munich: RFE/RL, Inc.)

Radu, Michael, ed., *Eastern Europe and the Third World: East vs. South* (New York: Praeger, 1981).

Russell, Jeremy, "Energy Considerations in Comecon Policies," *World Today*, February 1976.

———, *Energy as a Factor in Soviet Foreign Policy* (Lexington, Mass.: Lexington Books, 1976).

Saunders, Christopher T., ed., *East and West in the Energy Squeeze: Prospect for Cooperation* (New York: St. Martin's Press, 1980).

Sipos, Sandor, "Energy Cooperation between East and West," paper presented at Forum European, Paris, 23 April 1987.

Smith, Alan H., "Plan Coordination and Joint Planning in CMEA," *Journal of Common Market Studies*, September 1979.

Smith, Arthur, "The Council for Mutual Economic Assistance in 1977: New Economic Power, New Political Perspectives and Some Old and New Problems," in U.S. Congress, Joint Economic Committee, *Eastern European Economies Post-Helsinki* (Washington, D.C.: GPO, 1977).

Statisticheskii ezhegodnik stran-chlenov Soveta Ekonomicheskoi Vzaimopomoshchi (Moskva: Financy i Statistika). Annual edition.

Stein, Jonathan, *The Soviet Bloc, Energy and Western Security* (Lexington, Mass.: Lexington Books, 1983).

Stern, Jonathan, *Soviet Natural Gas Development to 1990: Implications for the CMEA and the West* (Lexington, Mass.: Lexington Books, 1980).

———, "CMEA Oil Acquisition Policy in the Middle East and the Gulf: The Search for Economic and Political Strategies," in U.S. Congress, Joint Economic Committee, *Soviet Economy in the 1980's: Problems and Prospects*, Part 1 (Washington, D.C.: GPO, 1982).

Thornton, Judith, "Chernobyl' and Soviet Energy," *Problems of Communism*, November/December, 1986.

Trend, Harry, "Economic Integration and Plan Coordination under COMECON," in Robert R. King and James F. Brown, eds., *Eastern Europe's Uncertain Future* (New York: Praeger, 1977).

United Nations Economic Commission for Europe, *Economic Survey of Europe* (New York: United Nations). Annual edition.

van Brabant, Jozef M., *Socialist Economic Integration: Aspects of Contemporary Economic Problems in Eastern Europe* (New York: Cambridge University Press, 1980).

———, "The USSR and Socialist Economic Integration—A Comment," *Soviet Studies*, January 1984.

Vanous, Jan, "Eastern European and Soviet Fuel Trade, 1970–85," in U.S. Congress, Joint Economic Committee, *East European Economic Assessment*, Part 2 (Washington, D.C.: GPO, 1981).

———, "Soviet and East European Trade and Financial Relations with the Middle East," *Soviet–East European Foreign Trade*, Spring/Summer/Fall 1985.

Vneshniaia torgovlia SSSR (Moskva: Financy i Statistika). Annual edition.

Wallace, W.V., and R.A. Clark, *Comecon, Trade, and the West* (London: Frances Pinter, 1986).

Wasowski, Stanislaw, "The Fuel Situation in Eastern Europe," *Soviet Studies*, July 1969.

Watson, Robin, "The Linkage between Energy and Growth Prospects in Eastern Europe," in U.S. Congress, Joint Economic Committee, *East European Economic Assessment*, Part 2 (Washington, D.C.: GPO, 1981).

Wharton Econometric Forecasting Associates, Centrally Planned Economies, *Analysis of Current Issues*, 29 June 1984; 21 January 1987.

Wilczynski, J., "Atomic Energy for Peaceful Purposes in the Warsaw Pact Coun- tries," *Soviet Studies*, October 1974.

Wolf, Thomas A., "East–West European Trade Relations," in U.S. Congress, Joint Economic Committee, *East European Economies Post-Helsinki* (Washington, D.C.: GPO, 1977).

Zoeter, Joan Parpart, "USSR: Hard Currency Trade and Payments," in U.S. Congress, Joint Economic Committee, *Soviet Economy in the 1980's: Problems and Prospects*, Part 2 (Washington, D.C.: GPO, 1982).

Zybkov, A.I., ed., *Toplivno-cyrevaya problema v. usloviyakh sotsialisticheskoi ekonomicheskoi integratsy* (Moskva: Nauka, 1979).

Journals and Newspapers from Communist Europe* Cited in Notes

Bulgaria

> *Energetika*
> *Otechestven front*
> *Pogled*
> *Rabotnichesko delo*
> *Trud*

Czechoslovakia

> *Dokumenty charty*
> *Hospodarske noviny*
> *Jaderna energie*
> *Lidova demokracie*
> *Planovane hospodarstvi*
> *Praca*
> *Pravda* (Bratislava)
> *Pravda* (Plzen)
> *Rude pravo*
> *Smena* (Bratislava)
> *Svet hospodarstvi*
> *Tribuna*
> *Zemedelske noviny*
> *Zemedelsko zname*
> *Zivot strany*

---

*Place of publication is national capital unless otherwise noted.

East Germany

Energieanwendung (Leipzig)
Energietechnik (Leipzig)
Militaertechnik
Neues Deutschland
Presse Informationen
Wasserwirtschaft-Wassertechnik
Wirtschaftswissenschaft

Hungary

Figyelo
Heti Vilaggazdasag
Hetofi Hirek
Kozgazdasagi Szemle
Kulgazdasag
Kulpolitika
Magyar Hirlap
Magyar Kozlony
Magyarorzag
Nepszabadsag
Nepszava
Partelet
Penzugyi Szemle
Tarsadalmi Szemle

Poland

Dziennik Baltycki (Gdansk)
Glos wybrzeza (Gdansk)
Gosc niedzielny (Katowice)
Gwiazda morza (Gdansk)
Nowe drogi
Nowosci (Toryn)
Polityka
Polityka-Eksport-Import
Prawo zycie
Rynki zagraniczne
Rzeczpospolita
Rzeczywistosc

Trybuna ludu
Tygodnik
Tygodnik Kulturalny
Tygodnik powszechny (Krakow)
Wprost (Poznan)
Zycie gospodarcze
Zycie partii
Zycie Warszawy

Romania

Era Socialista
Revista Economica
Romania Libera
Scinteia
Viata Economica

Soviet Union

Argumenty i fakty
Ekonomicheskaia gazeta
Ekonomicheskoe sotrudnichestvo stran-chlenov SEV
Izvestiia
Kommunist
Krasnaia zvezda
Literaturna Ukraina (Kiev)
Literaturnaia gazeta
New Times
Planovoe khoziaistvo
Pravda
Radyanska Ukraina (Kiev)
Voprosy ekonomiki

Austria

Die Presse
Kurier
Profil

Luxembourg

Luxemburger Wort

Sweden

Dagens Nhyeter

United Kingdom

Financial Times
The London Times

United States

New York Times
Wall Street Journal
Washington Post

West Germany

Das Parlament
Die Tageszeitung
Die Welt
Die Zeit
Frankfurter Allgemeine
IWE Tagesdienst
Stuttgarter Zeitung

Translation Services

Foreign Broadcast Information Service
Joint Publications Research Service

Index

About the Author

John M. Kramer is professor and chairperson, Department of Political Science, Mary Washington College, Fredericksburg, Virginia. He received his B.A. in political science from La Salle University and his M.A. and Ph.D. degrees in international relations and Soviet area studies from the University of Virginia. Mr. Kramer has served as a research associate, Russian Research Center, Harvard University, a resident scholar at the United States Naval Staff College, and a senior fellow at the National Defense University. His publications have appeared in many professional journals, including *Slavic Review*, *Problems of Communism*, *Orbis*, and *The Journal of Politics*.